VISUAL QUICKSTART GUIDE

ACT! 4.0

Steven Frank

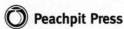
Peachpit Press

Visual QuickStart Guide
ACT! 4.0
Steven Frank

Peachpit Press
1249 Eighth Street
Berkeley, CA 94710
(510) 524-2178
(510) 524-2294 (fax)

Find us on the World Wide Web at: http://www.peachpit.com

Peachpit Press is a division of Addison-Wesley Longman Publishing Company

Copyright © 1998 by Steven Frank

Editor: Simon Hayes
Copy editor: Bill Cassel
Production coordinator: Amy Changar
Compositor: Owen Money
Indexer: Rebecca Plunkett

Notice of rights
All rights reserved. No part of this book may be reproduced or transmitted in any form or by any means, electronic, mechanical, photocopying, recording, or otherwise, without prior written permission of the publisher. For more information on getting permission for reprints and excerpts, contact Trish Booth at Peachpit Press.

Notice of liability
The information in this book is distributed on an "As is" basis, without warranty. While every precaution has been taken in the preparation of this book, neither the author nor Peachpit Press shall have any liability to any person or entity with respect to any loss or damage caused or alleged to be caused directly or indirectly by the instructions contained in this book or by the computer software and hardware products described herein.

ISBN: 0-201-35355-5

0 9 8 7 6 5 4 3 2 1

Printed and bound in the United States of America

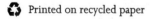 Printed on recycled paper

Dedication

To my keyboard, without whom this book
could never have been written.

Acknowledgments

Many people worked very hard to bring this book from the initial "Hey, what do you think about doing an ACT! book?" stage to the finished product that you hold in your hands. I'd like to thank my brother and sister-in-law, Mike and Robin, for keeping me locked in the attic until the book was done; Rachel, for sharing her crayons and "akkles" with me (that'd be "apples" to you and me); and little Jennifer, for the enthusiastic cooing and for waiting until her mom and dad got home to create "diaper situations" <shudder>.

Mind-boggling thanks go out to Simon Hayes, a giant among editors, for all of his helpful suggestions, timely advice, and (most of all) for laughing at my polar bear joke. Thanks to our great copyeditor Bill Cassel for his erudition and attention to detail (and for knowing who Heat Miser and Snow Miser were), and to Amy Changar and her production crew for turning a bunch of text and graphics into an actual book!

Special thanks to Rick Rhoades at Symantec for revealing all of the secrets of Actdiag to me (as well as for answering my many other ACT! questions).

About the author

Steven Frank is an independent computer consultant, trainer, and author. Steve is the coauthor of *Kai's Power Tools Studio Secrets* and *Illustrator 7 Complete*. He has also contributed to *The Macintosh Bible, Photoshop 4 Complete*, and numerous industry periodicals. In addition to mainstream computer books, Steve has designed and authored software manuals and custom training materials for numerous national training organizations and Fortune 500 companies.

When not chained to his keyboard, Steve travels throughout the U.S. conducting training seminars and workshops on ACT!, computer graphics and Web design, and general business software. Steve can be contacted via e-mail at *steve@bezier.com*.

TABLE OF CONTENTS

Chapter 4: **Working with Groups** **51**

Chapter 5: **Lookups and Queries** **63**

Chapter 6: **Activities and Schedules** **89**

TABLE OF CONTENTS

TABLE OF CONTENTS

INTRODUCTION

Welcome to the *ACT! 4.0 Visual QuickStart Guide*, the fastest and easiest way to learn the latest version of Symantec's de facto standard in contact-management software. By reading about the various features of ACT! and following the clear, concise step-by-step instructions for performing each task, you'll be using ACT! to its fullest potential in no time at all.

Who this book is for

The ACT! software program itself is meant to be used by virtually anyone, from salespeople to stockbrokers, real estate agents to writers, small business owners to corporate CEOs. Unlike many software programs on the market, you don't have to be a "computer person" in order to use it effectively.

With this in mind, we have written this book to be useful for a broad spectrum of ACT! users. The language used throughout the book is just regular, everyday stuff, so you won't need to keep referring to a glossary of terms or an encyclopedia of computer technology every five minutes. This book covers every aspect of ACT!, from the absolute basics to the most sophisticated administrative tasks. We have even tried to sprinkle in a few laughs along the way.

So whether you are brand new to ACT!, an old pro, or even just someone looking for a book or two to raise their monitor to a more comfortable viewing height, this book is for you.

How this book is structured

ACT! 4.0 Visual QuickStart Guide is designed (like all Visual QuickStart Guides) to be very modular. Each chapter discusses a different aspect of ACT!, and within each chapter are discrete sections (each clearly marked with edge-of-the-page labels) to help you understand and perform specific tasks. All you have to do is locate the correct chapter and then flip through the pages until you find the task that you need to perform. Once you've found it, read a little bit about it and just follow the steps to accomplish the task.

We've included a generous number of illustrations for each task section so that you won't ever get lost. All you have to do is check to make sure your screen looks like the illustration we've provided and you'll know that you are right on track.

This book starts with the simplest ACT! 4.0 topics and tasks, and gradually moves on to more advanced topics. The early and middle chapters will be most beneficial to beginning ACT! users, while later chapters will probably be more useful to experienced ACT! users or anyone who has to administer ACT! databases or provide support to ACT! users.

At the very end of the book are three appendices covering topics that don't quite fit into the task-oriented, step-by-step approach of the regular chapters. (Actually, at the *very* end of the book is the back cover, but you know what we mean.)

1

ACT! BASICS

This first chapter is designed for those readers who are new to ACT!, or even to the concept of contact management in general. Included in this chapter are the answers to such burning questions as "What is ACT!?", "What does A-C-T stand for?", and "How can I get started as quickly as possible?" If you are an experienced ACT! user, you can skip this chapter and go straight to Chapter 2 (or whatever chapter contains the answers to your specific questions). If you are new to ACT!, read on and be prepared for a great ACT! experience.

What is ACT!?

ACT! is the leader in a small but extraordinarily useful segment of the software market: contact management. Unlike the vast majority of traditional business software, which is designed to create something tangible (a letter, report, budget, chart, or presentation), ACT! is designed to allow you to create and enhance something intangible—relationships. ACT! assists you with just about everything that has anything to do with building and maintaining business relationships, from storing personal information to scheduling activities to sending letters and receiving phone calls. To quote ACT!'s own tag line, it helps you to "Turn contacts into relationships and relationships into results."

At its heart, ACT! is a database program like Microsoft Access or dBase, but ACT! is customized specifically for business contacts. Each of your contacts will have their own record in the database, and its built-in fields all pertain to contact information such as name, title, phone number, e-mail address, and so on. In addition to its database core, ACT! also has a built-in word processor so you can write letters and reports, an e-mail module for sending and receiving electronic correspondence, and a calendar/scheduling module for making and tracking appointments and other activities.

To install ACT!

1. Insert the ACT! CD-ROM into your computer's CD-ROM drive.

   When the ACT! CD is recognized by your computer, the installation screen (**Figure 1.1**) should appear automatically. If this screen does not appear automatically, double-click on your CD-ROM drive icon to bring up the installation screen.

Figure 1.1 The ACT! 4.0 CD splash screen.

ACT!, not Act or A.C.T.

Just in case you were wondering, the A-C-T in ACT! doesn't stand for anything at all. The capitalization of the entire word is simply a marketing ploy (and an effective one at that) to bring attention to the name of the product, as is the exclamation point at the end. Technically, the name of the product is ACT!, so it has to be written that way whenever it appears, leading to such unsightly and nonsensical punctuation arrangements as the previous section's title, "What is ACT!?", and references to things like "ACT!'s toolbar." By the same token, the product name is pronounced "act," not "A-C-T." (Perhaps the name is meant to be shouted, as indicated by the "!", but let's not get ridiculous about it.)

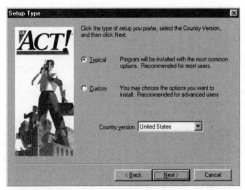

Figure 1.2 Select the type of ACT! installation you want.

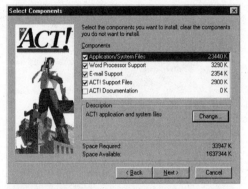

Figure 1.3 Selecting a Custom install gives you total control over exactly what is installed.

2. Click on **Install ACT!**.

When you click on any of the choices from this installation screen, additional options will appear in the second (blue) column. In this case, only one option appears, and that's "ACT! 4.0 for Windows 95/NT."

3. Double-click on **ACT! 4.0 for Windows 95/NT**.

4. Click on the **Next** button.

5. Read the enlightening and entertaining license agreement and click on the **Next** button.

6. Type in your name and company name, then click the **Next** button.

7. If desired, specify a custom location for the installation of the ACT! program by clicking the **Browse** button. Once you have specified a custom location (or if no custom location is desired), continue by clicking on the **Next** button.

If you do not specify a destination, ACT! will be installed into a new directory labeled "ACT" at the root level of your primary hard drive.

8. At the Select Type of Installation screen (**Figure 1.2**), click on the **Next** button for a typical United States installation.

Choosing the Custom Installation option will present you with an additional screen (**Figure 1.3**) where you can choose which ACT! components you want to exclude from the installation process (a typical installation includes all components). You can save some room on your hard drive by excluding certain components, but since a complete installation takes up less than 33 MB of hard-drive space there is very little reason to risk failing to install a component that you may need down the road.

WHAT IS ACT!?

You may also choose the installation appropriate for a different country by selecting it from the Country Version drop-down list.

9. If desired, change the name of the program folder used in your Start menu and click the **Next** button.

10. Click on the **Next** button to begin the installation process.

    A series of information screens will appear during the installation process to tell you all about the wonders of ACT!.

11. If you wish to skip the registration process, click on the **Skip** button and go to step 18. Otherwise, make sure that the correct country is showing in the Select Country drop-down list and click on the **Next** button.

12. Select your preferred registration method (Internet, Dial-up, or Printer) from the drop-down list and click on the **Next** button.

13. Fill in the User Information screen (**Figure 1.5**) and click on the **Next** button.

14. Select the appropriate responses in the Marketing screen (**Figure 1.6**), then click on the **Next** button.

15. Complete the Computer Info screen as well and click on the **Next** button.

16. Click on the **Start** button to begin the registration process.

    If you selected either Internet or Dial-up as your registration method, your modem will fire up and send off your registration data. If you selected Printer, the information will be printed out and you can mail it in.

17. Once the information is sent or printed, click on the **Continue** button.

18. Click on the **Finish** button to finish the installation process and return to your desktop.

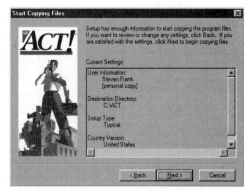

Figure 1.4 This is your last chance to make sure you selected the correct installation options.

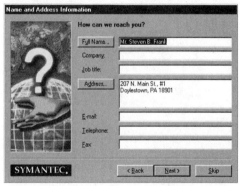

Figure 1.5 Complete the user information.

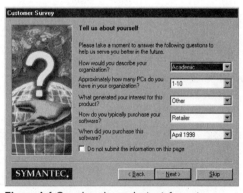

Figure 1.6 Complete the marketing information.

WHAT IS ACT!?

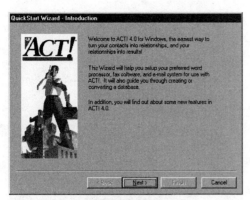

Figure 1.7 The ACT! QuickStart Wizard.

Setting up ACT!

The first time you launch ACT! after installing it, you will be presented with a series of dialog boxes that walk you through the process of setting up ACT! for your use. This includes creating your first database or converting an existing database to ACT! 4.0 format.

If you are a new ACT! user, this initial walk-through is a great way to make sure that your system is correctly configured for ACT!, as well as a way to create a database. After this initial walk-through, however, it will usually be faster to just create new databases manually (as explained in Chapter 2, *Database Creation*).

To set up ACT! for your use

1. Start the ACT! program.

   The first dialog box of the QuickStart Wizard will appear (**Figure 1.7**).

   If you have an existing database, you can access the QuickStart Wizard by selecting **QuickStart Wizard** from the Help menu.

2. If you want to check for updates to your version of ACT!, click on the **Connect** button and follow the prompts in the resulting dialog boxes. Otherwise, just click the **Next** button to continue.

3. Click **Next** again.

4. Select your preferred word processing and fax software from the drop-down lists and click **Next**.

5. Select the e-mail system you use from the listed choices (Internet Mail will work fine if you have e-mail through your Internet service provider) and click **Next**.

6. Select your e-mail account and click the **OK** button.

7. Enter or change any necessary information in the E-mail Setup Wizard screen (**Figure 1.8**) and click the **Next** button.

New terms you should know...

Database: A collection of related data. In ACT!, a database contains all the information related to your business contacts.

Record: In ACT!, a record is a set of information about one specific person. Each contact has his or her own record in an ACT! database.

Field: A category of information that appears in each record, like Name or Phone Number. While the field name is the same in all records, the information within the field will change from record to record.

8. Click the **Next** button (*not* the Finish button) to continue past e-mail setup.

9. If you have an existing database, ACT! will present you with a dialog box letting you know that it has found the existing database. Click the **Next** button to move past this screen.

10. At the Convert or Create screen, choose whether you want to convert a database, create a new database, or skip the conversion process, then click **Next**.

11. The next few screens you will see will vary depending on whether you chose to convert an existing database, or created a new database. Answer the (very simple) questions to complete the conversion or creation process.

✔ Tip

■ You cannot convert an open database, so if you want to convert your primary database to ACT! 4.0 format, close the database (which opens automatically when you launch ACT!) *before* selecting QuickStart Wizard from the Help menu.

Figure 1.8 All of this data needs to be correct if you want to send and receive e-mail while using ACT!

SETTING UP ACT!

The ACT! display

ACT! version 4.0, like its predecessor, offers numerous ways to view different aspects of your data, as well as several separate sets of controls for tasks and views. This can sometimes lead to a bit of confusion, especially for the new user. All of these views are discussed in detail in Chapter 7, *ACT!'s Many Views*, but a brief overview is in order here. **Figure 1.9** identifies the significant features of the main ACT! window.

THE ACT! DISPLAY

The menu bar contains menus and commands for just about every ACT! task you will perform.

The toolbar consists of 17 buttons that give you quick access to common commands.

Field labels identify ACT!'s data fields.

Data fields contain information about your contacts.

The view tabs can be used to view different types of information about the current contact.

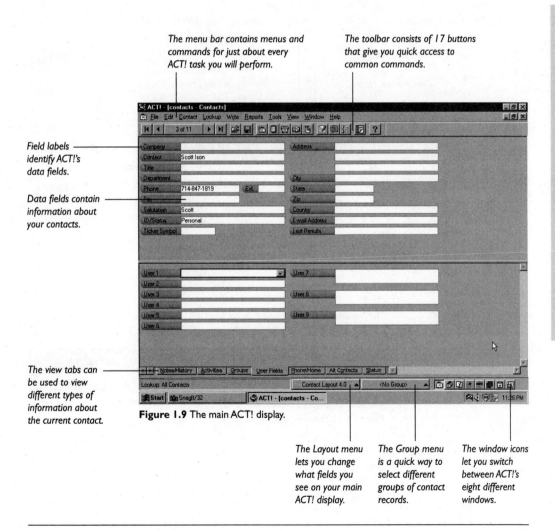

Figure 1.9 The main ACT! display.

The Layout menu lets you change what fields you see on your main ACT! display.

The Group menu is a quick way to select different groups of contact records.

The window icons let you switch between ACT!'s eight different windows.

ACT!'s toolbars

The main ACT! display has a toolbar across the top of the screen, as well as a row of viewing tabs in the lower-left area of the display and a set of window icons in the lower-right corner. **Figures 1.10–1.12** identify the various buttons and tabs within these three screen elements.

Contact List   Groups
Contact info   Daily calendar

Task List
E-mail

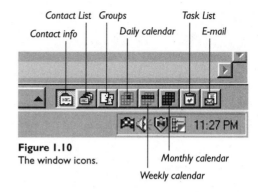

Figure 1.10
The window icons.

Monthly calendar
Weekly calendar

Schedule a phone call
Schedule a meeting
Schedule a to-do activity
Write a letter
Send a fax
Dial the phone

Go to the first record in the database
Go to the previous record
Record number out of total number of records
Go to the next record

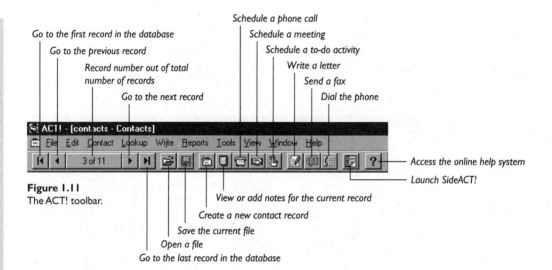

Access the online help system
Launch SideACT!

Figure 1.11
The ACT! toolbar.

View or add notes for the current record
Create a new contact record
Save the current file
Open a file
Go to the last record in the database

The first three tabs let you view different types of information about the selected contact.

The last four tabs show different sets of user fields.

Figure 1.12 The view tabs.

Navigation buttons

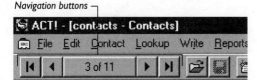

Figure 1.13 ACT!'s navigation buttons.

Getting around in ACT!

As you read through this book, you will learn all sorts of techniques for finding, sorting, and grouping contact records. Since this is the *ACT! Basics* chapter, we should probably talk about the non-shortcut, guaranteed-never-to-fail method for navigating from one record to another.

As shown earlier in the chapter, the Previous Record and Next Record buttons (**Figure 1.13**) are located in the toolbar. By clicking on these buttons, you can quickly flip through page after page of contact records in your database. You can also use the First Record and Last Record buttons to jump to the beginning or end of your database and then flip through them from there, which can be faster than just plodding through all of the records in order.

✔ Tip

- The keyboard shortcut for the Previous Record button is Ctrl-Page Up and the keyboard shortcut for the Next Record button is Ctrl-Page Down.

GETTING AROUND IN ACT!

Working with ACT!

As with any task, an understanding of how the process is designed to work will help you to use the product to its fullest extent, while at the same time eliminating, or at least reducing, any obstacles that might frustrate you along the way. There are many different approaches to ACT!, but they all follow the same basic steps.

The ACT! workflow

1. Create the database, including your own record (referred to as "My Record" within ACT!).

2. Enter information for your clients, prospects, business associates, and others you wish to store information about.

3. Create groups and add contacts as desired to make it easier to schedule activities or locate specific sets of contacts.

4. Schedule any appointments or other activities as they arise.

5. Write letters, send e-mail or faxes, and make and receive phone calls, using ACT! to simplify and record all of these activities.

6. Generate reports, to-do lists, and calendars to reflect past and upcoming activities and other contact information.

7. Back up your contact information or share it with colleagues as required or desired.

WORKING WITH ACT!

New terms you should know...

Group: A collection of contact records. Groups can be used to easily view a subset of records or to schedule activities with multiple contacts.

Report: An ACT!-generated document summarizing activities, contact information, etc.

Avoiding common mistakes

While ACT! is a fairly intuitive and easy-to-use program, there are times when using it can be somewhat frustrating. Some of these frustrations can't be avoided completely, but they can be greatly reduced with a little bit of database planning and a strategy for consistent data entry.

Your first temptation may be to sit down in front of ACT! and immediately start pouring in contact data so you can be up and running as quickly as possible. While your enthusiasm is admirable, a little forethought will serve you much better in the long run. Before you start entering data, think about what data you will need to store and how you will want to access it. Your database design should be driven by how you will use your contact data in the future, not what data you have in front of you now.

In general, always break up data into the smallest logical blocks. For example, separate a Bank field that contains name and location (PrimeFund Bank, St. Louis) into two separate fields for Bank Name and Bank Location. This will allow you, for example, to locate all contacts who bank in a certain city, regardless of what bank they use, or all those who use a certain bank, regardless of location.

Secondly, all information must be entered in a consistent fashion. If half of your New Jersey customers have "NJ" in their State fields, but most of the rest are entered as "N.J." and a few others are entered as "New Jersey," it will be difficult to locate all of the customers who live in that state south of New York and east of Pennsylvania. ACT! has some built-in ways to avoid this (as you will see in the next chapter) but it helps if you go into the job with consistency in mind.

Lastly, watch out for simple typos like extra spaces or transposed letters. Humans may not notice these mistakes, but ACT! most assuredly will.

AVOIDING COMMON MISTAKES

What's new in ACT! 4.0

When ACT! moved from version 2.0 to version 3.0, the most obvious difference was a completely new interface. The move from version 3.0 to version 4.0 is much more subtle, with very few obvious changes to the main interface, but quite a few new features and capabilities, as well as some enhancements to underlying interface elements (an interfacelift, as it were).

Here are the new features and enhancements that Symantec has made with version 4.0 of ACT!:

Better Internet capabilities. ACT! can access popular Internet business sites and Internet directories (such as Yahoo!, WhoWhere and Bigfoot) by automatically launching your default Web browser and feeding it the information it needs to take you where you need to go. *Find out more about this new feature in Chapter 13,* Productivity Power Tools *on page 227.*

Easier e-mail. A source of frustration in version 3.0, setting up e-mail addresses is now much easier. ACT! also now supports Eudora Pro and (best of all) direct Internet e-mail! *Find out more about this new feature in Chapter 11,* Staying in Contact *on page 185.*

SideACT!. With SideACT! you can now enter activity data without having to launch the full ACT! application. Data entered into SideACT! can be easily transferred to your ACT! 4.0 database, where it will appear on calendars and the Task List just as if the data had been entered directly in ACT!. *Find out more about this new feature in Chapter 12,* SideACT! *on page 213.*

Easier backup. Version 4.0 of ACT! more options for backing up database data, as well as envelopes, labersl, layouts and reports. *Find out more about this new feature in Chapter 14,* Security and Backup *on page 253.*

Improved WinFax integration. If you use WinFax Pro to send faxes from ACT!, you will find that the two programs are now even more closely integrated. *Find out more about this new feature in Chapter 11,* Staying in Contact *on page 185.*

Easier data synchronization. Another big source of frustration in version 3.0, ACT! now has an excellent Synchronization Wizard to make it as easy as possible to synchronize your data with other users. *Find out more about this new feature in Chapter 17,* Synchronizing Data *on page 291.*

Improved display and printing. New menu commands and interface elements make it easier to see, sort, filter and print your contact, activity and group information. *These new menu commands and interface elements are discussed throughout this book.*

Enhanced lookups. A new "tag" mode in the Contact List view and the ability to lookup by example in the Contact List, Task List, calendar windows and e-mail window give you much more flexibility and power in performing custom lookups. *These features are discussed in chapters 5,* Lookups and Queries *(page 63) and 7,* ACT!'s Many Views *(page 109).*

Easier to learn and use. ACT! 4.0 has a Setup Wizard to help you setup ACT!, online training in places to help you learn new features, and new keyboard commands and shortcut menus to make ACT! easier to work with on a day-to-day basis. *These features are discussed throughout this book.*

WHAT'S NEW IN ACT! 4.0

2

DATABASE CREATION

As we saw in Chapter 1, ACT! is, at its heart, a database program. That is, it is a collection of related data about your business contacts. The first step in using ACT!, then, is to create your initial database. Once you have created your database, you may never need to create another one. For the vast majority of ACT! users, making modifications to their initial database is enough, and they may never create another database as long as they use the program.

One common question new ACT! users have is whether it is better to create a single database for all of your contacts or to create separate databases for different types of contacts (prospects and customers, business and personal, etc.). The answer is unequivocally *one single database*. It is easy to create a field (or use the existing ID/Status field) to distinguish between types of contacts. Having all your contacts in one database makes it easy to work with all contacts, or just the ones you need at the moment. Having contacts split into multiple databases makes locating and working with these contacts an unwieldy and often torturous task.

It is critical to set up the database in a logical fashion. This means thoughtfully planning the fields you will need and setting up those fields to make data entry as easy and foolproof as possible.

Creating a database

After you create your database the first time you launch ACT!, the QuickStart Wizard never appears again (unless you select it yourself from the Help menu). If you need to create another database, you can use the QuickStart Wizard or create it manually. While the QuickStart Wizard is easy and friendly, it is generally faster to just create additional databases yourself.

Usually, you will not need to have more than one database, so this is a task that in all likelihood will not come up very often. The exception to this is if you're a database administrator who may need to create different databases for different departments or offices.

To create a database

1. From the File menu, select the **New** command.

2. At the New dialog box (**Figure 2.1**), select **ACT! Database** from the list of file types and click the **OK** button.

3. Type a name for your new database and click the **Save** button.

4. If necessary, modify the contents of the Enter "My Record" Information dialog box (**Figure 2.2**) and click the **OK** button.

5. Click the **Yes** button to confirm that the information you just entered is correct.

Figure 2.1 The New File dialog box.

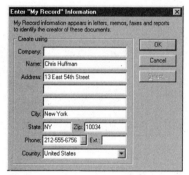

Figure 2.2 Enter your own data here.

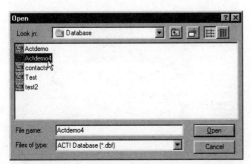

Figure 2.3 Open ACT! databases using this standard Open dialog box.

Opening a database

Since you will be working almost exclusively in a single database, you will rarely need to open another database. About the only time this will come up is when you are looking in an old or archive database, or when a colleague sends you a database containing some or all of his or her contacts.

To open a database

1. From the File menu, select the **Open** command.

2. If necessary, navigate to the drive and folder containing the database file.

3. Select the desired database file and click on the **Open** button (**Figure 2.3**).

✔ Tip

- Since ACT! always automatically opens the most recently viewed database, you will need to reopen your primary database the next time you launch ACT!

Renaming fields

All of the fields in your ACT! database can be renamed. For the most part, the fields that are already named to begin with can usually stay the same, though you might want to change one or two that you don't use (the Country field, for example, if all of your contacts are domestic). The prime candidates for renaming are the User 1 through User 15 fields, which are custom fields that you can use for anything you want.

Whenever you rename a field in an existing database (especially when renaming non-User fields), be aware that you may be affecting reports or other document templates that expect certain information to be stored in certain fields. Also, if you are part of a group that uses ACT!, be sure to communicate with your colleagues so that you will all be using the same fields for the same information. This will allow you to share data with far fewer headaches.

To rename a field

1. Click in the field you want to rename.

   This is not a necessary step, but it automatically selects the correct field in the Define Fields dialog box, so it is usually a timesaver.

2. From the Edit menu, select the **Define Fields** command.

3. If you did not do step 1, scroll through the list of fields on the left of the dialog box and click on the desired field.

4. Select the text in the Field Name box (**Figure 2.4**).

5. Type the desired new name for the field and click the **OK** button.

   The old field name has now been changed to the new name (**Figure 2.5**).

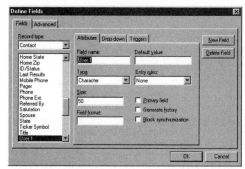

Figure 2.4 The Field Name box within the Define Fields dialog box.

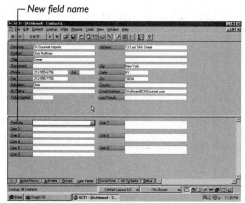

Figure 2.5 The ACT! display now shows the new field name.

Drop-down tab ⌐

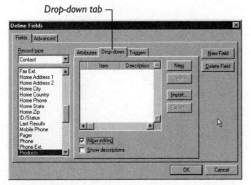

Figure 2.6 The Drop-down tab in the Define Fields dialog box.

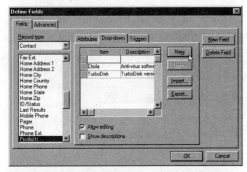

Figure 2.7 You can create lists in the Define Fields dialog box.

Creating drop-down lists

Drop-down lists can be a tremendous aid to accurate data entry, as there is no chance of a typo or misspelling when you're selecting from a list of choices. This is important, since inaccurate data entry will lead to reports that are inaccurate or incomplete or to contacts that end up missing from lookups and mass mailings.

To add a drop-down list to a field

1. Click in the field you want to add the drop-down list to.

2. From the Edit menu, select the **Define Fields** command.

3. Click on the Drop-down tab in the top-center of the dialog box (**Figure 2.6**).

4. Click on the **New** (not New Field) button.

5. If you like, you can start entering list items by typing directly into the Item and Description columns (**Figure 2.7**), or you can edit the list from the main database view (which is probably easier; see *Editing Drop-Down Lists*, later in this chapter).

New terms you should know...

Lookup: A search for contacts based on data in specific fields, such as City, State, ID/Status, and so on.

Removing drop-down lists

Most of the fields in ACT! already contain drop-down lists. You may find that want to use some of these fields without the lists.

To remove a drop-down list from a field

1. Click in the field from which you want to remove the drop-down list.

2. From the Edit menu, select the **Define Fields** command.

3. Click on the **Drop-down** tab in the top-center of the dialog box (**Figure 2.8**).

4. Click on the gray box to the left of the first row of list items.

5. Scroll down and Shift-click on the gray box to the left of the last row of list items (**Figure 2.9**). This should select all list items.

6. Click on the **Delete** (not Delete Field) button (**Figure 2.10**).

7. At the warning dialog box, confirm that you do indeed want to delete the selected items.

8. Click on the check mark in the Allow Editing box to remove it (**Figure 2.11**).

   With no entries and no editing allowed, the field will not display a drop-down list.

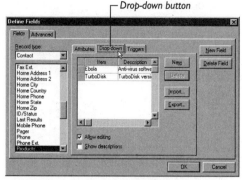

Drop-down button

Figure 2.8 The Drop-down tab in the Define Fields dialog box.

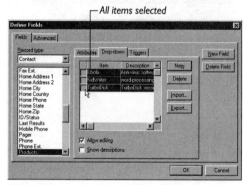

All items selected

Figure 2.9 All items in the drop-down list must be selected.

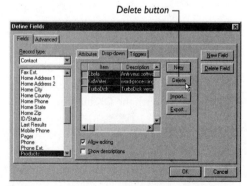

Delete button

Figure 2.10 Click the Delete button to remove the list items.

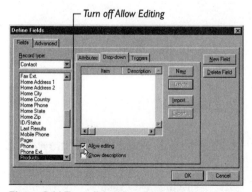

Turn off Allow Editing

Figure 2.11 Turn off the Allow Editing option.

Drop-down list —

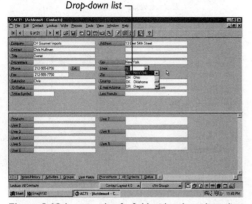

Figure 2.12 An example of a field with a drop-down list.

Edit List item —

Figure 2.13 The Edit List item lets you, um, edit the list.

Figure 2.14 New items can be added to the list from this dialog box.

Editing drop-down lists

Once you have added drop-down-list capabilities to a field, you will need to edit the contents of that list to reflect the entries that you use most often.

Drop-down lists can contain both list *items* and item *descriptions*. The items are the actual data that will be placed into the field, while the descriptions are simply text that helps identify each list item. For example, the State field drop-down list (**Figure 2.12**) contains two-letter state abbreviations (the list items) and full state names (the list descriptions) to help you identify what state each abbreviation stands for.

To edit a drop-down list

1. Click in the field for which you want to edit the drop-down list.

2. Click on the **Down Arrow button** on the right side of the field to activate the drop-down list.

3. Scroll to the bottom of the list and click on the **Edit List** item (**Figure 2.13**).

4. From the Edit List dialog box, select the list item you want to work with and click on the **Add, Modify,** or **Delete** button, depending on what you want to do.

   If you want to add an item to the list, click on the **Add** button, type the new item and description (if desired) (**Figure 2.14**), and click the **OK** button.

   If you want to change a list item, select it, click on the **Modify** button, make your change, and click the **OK** button.

   If you want to remove a list item, select it and click the **Delete** button.

5. Click the **OK** button when you are finished editing the list.

Setting default values

If your database is going to have any fields that will contain the same value most of the time, it will probably save you time and potential data-entry mistakes if you set default values for those fields. Each new record will have the default values automatically entered into the fields. You can, of course, change the values if necessary.

To set a default value for a field

1. Click in the field for which you want to set the default value.

2. From the Edit menu, select the **Define Fields** command.

3. Click in the **Default Value** text box and type in the value you want to be the default value for this field (**Figure 2.15**).

4. Click the **OK** button.

Default Value text box ¬

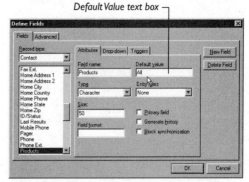

Figure 2.15 Whatever you type in the Default Value text box becomes the new default value for the selected field.

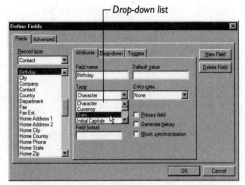

Figure 2.16 This drop-down list contains all of the possible data types for the selected field.

Setting field data types

The type of data entered into a field can affect how that field is sorted and how searches are performed within that field. Also, setting a field to accept only a certain data type can help eliminate data-entry inconsistencies. For example, setting a Delivery Date field to accept only date-type data will prevent someone from entering "Jan. 15" instead of "1/15/98."

To change a field's data type

1. Click in the field you want to work with then from the Edit menu, select the **Define Fields** command.

2. Click on the **down arrow** in the Type drop-down list.

3. Select the desired data type for this field (**Figure 2.16**).

   Character allows any combination of letters, numbers, and symbols.

   Currency allows only numerals and automatically formats the data as currency.

   Date allows only numerals and formats the data as a date. A drop-down list is also added from which a date can be selected.

   Initial Capitals allows only text and automatically capitalizes the first letter of each word.

   Lowercase and *Uppercase* allow only text and automatically format all text to either all lowercase or all uppercase, respectively.

   Numeric allows only numerals.

   Phone allows only numerals and automatically formats the data as a phone number.

   Time allows only numerals and A or P. A drop-down list is also added.

   URL Address will automatically launch your Web browser and take you to the indicated Web site when you click on the field.

4. Click the **OK** button.

Formatting field data

Another way to foster accurate data entry is to pre-format field data by using placeholder characters to represent the actual data that can be entered and how it should appear in the field. This creates a template for the data to be entered into.

Another formatting option is to change the size of the field, limiting the number of characters that can be typed into that field.

To create a field format

1. Click in the character field you want to work with (numeric fields cannot be formatted).

2. From the Edit menu, select the **Define Fields** command.

3. Click in the **Field Format** text box.

4. Type in the format you want to set for this field, using the "@" symbol to specify alphabetic characters, the "#" symbol for numerals, or the "%" symbol for either (**Figure 2.17**).

   For example, a field format of "@@@-###-##" would turn "Government12345" into "Gov-123-45".

5. Click the **OK** button.

   Field formatting is indicated with the underscore character in place of the @, #, or % placeholders (**Figure 2.18**).

To change a field's size

1. From the Edit menu, select the **Define Fields** command.

2. Select the text in the **Field Size** text box (**Figure 2.19**) and replace it with the desired maximum number of characters, from 1 to 254 for character fields and from 1 to 19.5 for numeric fields. (19.5 means 19 whole-number digits and 5 decimal digits.)

FORMATTING FIELD DATA

Field Format text box

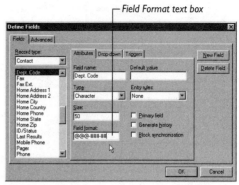

Figure 2.17 A sample field format created with placeholder symbols.

Formatted field

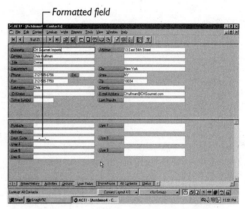

Figure 2.18 How a formatted field looks before data is entered.

Field Size text box

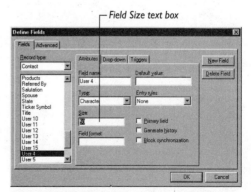

Figure 2.19 The Field Size text box in the Define Fields dialog box.

Figure 2.20 ACT! will not allow you to move to a different record until you have entered data in a required field.

Entry Rules drop-down list

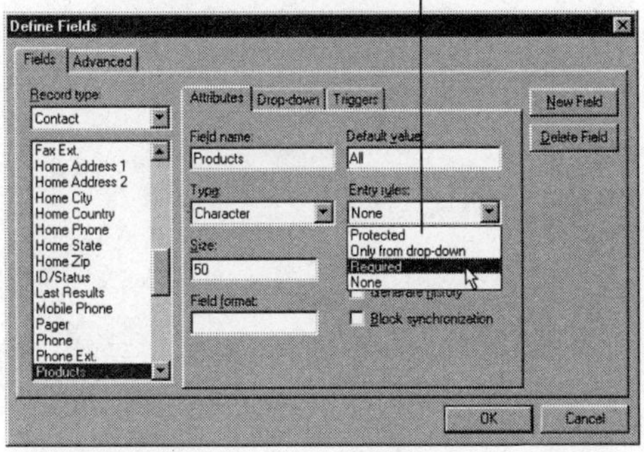

Figure 2.21 The Entry Rules drop-down list in the Define Field dialog box.

Setting data-entry rules

Anotherway to help ensure consistent data entry and maintain a maximum level of data reliability is to set data-entry rules for your fields. Each field's entry rules can be set to Protected, Only from drop-down, Required, or None.

Protected fields cannot be changed. This is ideal for data fields whose content is critical and is entered during the initial creation of the database.

Only from drop-down means that data cannot be typed into the field. All data must be entered by being selected from the field's drop-down list.

Required fields cannot be left blank. You are required to enter some value into the field (see **Figure 2.20**).

None means (obviously) that there are no data-entry rules for the field. This is the default setting for all fields.

To set data-entry rules for a field

1. Click in the field you want to work with.

2. From the Edit menu, select the **Define Fields** command.

3. From the **Entry Rules** drop-down list, select the desired rule for this field (**Figure 2.21**).

4. Click the **OK** button.

Creating a primary field

Primary fields are fields whose contents will be duplicated when a record or a group is duplicated (see **Figure 2.22**). Likely candidates for primary fields would be Sales Rep (since the same rep would most likely handle a second or third contact within the same company), Region, and other general classifications.

To define a field as a primary field

1. Click in the field you want to define as a primary field.

2. From the Edit menu, select the **Define Fields** command.

3. Click on the **Primary Field** checkbox to select it (**Figure 2.23**).

4. Close the dialog box by clicking the OK button.

✔ Tips

■ The default primary contact fields include Company, Address 1, Address 2, Address 3, City, State, Zip, Phone, and Fax.

■ The default primary group fields include Company, Address 1, Address 2, Address 3, City, State, Zip, Country, Description, and Division.

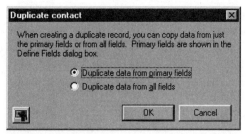

Figure 2.22 Duplicating primary fields.

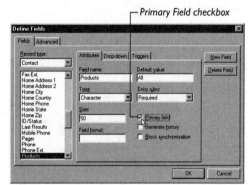

Figure 2.23. Clicking the Primary Field checkbox turns the Primary Field option on or off.

CREATING A PRIMARY FIELD

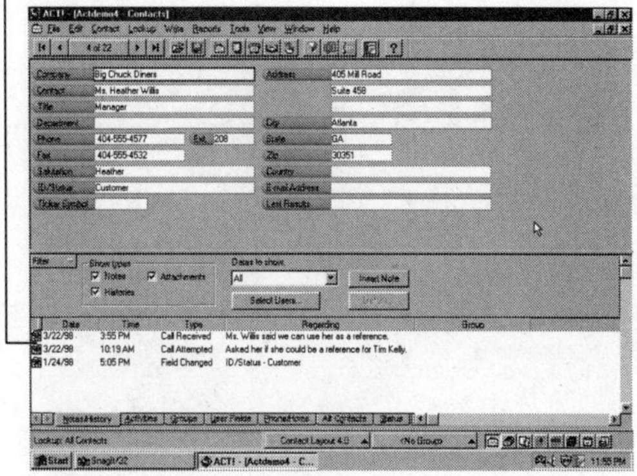

History entries

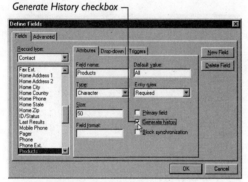

Figure 2.24 History entries for a contact record.

Generate History checkbox

Figure 2.25 Click on the Generate History checkbox to turn this option on or off.

Creating a history field

If you have a field whose content is important enough that you need to keep a record of when it changes, you can define that field as a history field. Whenever the content of a history field is changed, an entry is added to that contact's Notes/History tab indicating which field was changed, the date when the change was made, and what the field data was changed to (**Figure 2.24**).

To define a field as a history field

1. Click in the field you want to work with.

2. From the Edit menu, select the **Define Fields** command.

3. Click on the **Generate History** checkbox (**Figure 2.25**) to select it.

4. Click the **OK** button.

Creating a new field

While ACT! comes with enough predefined fields for most standard business needs and 15 user fields for you to customize as you see fit, you may still have to create additional fields to meet your needs.

Creating new fields is simple. Being able to actually use these new fields is a bit more involved. Once the fields are created, they must be added to a layout before you can access them. The following steps will take you through the process of creating new fields. To add them to your layouts, refer to *Adding and removing fields* in Chapter 13.

To create a new field

1. From the Edit menu, select the **Define Fields** command.

2. From the **Record Type** drop-down list, select either **Contact** or **Group**, depending on whether you want to create a new contact record or a new group record (**Figure 2.26**).

3. Click on the **New Field** button (**Figure 2.27**).

4. Name the new field and change any other relevant field attributes such as data type, entry rules, etc.

5. Click the **OK** button, and you're done.

✔ Tip

■ By default, all new fields will be contact fields. Unless you are familiar with groups and specifically want to create a new group field, you will never need to change the record type.

Record Type drop-down list

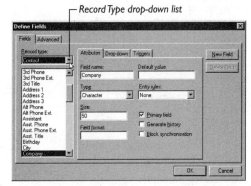

Figure 2.26 The Record Type drop-down list lets you create either new contact fields or new group fields.

New Field button

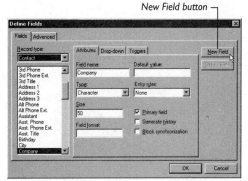

Figure 2.27 The New Field button makes it easy to create as many new fields as you need.

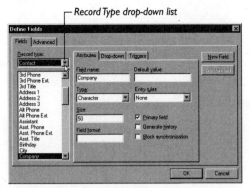

— Record Type drop-down list

Figure 2.28 The Record Type drop-down list lets you delete either contact fields or group fields.

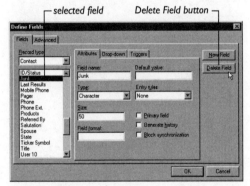

— selected field   Delete Field button —

Figure 2.29 One click on the Delete Field button and it's curtains for the selected field.

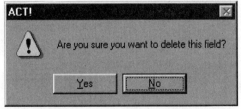

Figure 2.30 Are you really, really sure you want to permanently delete the selected field and its contents?

Deleting a field

All ACT! databases are made up of a group of "core" fields, other default (but not strictly necessary) fields, the 15 user fields, plus any new fields you create. The core fields include Contact, Title, Address, Phone, and Fax fields, as well as Creation Date, ID/Status, and a bunch more (a complete list is available in the online help under "Contact Database field attributes"). Except for the core fields, you can delete any fields that you don't want or need anymore.

To delete a field

1. From the Edit menu, select the **Define Fields** command.

2. From the Record Type drop-down list, select either **Contact** or **Group**, depending on whether you want to delete a contact record or a group record (**Figure 2.28**).

3. From the scrolling list of fields, select the field you want to delete.

4. Click the **Delete Field** button (**Figure 2.29**).

5. Click the **Yes** button in the confirmation dialog box (**Figure 2.30**).

   The field is permanently deleted from the database. This does not (oddly enough) remove the field from any layouts on which it appears. You will have to do this yourself. To learn how, refer to *Adding and removing fields* in Chapter 13 (page 231).

✔ Tip

■ Be warned that deleting a field will irretrievably delete all data contained in that field. Don't delete fields unless you have a good reason and are sure you know what you are doing.

3

MANAGING RECORDS

Everything that ACT! does depends on the creation and maintenance of accurate records. By maintaining accurate data for all of your contacts, you can easily write letters, send e-mail, make and log phone calls, schedule activities, and generate detailed reports.

This chapter covers such important data-management topics as creating and deleting records, attaching files, working with notes and history, and using Contact Lists.

Modifying "My Record"

As mentioned earlier, all of your own information is stored in a contact record referred to as "My Record." It is important to keep the information in "My Record" accurate, as practically all reports, letters, form letters, faxes, and e-mail created in ACT! use this information in one way or another. Probably the best example of this is the sender information on a business letter or fax cover sheet (**Figure 3.1**), which is taken directly from the appropriate fields in "My Record."

You can easily access the "My Record" record from the Lookup menu.

Changing user data in "My Record"

1. From the Lookup menu, select the My Record command (**Figure 3.2**).

2. Change any erroneous or out-of-date information in any of the fields in "My Record."

   Text can be selected, deleted or edited using the same techniques you would use in any word processor. This is a simple task, but an important one, as many a tree has died to produce 1,000 copies of a form letter with an *incorrect* return address or phone number. Many ACT! users are good at keeping contact records up-to-date, but forget to check their own.

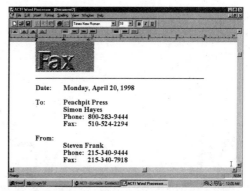

Figure 3.1 The top of a fax cover sheet, with data from both the contact record and "My Record."

Figure 3.2 The My Record command is the first item in the Lookup menu.

New Contact button

Figure 3.3 The New Contact button in the toolbar.

Creating new contacts

Adding a contact to your database is very easy. If you just want a new blank record to enter data into, you can create one either with a menu command or by using the main ACT! toolbar.

Adding a new contact record

1. Do one of the following: Click on the **New Contact** button (**Figure 3.3**), hit the **Ins** (Insert) key on the keyboard, or select the **New Contact** command from the Contact menu.

2. Enter all available information for your new contact into the appropriate fields.

Printing contact data

ACT! offers quite a few ways for you to print out information regarding your contacts. The majority of these involve printing ACT! reports (which are discussed in detail in Chapter 10: *Reports*). Without knowing anything about reports, though, you still have several options for getting your contact data on paper. You can print a quick report of all the information for any of the contacts in your database; you can print an address book for use in any of several commercial organizers, such as Daytimer or Rolodex; or you can print labels or envelopes for mass mailings.

To print data for a single contact

1. Locate the contact record you want to print.

   Using the navigation buttons (**Figure 3.4**) or the Contact List (discussed later in this chapter) are probably the easiest ways to find a particular record.

2. From the File menu, select the **Print** command.

3. At the Print dialog box, select **Reports** from the Printout Type drop-down list (**Figure 3.5**).

4. Select **Contact Report** from the list of available reports (**Figure 3.6**) and click the **OK** button.

5. At the Run Report dialog box, select the **Current Contact** option (**Figure 3.7**) and click the **OK** button.

   The other options in this dialog box are discussed in Chapter 10, *Reports* on page 165.

Navigation buttons

Figure 3.4 Use these navigation buttons to move from one record to another.

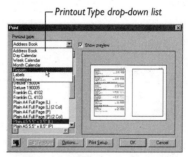

Printout Type drop-down list

Figure 3.5 Select the type of printout you want from this list.

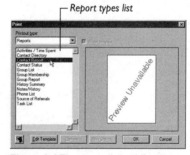

Report types list

Figure 3.6 These are all the different report types available.

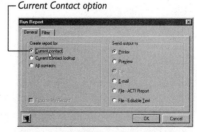

Current Contact option

Figure 3.7 Choose this option to print the report for just the current contact.

PRINTING CONTACT DATA

— *Address Book formats list*

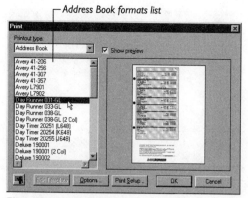

Figure 3.8 This list contains all the different address book formats ACT! can print.

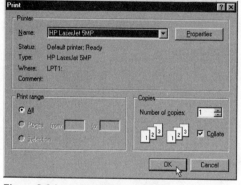

Figure 3.9 A standard Print dialog box.

To print an address book of all contacts

1. From the File menu, select the Print command.

   The Print dialog box appears with "Address Book" already selected as the printout type.

2. Scroll down the list, if necessary, and select the layout that most closely matches the address book or organizer format that you use (**Figure 3.8**).

   The preview window shows you how the address book will look when printed. This preview can also help you determine how best to feed any special paper you might want to use into the printer.

3. Click the OK button.

4. At the Print dialog box (**Figure 3.9**), click the OK button.

PRINTING CONTACT DATA

Duplicating contacts

Occasionally, you will want to create a duplicate entry for a contact. Perhaps you want to have two separate entries for a friend of yours who is also a customer (allowing you to keep personal activities and notes out of your business-related reports). You might also have two different contacts whose information is virtually identical. It would then be easier to duplicate one contact and change only the name and perhaps phone extension, rather than creating an entirely new entry.

When duplicating contacts you have the option to only copy the primary fields, which contain the data most likely to be shared by more than one contact. This is ideal when you have two contacts at the same company. In this case, the new contact is based on an existing contact, but not all of the contact information is duplicated.

To duplicate a contact

1. From the Contact menu, select the Duplicate Contact command.

2. From the Duplicate Contact dialog box (**Figure 3.10**), select the Duplicate data from all fields option and click the OK button.

To base a new contact on an existing contact

1. From the Contact menu, select the Duplicate Contact command.

2. Select the Duplicate data from primary fields option in the resulting Duplicate Contact dialog box (**Figure 3.11**) and click OK.

✔ Tip

■ The default primary fields are Company, Address 1, Address 2, Address 3, City, State, Zip, Phone, and Fax.

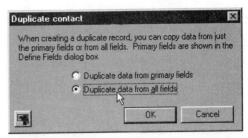

Figure 3.10 The Duplicate Contact dialog box used to duplicate all fields.

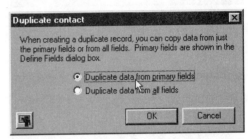

Figure 3.11 The Duplicate Contact dialog box used to duplicate data only from the primary fields.

DUPLICATING CONTACTS

Figure 3.12 Click the Contact button to ensure that only records for the active contact will be deleted.

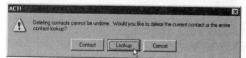

Figure 3.13 Click the Lookup button to delete the entire active lookup.

Deleting contacts

While we would always hope that business relationships last forever, it is inevitable that the time will come when you will have to delete contacts from your database. Deleting contacts is easy. In fact, it is sometimes too easy, and you can unwittingly and permanently remove a group of contacts from your database when you only wanted to remove a single contact. This is because the same process can be used to delete either a single contact or an entire group of contacts. With a little forethought, though, you can safely remove exactly the contacts you want.

To delete a single contact

1. From the Contact menu, select the **Delete Contacts** command.

2. At the resulting dialog box (**Figure 3.12**), click the **Contact** button.

3. A warning dialog box will come up. This is your last chance to change your mind before the selected contact is forever deleted from your database. After making sure that you're deleting the right thing, click the **Yes** button.

To delete a group of contacts

1. Create a lookup of all the contacts you no longer want.

   This can be accomplished with the Lookup menu, by running a query, by selecting an existing group, or from the contact list or one of the calendars. See Chapter 5: *Lookups and Queries*.

2. From the Contact menu, select the **Delete Contacts** command.

3. Click the **Lookup** button in the resulting dialog box (**Figure 3.13**).

4. Click the **Yes** button in the warning dialog box.

✔ Tips

■ Because deleted records cannot be retrieved, do not delete groups of records unless you are *absolutely* sure the group contains only records you no longer want. You might want to view the group in the Contact List window (see *Viewing Contact Lists*, later in this chapter) or even print a report to confirm that the current lookup contains only unneeded records.

■ Pressing the Ctrl-Delete key combination on your keyboard has the same effect as selecting the Delete Contacts command.

DELETING CONTACTS

Editing multiple contacts

From time to time, events will occur that will necessitate your editing a group of contacts. For example, one company you work with may be bought by another company. You would then need to change the company name, and perhaps the address and phone number as well, for several of your contacts. Rather than waste time editing each individual contact, you can have ACT! replace data in a selected set of contacts with one command.

This process involves performing a lookup, which is discussed in detail in Chapter 5: *Lookups and Queries*. If you are not yet familiar with lookups, please review Chapter 5 before attempting this task. Otherwise you risk permanently altering data *in your entire database!*

Replacing data in multiple records

1. Perform a lookup to select the records that contain the data you wish to change.

2. From the Edit menu, select the **Replace** command.

   A Replace window with blank fields will appear (**Figure 3.14**).

3. Enter the new data in the desired field.

4. From the Replace menu, select the **Apply** command or click on the **Apply** button (**Figure 3.15**).

5. At the warning dialog box (**Figure 3.16**), click the **Yes** button.

   The new data replaces the old data for all records in the lookup.

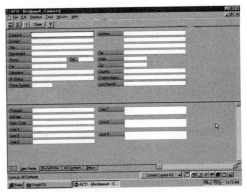

Figure 3.14 Enter the new information into the appropriate field(s) in this window.

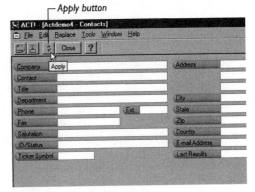

Figure 3.15 The Apply button.

Figure 3.16 Last chance to change your mind...

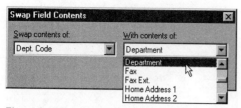

Figure 3.17 The Swap Field Contents dialog box.

Swapping field data

You may encounter a situation where you have been using one field to store a certain type of data, but then need to swap this field with another field. The most common example of this would be when you store a certain type of data in one user field, but your colleagues store that same data in a different user field. To bring everyone together, you will need to swap the data in the two fields in your database so that you and your colleagues are both storing the same data in the same fields. Be aware that swapping field data always affects the entire database, not just the selected contact record.

Swapping data between two fields

1. From the Edit menu, select the **Replace** command.

2. From the Replace menu, select the **Swap Fields** command.

3. At the Swap Field Contents dialog box (**Figure 3.17**), select the two fields you want to swap from the drop-down lists. It makes no difference which field you choose first.

4. Click the **OK** button.

Attaching files to contact records

The many fields in an ACT! database are designed for storing small blocks of information. From time to time, you will need to be able to store information that doesn't fit into ACT!'s fields. For example, you may regularly need to refer to a Microsoft Excel price sheet for a client, or perhaps a lengthy word-processing document. ACT! allows each contact record to have an unlimited number of document files attached to it. When you double-click on the attached file from within ACT!, the document is opened using the software program that created it.

To attach a file to a contact record

1. From the Contact menu, choose the **Attach File** command.

2. Navigate through the resulting standard Open File dialog box to locate the desired data file.

3. Select the desired file and click the **OK** button, or simply double-click the desired file.

   The attached file(s) will appear in the Notes/History view (**Figure 3.18**).

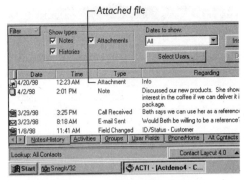

Attached file

Figure 3.18 The Notes/History view showing attached files.

— Notes/History tab

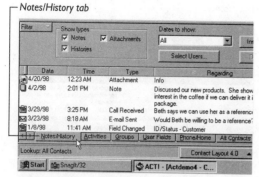

Figure 3.19 The Notes/History tab gives you access to all attached files.

Opening attached files

Once files have been attached to a contact record, they can easily be opened, edited, and printed from the Notes/History view.

To open an attached file

1. Go to the contact record to which the file is attached.

2. Click on the **Notes/History** tab located in the lower-left corner of the display (**Figure 3.19**).

3. If necessary, use the scroll bar on the far right of the window to locate the attached file you want to open.

4. Double-click on the icon for the desired file. The file will be opened using the software program that created it, just as if you had double-clicked on the file icon from the desktop.

5. When you are done with the file, simply exit whatever program you are in to return to ACT!

Removing attached files

Once an attached file is no longer needed, you can remove it from the contact record's Notes/History listing.

To remove an attached file

1. Go to the contact record to which the file is attached.

2. Click on the **Notes/History** tab located in the lower-left corner of the display.

3. If necessary, use the scroll bar on the far right of the window to locate the attached file you want to remove.

4. Click on the icon at the far left of the entry line to select the desired file (**Figure 3.20**).

5. Hit the **Delete** key.

6. At the resulting warning dialog box (**Figure 3.21**), click the **Yes** button.

Entry icon

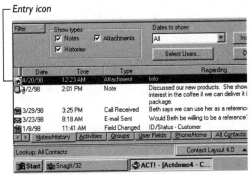

Figure 3.20 Click on the icon for the entry to select the entire entry.

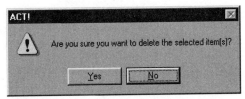

Figure 3.21 Click this Yes button to remove the attached file.

Notes/History tab

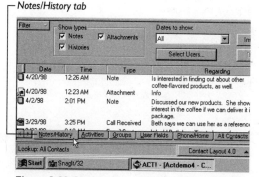

Figure 3.22 Click the Notes/History tab to view all note or history entries.

Scroll bar

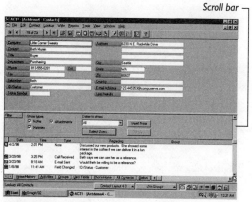

Figure 3.23 Use this scroll bar to see more entries.

Viewing notes and history

ACT! stores all history entries and user-created notes in the appropriately named Notes/History view. These entries can easily be viewed, edited, and printed from the Notes/History view tab.

To view a record's notes or history

1. Locate the record for the contact whose notes or history you want to see.

2. Click on the **Notes/History** tab in the lower-left corner of the display (**Figure 3.22**).

    All notes, history entries, and attached files are displayed in reverse chronological order, with the most recently added items at the top of the list.

3. To view entries not currently visible, use the scroll bar at the far right of the Notes/History display (**Figure 3.23**).

✔ Tip

■ A sent document, sent e-mail, made or received phone call, and any changes made to a field designated as a history field are all worthy of a place in history (well, in ACT!'s history file, at least). These actions are stored as history entries in the database's Notes/History file. To designate a field as a history field (and thus record all changes made to the field), see *Creating a history field* in Chapter 2.

Filtering notes and history

As you work with contact records, their Notes/History display will fill up with notes that you have written, attached files, and all the changes that you will undoubtably be making to fields designated as history fields. With older records, it can sometimes be time-consuming to scroll through the Notes/History display to locate a particular entry.

ACT! gives you a way to reduce the amount of data displayed in the Notes/History view (as well as several other views, as discussed throughout this book). This is called filtering and is easily accomplished by selecting options from the top of the Notes/History display.

To filter out notes and history entries

1. Click on the **Notes/History** tab.

2. To filter out certain types of entries, click on the Notes, Histories, or Attachments checkboxes (**Figure 3.24**) to deselect those items and hide them from view.

3. If you want to see notes and history entries for a specific date range, select an entry from the Dates to Show drop-down list.

   If you select Date Range, you will be presented with a dialog box (**Figure 3.25**) in which you can specify an arbitrary range of dates.

4. To see only entries made by specific users of the database, click on the **Select User** button and select the desired users from the resulting dialog box.

   This only applies to multiuser databases, of course.

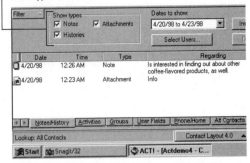

Show Types checkboxes

Figure 3.24 Use these checkboxes to hide or show different entry types.

Figure 3.25 You can view the entries for a very specific range of dates.

New terms you should know...

Filtering: The process of hiding entries or records that do not meet specified criteria. Filtering is a temporary process that affects what data is displayed, but does not affect the actual contents of the database.

Multiuser database: A database that is located on a network and can be accessed by more than one user. All records created and entries made are "tagged" as belonging to a specific user, but are usually visible to everyone.

Insert Note button ─┐

Figure 3.26 Click the Insert Note button to quickly add notes to your contact's Notes/History view.

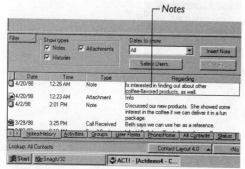

Figure 3.27 Any information typed in a note is readily available.

Adding notes

In the course of any business relationship, you will learn innumerable small but important details about your client or customer. ACT! lets you keep track of all those details by making notes within each contact's record. Rather than going into any of ACT!'s fields, these notes are stored separately, and can be opened, viewed, edited, and printed from the Notes/History view.

Adding a note to a record

1. Locate the record to which you want to add a note.

2. Click on the Insert Note button (**Figure 3.26**).

    ACT! will open the Notes/History view in the bottom half of the display. Your new note will be created and selected.

3. Type your information in the Regarding column for the note (**Figure 3.27**).

✔ Tip

■   You are not limited in any way in the length of your notes. As you type, your text will wrap within the Regarding column to as many lines as you need.

Printing notes and history entries

Quite often you may need to refer to contact notes or history entries when you are not at your computer. The notes and history data can easily be printed with the Print command.

To print contact notes and history entries

1. Locate the contact record whose notes and history you wish to print.

2. From the File menu, select the Print Notes/Histories command (**Figure 3.28**).

3. At the Print dialog box click OK.

Figure 3.28. In version 4.0 of ACT! it's this easy to print your Notes/History entries..

Notes/History tab

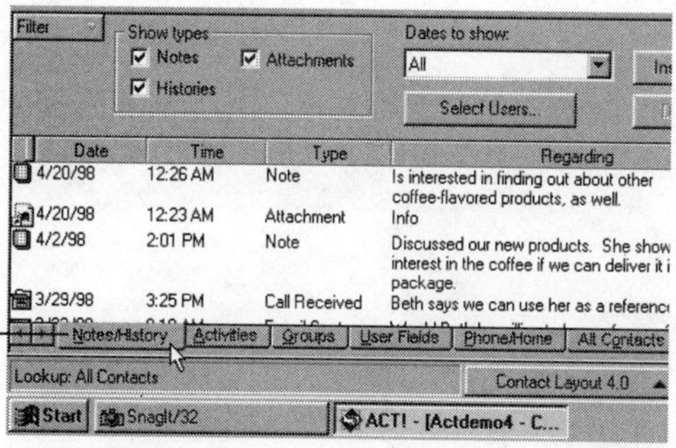

Figure 3.29 The Notes/History tab gives you access to all notes and history entries associated with the selected contact.

Editing notes and history entries

Once created, contact notes can easily be edited to ensure that the information is always accurate and up-to-date. Likewise, history entries can be edited to remove or correct erroneous information.

To edit a note or history entry

1. Locate the record for the contact whose note or history you wish to edit.

2. Click on the **Notes/History** tab in the lower-left corner of the display (**Figure 3.29**).

3. If necessary, use the scroll bar on the right side of the display to locate the note or history entry you want to edit.

4. Edit the text in the Regarding column as you would in any word processor.

✔ Tip

■ There is no need to save your changes when you are done editing a note. Simply move on to another contact record and your changes are saved to disk.

EDITING NOTES AND HISTORY ENTRIES

Removing notes and history entries

From time to time, you may decide that you no longer need old information and want to remove a note from a contact record.

History entries can also be removed, although this does defeat the whole purpose of maintaining a history file. Usually, you will need to remove history entries early in your ACT! career, when you may accidentally create multiple or inappropriate history entries.

Removing a note or history entry from a contact record

1. Locate the record for the contact whose note or history entry you wish to remove.

2. Click on the Notes/History tab in the lower-left corner of the display.

3. If necessary, use the scroll bar on the right side of the display to locate the entry you want to delete.

4. Click on the entry icon at the far-left edge of the note or history listing (to the left of the date) (**Figure 3.30**).

   This selects the entire note or history entry as a single object.

5. Hit the Delete key on the keyboard.

6. At the warning dialog box (**Figure 3.31**), click the Yes button.

   The selected entry is permanently removed from the contact record.

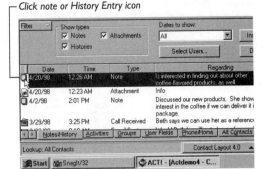

Click note or History Entry icon

Figure 3.30 Click the note or history entry icon to select the entire note.

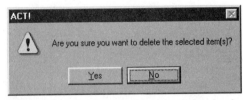

Figure 3.31 Deleted entries cannot be retrieved, so be sure before clicking this Yes button.

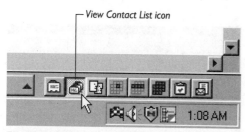

Figure 3.32. The View Contact List icon.

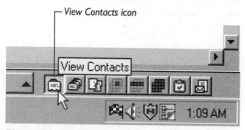

Figure 3.33. The View Contacts icon.

Figure 3.34. Single-clicking this gray box selects the contact. Double-clicking takes you back to the Contact view for that contact.

Viewing Contact Lists

While it is easy to move from one record to another using the navigation buttons in the toolbar, it is often easier to locate a particular contact by simply looking at a list of all contacts. Once you locate the record you want, you can bring it up up directly from the list. In fact, it is often unnecessary to bring up the contact's record, since the Contact List contains the most commonly needed data, such as phone and fax numbers.

To view the Contact List

1. Click on the **View Contact List** icon near the lower-right corner of the display (**Figure 3.32**).

2. If necessary, use the scroll bar on the right side of the window to view additional contacts.

   By default, all contacts are sorted in ascending alphanumeric order by company name. If you want to change this sorting, see *Sorting Contact Lists*, next.

3. If necessary, use the horizontal scroll bar to view additional columns of data, such as City, State, and Zip, which are usually not visible in the window.

4. To return to the Contact view, simply click on the **View Contacts** icon (the first of the view icons) (**Figure 3.33**).

✔ Tip

- To immediately return to the Contact view of *a particular record*, simply double-click on the gray selection box for the record that you want to view at the far-left edge of the window (**Figure 3.34**).

VIEWING CONTACT LISTS

Sorting Contact Lists

By default, all entries in the Contact List view are sorted in ascending alphanumeric order by company name. There will undoubtedly be times when it will be more convenient for you to have your contacts listed in some other order: by name to make it easier to find a particular person, by title if you need to call only certain decision-making contacts, or by city, state, or ZIP code if you need to look for contacts in a specific geographical location.

To sort entries in the Contact List view

1. Click on the View Contact List icon near the lower-right corner of the display

   Note the triangle in the column heading for Company (**Figure 3.35**). The triangle indicates the column that the list is currently sorted by.

2. Click on any other column heading to sort your contacts in ascending alphanumeric order by the information in that column.

3. Click again on the column heading to reverse the sort order, sorting your contacts by the information in that column in *descending* alphanumeric order.

   The triangle sort indicator will turn down to indicating a descending sort order.

Triangle

Figure 3.35 The triangle always lets you know by which column your list is sorted.

WORKING WITH GROUPS

Don't underestimate the power of groups

Many ACT! users never fully tap the potential power and convenience of groups in their databases. You can create groups for every conceivable purpose. Here are some possibilities:

- Create groups for different mailings that need to be sent out. Some contacts might receive all mailings, some might not want to receive any, and some will get only holiday cards, while others might subscribe to a newsletter.

- Create groups for the different relationship levels that occur in business. You might have groups of your top ten customers, your hottest prospects, and those "problem" customers who require special attention.

- Create groups to separate contacts in different industries or aspects of business. For example, you could have groups for all contacts in the computer, banking/finance, marketing, manufacturing, and media industries. This way you could pass along interesting news and possible opportunities to the kinds of contacts who would benefit most from that knowledge.

One of the many great features of ACT! is the ability it gives you to create and use permanent groups of contact records. Groups allow you to create and save custom subsets of your contact records. By placing certain records in a group, you can easily select just those records when you need to. You can then print reports for all the records in the group, send form letters or mass faxes to group members, and even create fields to store data that is specific to that group.

ACT! also enables you to write group notes, record group history entries, and even schedule group activities.

Creating groups

Before you can add a contact to a group or schedule any group activities, you must first create the group. Creating groups is a fairly easy process and is done from the Groups window.

To create a group

1. Click on the **View Groups** icon in the lower-right corner of the display (**Figure 4.1**). This will bring up the Groups window (**Figure 4.2**). This window is divided into three parts. On the left is a list of all existing groups. To the right of that are the name and description of the currently selected group, and below that are the group fields.

2. Click on the **New Group** button on the toolbar at the top of the display (**Figure 4.3**).

3. Type the new group name, replacing the selected text "Untitled" in the Group Name text box.

4. Hit the **Tab** key and type in a description for the group.

5. To return to the Contact window, click on the **View Contacts** button (**Figure 4.4**).

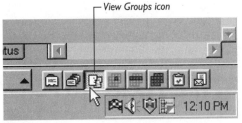

Figure 4.1 Click the View Groups icon to open the Groups window.

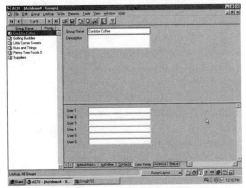

Figure 4.2 All the work that you do with groups will be done within this Groups window.

Figure 4.3 Click this button to create a new group.

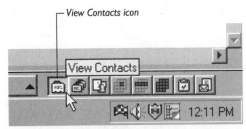

Figure 4.4 The View Contacts icon takes you back to the default (Contacts) window.

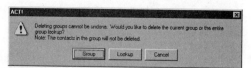

Figure 4.5 What exactly do you want to delete?

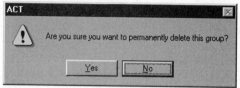

Figure 4.6 Are you sure you want to delete the group?

Deleting groups

Whether a group has outlived its usefulness or you simply made a mistake when creating the group, there will be times when you will need to delete groups. Deleting groups only deletes the group as an organizational entity; the members of the group (that is, your individual contact records) are not affected at all.

To delete a group

1. Click on the **View Groups** icon in the lower-right corner of the display.

2. In the group list on the left side of the display, click on the group you want to delete.

3. From the Group menu, select the **Delete Group** command.

4. In the warning dialog box that appears (**Figure 4.5**), click on the **Group** button.
   Clicking the Lookup button would delete all of the *contacts* in the group, so be careful!

5. In the next warning dialog box (**Figure 4.6**), click the **Yes** button.
   The group (but not the contact records belonging to that group) is permanently removed from your database.

✔ Tip

- Instead of selecting Delete Group from the Group menu, you can use the Ctrl-Delete keyboard shortcut.

DELETING GROUPS

Adding contacts to groups

While creating and removing groups provides hours of fun, groups are much more useful if they contain contacts. Contacts can only be added to groups from within the Groups window. Note that a particular contact can be a member of any number of groups.

To add a contact to a group

1. Click on the **View Groups** icon in the lower-right corner of the display.

2. Select the group to which you want to add the contact from the list on the left side of the display.

3. Click on the **Group Membership** button (**Figure 4.7**).

   This brings up the Group Membership dialog box (**Figure 4.8**).

4. In the upper-left corner of the Group Membership dialog box, choose whether you want to select contacts from **All Contacts**, the **Current Lookup**, or a **Selected Group**.

   This determines which contacts are displayed in the contact list in the lower-left corner of the dialog box. If you choose the Selected Group option, a drop-down list of existing groups will become active. You can then select the group from which you want to view contacts.

5. Click on the desired contact from the list in the lower-left corner of the dialog box.

6. Click on the **Add** button.

Add/Remove Contacts button

Figure 4.7 Click this button if you want to add contacts to or remove contacts from a group.

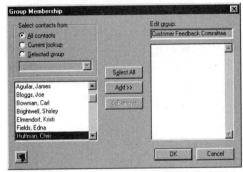

Figure 4.8 All group membership changes are made from this dialog box.

✔ Tip

■ The absolute best way to add a large number of contacts to a group is to select all desired contacts by performing a lookup *before* bringing up the Groups window. If you do this, you can simply select the Current Lookup option in the Group Membership dialog box and click on the Select All button; a single click of the Add button will then add all the contacts in the lookup to the group.

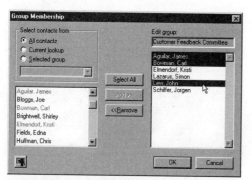

Figure 4.9 Select group members to be removed from the list of current group members on the right side of the dialog box.

Remove button ⌐

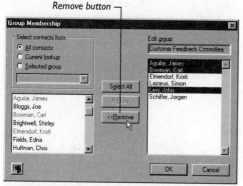

Figure 4.10 Click the Remove button to remove the selected contact(s) from the group.

Removing contacts from groups

The flip side of adding a contact to a group is, of course, removing that contact from the group. Removing a contact from a group does not affect the contact record itself in any way. In order to remove a contact from a group, you must access the Group Membership screen, which is located in the Groups view.

To remove a contact from a group

1. Click on the **View Groups** icon in the lower-right corner of the display.

2. From the list on the left side of the display, select the group from which you want to remove the contact.

3. Click on the **Group Membership** button. This brings up the Group Membership dialog box.

4. From the list on the right side of the Group Membership dialog box, select the contact or contacts that you want to remove from the group (**Figure 4.9**).

5. Click on the **Remove** button (**Figure 4.10**).

✔ Tip

■ You can hold down the Shift or Control keys while clicking to select multiple contacts. When you click the Remove button, all the selected contacts will be removed at once.

Viewing group information

The Groups window, like the Contacts window, has a set of view tabs along the bottom of the display. These tabs work in much the same fashion as the view tabs in the Contacts window.

To view group information

1. From the list on the left side of the Groups window, select the group whose information you want to view.

2. Click on the **Notes/History** tab to see all notes, history entries, and attached files for the group.

3. Click on the **Activities** tab to see all scheduled meetings, phone calls, and to-do activities for the group.

4. Click on the **Contacts** tab to see the name, company, phone number, and title information for all contacts in the group (**Figure 4.11**).

5. Click on the **User Fields** tab to see any information you have entered in any of the available group user fields.

6. Click on the **Address** tab to see or change the address information for the group itself (**Figure 4.12**).

7. Click on the **Status** tab to see or change group status information (**Figure 4.13**).

Figure 4.11 The Contacts view shows information about the contacts in the selected group.

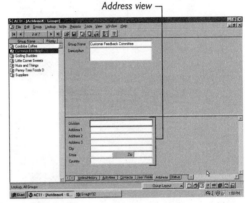

Figure 4.12 The Address view contains group address information.

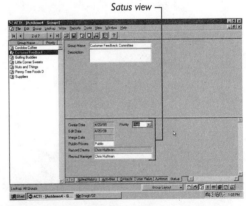

Figure 4.13 The Status view contains group status information.

Figure 4.14 Files can be attached to group records in the same way that they are attached to contact records.

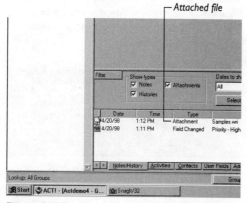

Figure 4.15 The Notes/History view with the attached file listed.

Attaching files to groups

Files can be attached to group records just as they can be attached to contact records. You attach files to groups for the same reason you attach them to contact records: You need to access information that doesn't fit into any of the group user fields.

To attach a file to a group

1. Click on the View Groups icon in the lower-right corner of the display.

2. From the list on the left side of the display, select the group to which you want to attach the file.

3. From the Group menu, select the Attach File command (Figure 4.14).

4. Navigate through the resulting standard Open File dialog box to locate the desired data file.

5. Select the desired file and click the OK button, or simply double-click the desired file.

   The attached file(s) will appear in the Notes/History view (Figure 4.15).

Removing attached files

Once an attached file is no longer needed, you can removed it from the group's Notes/History listing.

To remove an attached file from a group

1. Click on the **View Groups** icon in the lower-right corner of the display.

2. From the list on the left side of the display, select the group from which you want to remove the attached file.

3. Click on the **Notes/History** tab located at the bottom of the display (**Figure 4.16**).

4. Click on the gray box to the left of the attached file you want to remove.

5. Hit the **Delete** key.

6. At the resulting warning dialog box (**Figure 4.17**), click the **Yes** button.

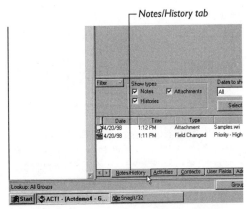

Notes/History tab

Figure 4.16 Click here to view the notes, history entries, and attached files for the group.

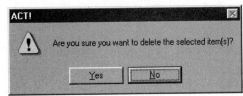

Figure 4.17 Last chance to change your mind...

REMOVING ATTACHED FILES

View/Add Notes button

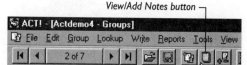

Figure 4.18 Click this button each time you want to add a note.

Note text

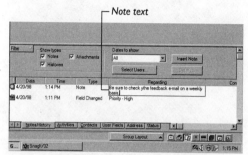

Figure 4.19 Your text is stored here for later viewing and editing.

Adding group notes

Just as you need to keep track of all sorts of miscellaneous bits of data about individual contacts, you will also need to do so for your groups. You can easily add notes to any group in the same way you add them to contact records.

To add a note to a group record

1. Click on the **View Groups** icon in the lower-right corner of the display.

2. From the list on the left side of the display, select the group for which you want to add the note.

3. Click on the **Insert Note** button (**Figure 4.18**).

   ACT! will open the Notes/History view for the selected group. Your new note will be created and selected.

4. Type your information in the Regarding column for the note (**Figure 4.19**).

   Your text will wrap within the Regarding column to as many lines as you need.

Editing group notes or history

Once created, contact notes can easily be edited to ensure that the information is always accurate and up to date. Likewise, history entries can be edited to remove or correct erroneous information.

To edit a group note or history entry

1. Click on the **View Groups** icon in the lower-right corner of the display.

2. From the list on the left side of the display, select the group for which you want to edit the note.

3. Click on the **Notes/History** tab in the lower-right portion of the Groups window.

4. Edit the text in the Regarding column as you would text in any word processor (**Figure 4.20**).

✔ Tip

■ There is no need to save your changes when you are done editing a note. Simply move on to another contact record and your changes are automatically saved to disk.

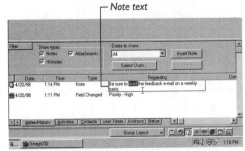

Figure 4.20 Use regular text-editing techniques to correct, add, or delete text in the note.

EDITING GROUP NOTES OR HISTORY

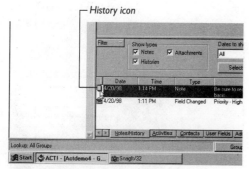

History icon

Figure 4.21 You must click the note or history icon itself to select the entire note or history entry.

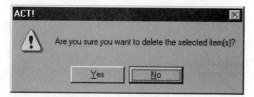

Figure 4.22 Deleted entries cannot be retrieved, so be sure of what you're doing before you click this Yes button.

Removing group notes or history

Group notes and group history entries can be removed from the listing when they are incorrect or no longer needed. For instance, it is possible that you might accidentally associate a note of a phone call you received with an entire group of 500 contacts, instead of with just one contact. In your next activity report, it would then appear that you had a much busier day than you actually did. This would be a perfect time to go in and delete the other 499 history entries.

To remove a note or history entry from a group

1. Click on the **View Groups** icon in the lower-right corner of the display.

2. From the list on the left side of the display, select the group for which you want to remove the note.

3. Click on the **Notes/History** tab in the lower-right portion of the Groups window.

4. Click on the entry icon at the far-left edge of the note or history entry (to the left of the date) (**Figure 4.21**).

   This selects the entire note or history entry as a single object.

5. Press the **Delete** key.

6. At the warning dialog box (**Figure 4.22**), click the **Yes** button.

   The selected entry is permanently removed from the group record.

REMOVING GROUP NOTES OR HISTORY

Renaming group fields

The six user fields in the User Fields tab can all be renamed to reflect the data that you want to store in them.

To rename a group field

1. Click on the **View Groups** icon in the lower-right corner of the display.

2. From the list on the left side of the display, select the group for which you want to rename the field.

3. If necessary, click on the **User Fields** tab at the bottom of the display to make the user fields visible (**Figure 4.23**).

4. Click in the field you want to rename.

5. From the Edit menu, select the **Define Fields** command.

6. Select the text in the **Field Name** box (**Figure 4.24**).

7. Type the desired new name for the field and click the **OK** button.

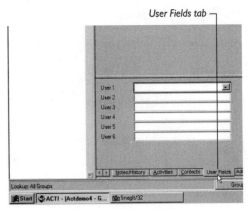

User Fields tab

Figure 4.23 Click the User Fields tab to view your group fields.

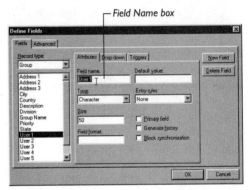

Field Name box

Figure 4.24 Type the new name for the selected field into the Field Name box.

LOOKUPS AND QUERIES

One of the many advantages of storing your contact data in ACT! is the ease with which you can sort and retrieve your data. This chapter focuses on three vital ACT! skills: sorting records, performing lookups, and creating advanced queries.

Sorting records

Sorting your records has the obvious benefit of making it easier to locate a particular record or group of records as you browse your database. Sort requests can be either simple single-level sorts or multi-level sorts (which are still pretty simple). A *single-level sort* is a sort that is based on just one field, such as a sort of all records by company name. A *multi-level sort* involves up to three different fields, such as a sort by state, then by city, then by company name.

ACT! provides two ways to sort your records. One is a shortcut using lookups that is called a "quicksort." The other uses a traditional sort command and dialog box.

To perform a quicksort with a lookup

1. From the Lookup menu, select the field that you want to sort by (Company, First Name, Last Name, Phone, City, State, Zip Code, ID/Status) (**Figure 5.1**).

2. Do *not* enter any information in the Lookup dialog box.

3. Click the **OK** button.

   ACT! automatically sorts all found records whenever a lookup is performed. By specifying no search criteria, you ensure that all records will be found, and ACT! will perform a quick multi-level sort on the records.

To perform a standard sort

1. From the Edit menu, select the **Sort** command.

2. In the resulting Sort Contacts dialog box (**Figure 5.2**), select the field that you want to sort by from the first drop-down list (the one labeled "Sort Contacts by").

3. If necessary, click on either the **Ascending**

Figure 5.1 Select any field from the Lookup menu for a quicksort.

Figure 5.2 You can sort your contacts by up to three different fields.

New terms you should know...

Sort: A temporary reordering of your contact records. Sorts are most useful to help locate a particular record or to put your records in a certain order for printing.

Lookup: A temporary selection of records that match specified criteria. Lookups are also useful when you're locating or printing records.

Query: An advanced form of lookup. Unlike lookups and sorts, queries can be saved to disk and reused.

Descending sort option ¬

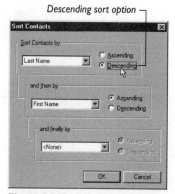

Figure 5.3 The default sort order is ascending, but it can be changed.

or the **Descending** option (**Figure 5.3**) to change the direction of the sort (ascending is 0–9, a–z; descending is z–a, 9–0).

4. If you want to further refine the sort, select a second sort field from the second drop-down list (the one labeled "and then by").

5. Select the Ascending or Descending option for the second sort field, if necessary.

6. Finally, if you want to refine the sort still further, select a third field from the third drop-down list (the one labeled "and finally by").

7. Again, select the Ascending or Descending option for the third field, if you have used a third field.

8. Click the **OK** button.

Quicksort default sort orders

Whenever you use a lookup to perform a quicksort of your records, ACT! uses a predefined field hierarchy to determine the sort order. This hierarchy is as follows:

- **Lookup by Company**: Company, Last Name, First Name

- **Lookup by First Name**: First Name, Last Name, Company

- **Lookup by Last Name**: Last Name, First Name, Company

- **Lookup by Phone**: Phone Number, Last Name

- **Lookup by City**: City, Company, Last Name

- **Lookup by State**: State, City, Company

- **Lookup by Zip Code**: Zip Code, City, Company

- **Lookup by ID/Status**: ID/Status, Company, Last Name

SORTING RECORDS

Lookup basics

The whole point of using ACT! lookups and queries is to work with a subset of your contact records. While the lookup itself can't be saved, the subset of records created by the lookup can be saved (as a group) for later use, printed in any number of report formats, used for the generation of bulk mailings or broadcast faxes, and so on.

Your ACT! database has three levels. The first level is the database itself. This level obviously includes all the records in your database. The second level is the current group that you are looking at (as discussed in the previous chapter). When you are viewing a group of records you will almost certainly be looking at some sort of subset of your entire database. The third level is the current lookup that you have defined. A lookup is a subset of records from the *current group* only, *not* from the entire database.

By default, the current lookup will be All Contacts, as shown in the status bar (**Figure 5.4**). After you perform a lookup of your own, this will change to reflect the current lookup criteria (City, State, ID/Status, Custom, etc.).

✔ Tips

- Make sure that you are aware of what group of records you are working in. Select the No Group option from the group pop-up menu (**Figure 5.5**) to work with your entire database before performing a lookup.

- If you can't find a record that you want, make sure that you aren't still in a lookup you no longer need to be in. If the lookup indicator doesn't show "All Records," select the All Records command from the Lookup menu.

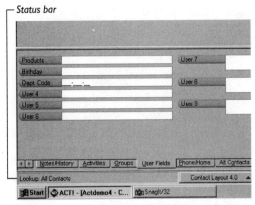

Status bar

Figure 5.4 The status bar displays the current lookup criteria field, if any.

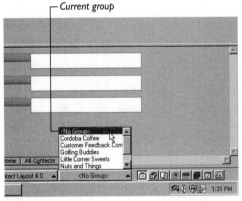

Current group

Figure 5.5 Only the current group is searched when you perform a lookup.

LOOKUP BASICS

Using quick lookups

ACT! offers three predefined lookups that can be performed in an instant with no input from you. These lookups let you jump to "My Record," remove any existing lookup criteria (to view all records again), or return to the last set of records you looked up. Because no input is required, these lookups are as easy as can be.

To locate "My Record"

1. From the Lookup menu, select the My Record command.

   Told you it was easy.

To view all records

1. From the Lookup menu, select the All Records command.

   This will remove all lookup criteria, allowing you to once again view all of the records in your database or group.

To return to the previous lookup

1. From the Lookup menu, select the Previous command (it's about two-thirds of the way down the menu).

   This changes the current lookup to whatever criteria you specified in to your last lookup. If you have not done a lookup since opening the database, the Previous command will be dimmed and unavailable.

✔ Tip

- Remember, if you are using a multiuser database, the "My Record" data will reflect the current user, as determined by the log-in name and password entered when the database was first opened. To view or change the data for another user, you will need to reopen the database and log in as that user.

Performing a simple lookup

The most common lookups that you will perform will be simple lookups based on a contact's name, company, city, etc. These are considered simple lookups because you are searching your database for information in a single field at a time, and because you are accessing the search field by simply selecting it from the Lookup menu.

To perform a simple lookup

1. From the Lookup menu, select the field that you want to use as the basis for your search.

   The available fields are Company, First Name, Last Name, Phone, City, State, Zip Code, and ID/Status.

2. Enter the information that you want to find in the resulting Lookup dialog box (**Figure 5.6**).

3. Click the **OK** button and ACT! will search your database for the information you entered.

✔ Tip

■ When looking up records by phone number, you must always include the area code. Thus, if you wanted to find all of your contacts whose phone numbers have a certain prefix, you would have to search for the area code and prefix, such as "714838" for the 714 area code and 838 prefix.

Figure 5.6 The Lookup dialog box with criteria entered to find all California contacts.

PERFORMING A SIMPLE LOOKUP

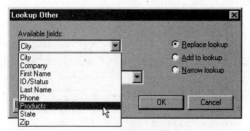

Figure 5.7 Use this dialog box to perform a lookup using indexed fields not listed in the Lookup menu.

Using indexed fields in a lookup

An *indexed field* is a field that ACT! uses to sort and track information about your contacts. By default, the indexed fields are just the fields listed in the Lookup menu. If you have created your own indexed fields (as discussed in Chapter 13, *Productivity Power Tools*), you can use them for fast lookups as well.

To perform a lookup using other indexed fields

1. From the Lookup menu, select the **Other Fields** command.

2. Select the desired field from the list of available fields in the Lookup Other dialog box (**Figure 5.7**).

3. Type the data you wish to find in the To Be Found text box.

   If the selected field has a drop-down list associated with it, you can also select the desired data from the same drop-down list in the Lookup Other dialog box.

4. Click the **OK** button.

Narrowing lookups

Simple lookups can help you to locate a sub-set of contact records, but you will often need to specify further data to focus your lookup on just the records you want to view. You can do this by performing an additional lookup and instructing ACT! to *narrow* the lookup, excluding all records that don't match the new criteria as well as the old criteria.

A good example of this is when you want to find all prospective clients (whose ID/Status will be "prospect") in a certain state.

To narrow a lookup

1. Perform any simple lookup to select contacts based on your first set of criteria. Now you are ready to further focus your lookup.

2. From the Lookup menu, select the second field that you want to search for information in.

3. Enter the information that you want to find in the resulting Lookup dialog box.

4. Select the **Narrow Lookup** option (**Figure 5.8**).

5. Click the **OK** button.

6. If desired, perform additional lookups with other fields, each time selecting the Narrow Lookup option to further focus your selection of records.

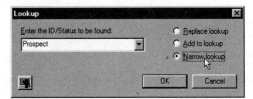

Figure 5.8 Each time you narrow a lookup, fewer records will be found.

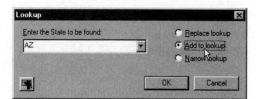

Figure 5.9 When you expand a lookup, more records will be found.

Expanding lookups

Just as you will sometimes need to focus your lookups to reduce the number of records you work with, you may also need to expand your lookups to include additional records. Expanding lookups lets you find contacts who meet any one of several specified search criteria. For example, you may need to work with all contacts from two or three different states or from several cities that you will be visiting.

To expand a lookup

1. Perform any simple lookup to select contacts based on your first set of criteria.

   You can now expand your lookup to include additional records.

2. From the Lookup menu, select the field for which you want to specify additional data.

   When expanding a lookup, you can enter data from another field or you can just enter a different value for the same field.

3. Enter the information that you want to find in the resulting Lookup dialog box.

4. Select the **Add to Lookup** option (**Figure 5.9**).

5. Click the **OK** button.

6. If desired, perform additional lookups with other fields, each time selecting the Add to Lookup option to further expand your selection of records.

Performing keyword lookups

If you need to search for a contact record based on data that is either in an unknown field or in a note or history entry, you can search for that record using a keyword lookup. A *keyword lookup* searches entire contact records for the specified information, rather than just a single field. Keyword lookups take longer than regular lookups, since ACT! has to read much more data when searching for your criteria, but often a keyword lookup will find a record when nothing else will.

Keyword lookups are ideal for when you want to find information that's part of a note, when you are looking for all records with whom you have scheduled a certain type of activity, or when you want to find all records that have a particular history entry.

To perform a keyword lookup

1. From the Lookup menu, select the **Keyword** command.

2. Enter the desired search string in the Look For text box at the top of the Lookup Keyword dialog box (**Figure 5.10**).

3. In the Look In section, choose whether you want ACT! to search **Contacts**, **Groups**, or both.

   The Groups option will only be available if you are in the Groups view.

4. If you want ACT! to search in your **Activities**, **Notes/History** entries, or **E-mail Addresses**, click on the desired option to select it.

5. Click the **OK** button.

   If you have a large database and have selected any of the options in step 4, your search may take a while.

Figure 5.10. Use the Lookup Keyword dialog box to search for any text string anywhere in a contact record.

PERFORMING KEYWORD LOOKUPS

Figure 5.11 You can use the asterisk character at the beginning of your search text, at the end, or at both the beginning and the end.

Using wildcards in keyword lookups

You can use the asterisk (*) wildcard character in keyword searches to represent any number of unknown or unspecified characters. The * wildcard can be used anywhere in a string of text.

An * at the beginning of a text string is used to search for all words that end with the typed characters. For example, "*ware" would find "software," "shareware," "freeware," and "courseware."

An * at the end of a text string is used to locate all words that begin with the typed characters. For example, "mic*" would find "microphone," "Michael," and "MicroSports."

An * at both the beginning and end of a text string will find any word that contains the specified characters anywhere within it. Thus, "*sal*" would find "salary," "resale," "universal," and "unsalted."

To perform a keyword lookup using wildcards

1. From the Lookup menu, select the **Keyword** command.

2. Enter the desired search string in the Look For text box at the top of the Lookup Keyword dialog box, using asterisks in place of any unknown characters (**Figure 5.11**).

3. In the Look In section, choose whether you want ACT! to search **Contacts, Groups**, or both.

4. If you want ACT! to search in your **Activities, Notes/History** entries, or **E-mail Addresses**, click on the desired option to select it.

5. Click the **OK** button.

Modifying a lookup with the Contact List

Lookups will always select all records that match the criteria you specify, but you may not always want to work with all of the records that ACT! finds. If, for example, you have a couple of clients who have specifically requested that they not receive any mailings, you would want to remove them from the lookup before printing labels or envelopes. Another scenario that presents itself from time to time is that a few of your clients have out-of-state addresses even though they do business in your home state. You'll probably want to include these clients whenever you send out mailings to all in-state clients. The easiest way to remove records from or add records to an otherwise acceptable lookup is with the Contact List.

You can also use the Contact List to create a lookup of records that have no logical relationship, but that you wish to work with as a group. It's impossible to create a collection of records that have no fields in common with the standard lookups, but you can easily do so with the Contact List.

To remove records from a lookup with the Contact List

1. Perform a lookup using single or multiple criteria and/or keywords.

2. Click on the **Contact List** icon near the lower-right corner of the display.

3. Select Tag Mode from the drop-down list in the upper-right corner of the display (**Figure 5.12**).
   The Tag mode is used to select or deselect records in a lookup.

4. Click in the empty space at the far left of any record entry that you do not want in the lookup.

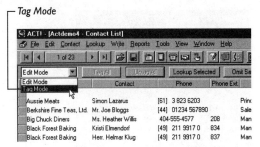

Tag Mode

Figure 5.12 Tag Mode lets you remove or add ("tag") individual contacts from a lookup.

"Tagged" record

Figure 5.13 Plus signs indicate "tagged" records, which are part of the current lookup.

Omit Tagged button

Figure 5.14 Use the Omit Tagged button to remove unwanted contacts from a lookup.

Plus signs (+) appear next to the records, indicating that they are tagged (**Figure 5.13**).

5. Click on the Omit Tagged button (**Figure 5.14**).

   All tagged records are removed from the current lookup.

6. Click on the Contact View icon to return to the normal Contact view.

To create a custom lookup with the Contact List

1. Make sure that all records that you will want to work with are part of the current lookup.

   This may be a matter of performing a very broad lookup or simply looking up all records.

2. Click on the Contact List icon.

3. If necessary, select Tag Mode from the drop-down list.

   You may also need to use the Untag All or Tag All buttons if you have a previously tagged records in the list.

4. Tag or untag records by clicking in the far-left column next to each record that you want to add or remove from the lookup.

5. Click on the Lookup Tagged or Omit Tagged button, depending on how you've tagged your records.

6. Click on the Contact View icon to return to the normal contact view.

Saving lookup records

Because so much work goes into creating a lookup, and because it's so useful to be able to go back to a successfully defined subset of records, it is important to save your lookups for later use. While the lookup itself can't really be saved, you can effectively save a lookup by creating a group of all records in the lookup.

To save a lookup as a group

1. Perform the lookup to select the records you want to work with.

2. Click on the View Groups icon (**Figure 5.15**) in the lower-right corner of the display.

3. Click on the New Group button in the toolbar (**Figure 5.16**).

4. Enter a group name and description that reflects the current lookup.

5. Click on the Group Membership button (**Figure 5.17**).

6. Click on the Current Lookup option in the upper-left corner of the Group Membership dialog box.

7. Click on the Select All button.

8. Click on the Add button.

9. Click on the OK button.

10. Click the View Contacts icon to return to the normal Contacts view.

    Once created, this group will be available from the Groups pop-up list at the bottom of the display.

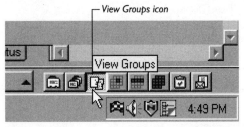

Figure 5.15 You must go to the Group view to save a lookup as a group.

Figure 5.16 As you might guess, the New Group button creates a new group.

Figure 5.17 Contacts can only be added to a group with this Group Membership button.

SAVING LOOKUP RECORDS

Figure 5.18 The Query window is basically a blank record where you enter search criteria.

Run button ─┐

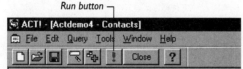

Figure 5.19 Click the Run button to search for all records meeting the specified criteria.

┌─ *Clear Query button*

Figure 5.20 To start over, click the Clear Query button.

✔ Tips

■ To clear all criteria and start fresh, simply click on the Clear Query button (**Figure 5.20**) in the toolbar. This will remove all data from all fields.

■ If you want to search for more than one value in the same field, separate the values with two vertical lines, like this: CA | | AZ. This will find all contacts in California or Arizona.

■ You can specify a range of values by typing two dots between the low and high values in the range, like this: 1/1/95..12/31/95. This will find all dates for the entire year of 1995.

Using Queries

If you need to create a very specific lookup using criteria from several fields, the fastest way to do so is with a custom multi-field lookup, also called a *query*. Not only is a query faster than narrowing a standard lookup, it also enables you to search for data in non-standard fields such as the user fields. A query is also the answer if you need to search for multiple criteria in multiple fields or for ranges of values.

To create a query

1. From the Lookup menu, select the **By Example** command.

   ACT! opens up a window with all database fields available for you to enter data into (**Figure 5.18**).

2. Click in the first field in which you want to search for data.

3. Enter the desired search text.

4. If you want to use additional fields, enter the desired search text in those fields as well. Only those records that match *all* criteria will be found.

5. Click on the **Run** button in the toolbar (**Figure 5.19**)—it looks like a green exclamation point.

   Once you run it, you can use the results of your query just as you would with a lookup.

Saving queries

Creating queries can be a lot of work, especially if they use multiple criteria or if you create advanced queries (Discussed later in this chapter). Once you've created and edited your queries, you will undoubtedly want to save some of them to disk for later use.

To save a query

1. In the Query window (which is where you should be after you have created and edited your query), select the **Save As** command from the File menu.

2. Enter a name for your query in the resulting Save As dialog box (**Figure 5.21**).

   Note that all queries are automatically placed in the Query folder within the Act folder on your hard drive.

3. Click the **OK** button.

To open a query

1. From the main ACT! display (in either the Contact view or Group view), select the **By Example** command from the Lookup menu.

   This takes you to the Query window.

2. From the File menu, select the **Open** command.

3. Select the query you want to open and click the **OK** button.

   ACT! will open the selected query in the Advanced Query window. From here you can run the query (using the Run button) or edit the query.

Figure 5.21 Queries are saved using standard Save As dialog boxes.

SAVING QUERIES

Figure 5.22 The Lookup menu modified to show saved queries

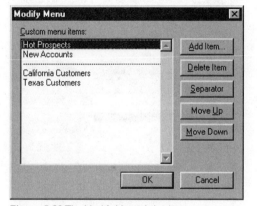

Figure 5.23 The Modify Menu dialog box

Locate/Select Saved Quries button

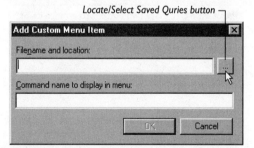

Figure 5.24 Oddly, this button is not clearly labeled. It is used, however, to locate and select saved queries

Modifying the Lookup menu

Because of the extremely useful nature of queries and the frequency with which you may need to run queries during the course of a typical ACT! session, it is often very useful to add queries to the Lookup menu (**Figure 5.22**).

In order for a query to be added to the menu, it must first have been converted to an advanced query and saved to disk, as discussed earlier in this chapter.

Once added to the menu, queries can be arranged and removed as needed.

To add a query to the Lookup menu

1. From the Lookup menu, select the **Modify Menu** command (it's at the bottom of the menu).

2. In the Modify Menu dialog box (**Figure 5.23**), click on the **Add Item** button.

3. In the Add Custom Menu Item dialog box, click on the button with the ellipses (the three dots) on it (**Figure 5.24**).

   This will give you a standard Open dialog box displaying the contents of the Query folder.

4. Select the query you want to add and click the **Open** button.

5. Enter a name for this query in the "Command name to display in menu" text entry box.

6. Click the **OK** button.

To remove a query from the Lookup menu

1. From the Lookup menu, select the **Modify Menu** command.

2. In the Modify Menu dialog box, select the query that you no longer want.

3. Click on the **Delete Item** button (**Figure 5.25**).

4. Click the **OK** button.

To rearrange the Lookup menu

1. From the Lookup menu, select the **Modify Menu** command.

2. Select the item that you want to move.

3. Click on either the **Move Up** button or the **Move Down** button (**Figure 5.26**) to reposition the item in the menu.

4. If you want to add a separator line in the menu, click on the **Separator** button.

The separator line does nothing but let you group different queries together to make it easier for you to find what you want.

5. If necessary, select the separator line and use the **Move Up, Move Down,** and **Delete Item** buttons to move or remove the separator line.

Delete Item button —

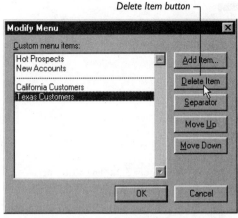

Figure 5.25 Delete unwanted items with this button.

Move Down button —

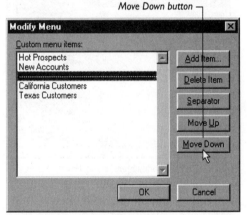

Figure 5.26 Use these two buttons to arrange items within the Lookup menu.

MODIFYING THE LOOKUP MENU

Understanding operators

A *logical operator* is a symbol that helps to define the relationship between specified criteria and the field to be searched. ACT! supports the following operators:

=	Equal to
<>	Not equal to
<	Less than
<=	Less than or equal to
>	Greater than
>=	Greater than or equal to
*	Unknown characters
..	Between

Ship Date = 10/1/96..10/31/96 or State = "CA" are examples of criteria using logical operators.

ACT! also lets you use Boolean operators to define the relationships between multiple fields or multiple criteria within the same field. ACT! supports the following Boolean operators:

AND	Conditions 1 and 2 are both true
&&	Another form of AND
OR	Either condition 1 or condition 2 is true
||	Another form of OR
AND_NOT	Condition 1 is true and condition 2 is false
OR_NOT	Condition 1 is true or condition 2 is false

ID/Status = "Client" AND Sales > 10000 and State = "CA" AND_NOT City = "Los Angeles" are examples of criteria using Boolean operators.

Creating advanced queries

ACT! has the capability to perform much more powerful and complex lookups through the use of advanced queries. An *advanced query* is a set of detailed instructions on exactly what criteria must be met in order for a record to be included in a lookup. With advanced queries, criteria can be specified using a set of programming-like syntax. This syntax allows for very complex instructions such as logical operators like greater than or less than, number or date ranges, Boolean operators such as AND, OR, and NOT (to find all California clients not in Los Angeles or San Francisco, for example), and fields that either are empty or contain any value at all. These queries can be relatively simple or as detailed and complex as you wish. They are most easily created by starting with a custom lookup and converting that lookup to an advanced query.

To create an advanced query

1. From the Lookup menu, select the **By Example** command.

2. Enter as many of your desired criteria as you can into the appropriate fields.

   Remember that you can use the || logical operator to specify multiple entries in the same field. For example, specifying "Prospect || Customer" in the ID/Status field would find all prospects or customers.

3. Click on the **Convert Query** button in the toolbar (**Figure 5.27**).

   Your custom lookup is converted into a text-based advanced query. In this new Query window you have a text document and a Query Helper dialog box (**Figure 5.28**). This advanced query can be run as is, or can be expanded, edited, and saved, as discussed on the following pages.

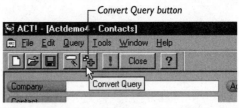

Convert Query button

Figure 5.27 Click this button to convert your simple queries into editable advanced queries.

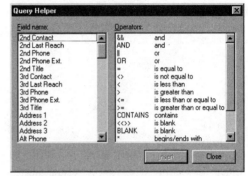

Figure 5.28 The Advanced Query window contains the text-based query instructions and the Query Helper dialog box.

Operators list ⌐ ┌ Insert button

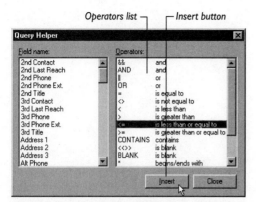

Figure 5.29 Insert fields and operators from the Query Helper dialog box to save typing time and avoid possible typos.

Editing advanced queries

You can edit advanced queries to create exactly the search criteria that you are looking for. ACT! makes editing advanced queries a little easier with the Query Helper dialog box, but the process is still a very exacting one, demanding patience, accuracy, and planning. To avoid frustration as much as possible, keep a couple things in mind:

First, syntax is everything. All instructions must be written *exactly* the way that ACT! expects them to appear. Pay special attention to the parenthetical notation used by ACT!. ACT! places double parentheses (with a space between them) around all criteria. This helps ACT! keep track of the order of operations when analyzing field content.

Second, once you have converted your query to an advanced query, most of the changes you will need to make will be simple ones such as changing logical operators or criteria. By using the Query Helper dialog box to insert field names and operators, you can protect yourself from possible typographical errors.

To edit an advanced query

1. Create or open an advanced query.

2. Select any incorrect operators in the advanced query text.

3. Select the correct operator from the list of operators in the Query Helper dialog box and click the **Insert** button (**Figure 5.29**). You can also just double-click on the desired operator.

4. Select any incorrect field names in the advanced query text.

5. Select the correct field name from the list of fields in the Query Helper dialog box and click the **Insert** button (or just double-click the field name).

6. Select any incorrect criteria and type in the new criteria to replace them.

7. Save the query (just in case), then click the **Run** button to test it.

8. If the query still isn't working the way you want it to, reopen the query, make any necessary changes, and run it again. Unfortunately, ACT! closes the query before actually finding the records, so you have to reopen the query every time you want to edit it.

✔ Tips

- The easiest way to avoid having to make a lot of changes to an advanced query is to enter as much information as possible in the fields of the Query window before converting the query to an advanced query.

- If you do need to make large changes in an advanced query, copy and paste as much information as possible to avoid typos and other user errors.

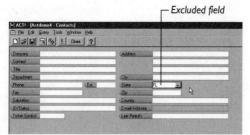

Excluded field

Figure 5.30 Enter the value you want to exclude.

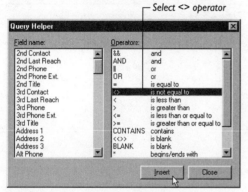

Select <> operator

Figure 5.31 The <>operator means "not equal to."

Excluding values in advanced queries

From time to time you will want to find records based not on what is in a field, but on what is not in the field. It is easier, for example, to search for all records that are not in the state of Florida than it is to search for all records in the other 49 states.

To exclude certain values

1. From the Lookup menu, select the **By Example** command.

2. Enter the value you do not want to find in the appropriate field.

    For the example used at the beginning of this page, we would enter **FL** in the State field (**Figure 5.30**).

3. Click on the **Convert Query** button.

4. Select the = logical operator in the advanced query text.

5. Select the <> operator from the list in the Query Helper dialog box and click on the Insert button (**Figure 5.31**).

    You could also double-click on the <> operator, or simply type it in.

    In the example we've used, the text would look like this:

    (("State" <> "FL"*))

    Your query will now find all records that do not contain the specified value.

Searching for blank fields

In addition to looking for certain values (or excluding those values), you can look for either all records where a particular field is empty or all the records where a particular field is not empty.

To find empty or non-empty fields

1. From the Lookup menu, select the **By Example** command.

2. Enter some text into the field you want to search for blanks or non-blanks.

   This is just placeholder text, so you could just type **abc** or anything at all.

3. Click on the **Convert Query** button.

4. Select the data you entered, including the quotation marks and the asterisk.

   For example, if you typed **abc**, you would need to select **"abc"***.

5. To search for all records where the specified field contains no data, select and insert the BLANK operator from the list in the Query Helper dialog box (**Figure 5.32**).

   The text should now look like this:

   (("Sample Field" = BLANK))

   This will locate all records where the field you specified is empty.

6. If you want to search for all records where the specified field does contain data, select the = operator in the query text and replace it with the NOT operator.

   The text should now look like this:

   (("Sample Field" NOT BLANK))

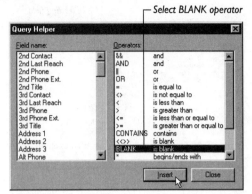

Select BLANK operator

Figure 5.32 Pretty self-explanatory; the BLANK operator finds records with no data in the specified field.

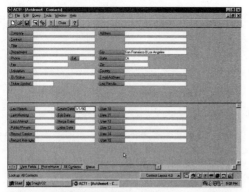

Figure 5.33 Almost all of the work is done in the standard Query window.

Figure 5.34 The finished advanced query, ready to be saved and tested

Using complex criteria in advanced queries

The real power of advanced queries comes into play when you start creating complex criteria. Complex criteria is any criteria that includes several fields, multiple criteria in a single field, or multiple Boolean operators. We will use an example exercise here to illustrate a typical process.

Your mission, should you choose to accept it, is to locate the records of all *customers* in *California* who are not in either of the major metropolitan areas (*San Francisco* and *Los Angeles*) and with whom we have been working with since 1990.

To create a complex set of criteria in an advanced query

1. From the Lookup menu, select the **By Example** command.

2. Enter as much information as possible into the appropriate fields.

    We would enter **CA** in State, **San Francisco && Los Angeles** in City, **Customer** in ID/Status, and **1/1/90** in Create Date (located on the Status tab) (**Figure 5.33**).

3. Click on the **Convert Query** button in the toolbar.

    Most of the work is done for us in the Advanced Query window. We just need to make a couple of minor adjustments.

4. Select and change any invalid operators.

    Since we specifically want to exclude San Francisco and Los Angeles customers, we need to change the = operators to <> operators.

    For the Create Date criterion, we also need to change the = operator to a >= operator.

5. Check your text for any typos, missing parentheses, or other problems (**Figure 5.34**).

ACTIVITIES AND SCHEDULES

In addition to its database capabilities, ACT! is also an outstanding scheduling tool. With its ability to track thousands of upcoming activities and to display these activities in multiple report and calendar formats, ACT! would be worth the price of admission just as a scheduling program.

ACT! allows you to schedule phone calls, meetings, and to-do activities for yourself or for other users in a shared database. You can easily edit these activities, set alarms for them, reschedule them, or clear them from your contact records.

Scheduling activities

You can easily schedule activities for any contact by clicking on the appropriate toolbar button (depending on whether you want to schedule a phone call, meeting, or to-do activity) and selecting options from the Schedule Activity dialog box.

Every activity must be assigned to a contact, so the easiest thing to do is to locate the contact you want to assign the activity to first, then schedule the activity.

To schedule an activity

1. Locate the contact record of the person for whom you want to schedule the activity.

   You can flip through your records one by one, use the Contact List view (page 49), or perform a quick lookup to get to the desired record (page 67).

2. Click on the **Schedule Call, Schedule Meeting,** or **Schedule To-Do** button (**Figure 6.1**), depending on the type of activity you want to schedule.

   This will bring up the Schedule Activity dialog box (**Figure 6.2**), from which you can set every parameter of the new activity.

   If you accidentally click on the wrong button (that is, you click on the Schedule Call button when you really just need to schedule a to-do activity), you can change the activity type using the **Activity Type** drop-down list.

3. Click on the **Date** list arrow and choose a date for the activity from the resulting calendar (**Figure 6.3**).

   If you need to schedule the activity for a different month, you can flip to the next or previous month using the arrows in the upper-right and upper-left corners of the calendar.

Figure 6.1 You can schedule all of your activities with these three buttons.

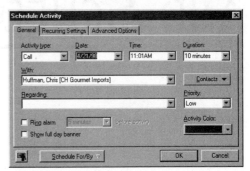

Figure 6.2 You select all settings for scheduled activities from this dialog box.

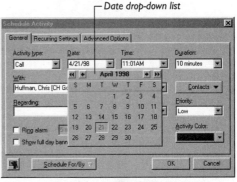

Figure 6.3 The drop-down list for dates is actually a mini-calendar.

New terms you should know...

Activity: An entry in an ACT! database denoting some sort of task that needs to be performed. ACT! divides activities into three categories: phone calls, meetings, and to-dos (or to-do activities).

SCHEDULING ACTIVITIES

Time drop-down list

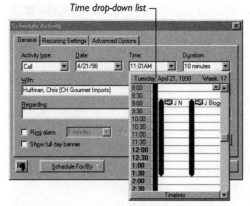

Figure 6.4 The drop-down list for times is a daily time sheet.

4. Click on the **Time** list arrow and choose a time for the activity from the resulting time sheet (**Figure 6.4**).

   Choose a time by clicking on the desired line. You can specify both time and duration from this time sheet by pressing on a time slot and dragging up or down to select several lines.

5. If the default duration (ten minutes for a call, one hour for a meeting, or five minutes for a to-do) needs to be changed, select the desired duration from the **Duration** drop-down list.

6. If desired, change the default priority by clicking on the **Priority** list arrow.

   Assigning different priorities simply changes the activity colors and lets you sort by priority or filter out unwanted priorities in reports and the task list (to see only high-priority activities, for example).

7. From the **Regarding** drop-down list, select the purpose of this activity.

   If none of the list items is appropriate, just type in what the activity is regarding.

8. Click the **OK** button.

Unattached activities

In ACT!, all activities must be assigned to a contact, even if there is no appropriate contact in your database. Activities that would fall into this category include things like dentist's appointments, calling Mom on her birthday, getting the car tuned up, and so on.

For the most part, these activities can be assigned to your own contact record (just select My Record from the Lookup menu before creating the activity). Another option is to create a dummy record or two for miscellaneous personal and business activities. By setting the ID/Status of these dummy records, you can determine whether or not the activities assigned to them will show up on your calendars or in your reports.

Modifying the activity Regarding list

You can edit the Regarding drop-down list within the Schedule Activity dialog box in the same way you'd edit any of the drop-down lists in the Contact view display.

To edit a drop-down list

1. Click on one of the three activity-scheduling buttons (**Schedule Call, Schedule Meeting,** or **Schedule To-Do**) to bring up the Schedule Activity dialog box.

   You may decide to edit the Regarding list while already in the process of scheduling an activity, in which case you will not need to follow this first step.

2. Click on the down arrow on the right side of the **Regarding** text box to activate the drop-down list.

3. Scroll to the bottom of the list and click on the **Edit List** item (**Figure 6.5**).

4. From the Edit List dialog box (**Figure 6.6**), you can add, modify, or delete items.

   If you want to add an item to the list, click on the **Add** button, type the new item and any desired description (**Figure 6.7**), and click the **OK** button.

   If you want to change a list item, select it, click the **Modify** button, make your change, and click the **OK** button.

   If you want to remove a list item, select it and click the **Delete** button.

5. Click the **OK** button when you are finished editing the list.

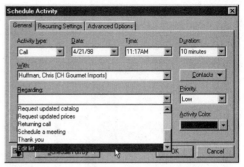

Figure 6.5 Like all drop-down lists, the Regarding list can be edited.

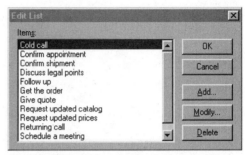

Figure 6.6 The Edit List dialog box

Figure 6.7 All new list items are added from here.

✔ Tip

- There are actually three separate drop-down lists—one for calls, one for meetings, and one for to-do activities. While all are accessed in the same way, the choices within the drop-down list will change depending on the type of activity you are scheduling. Make sure that you have selected correct activity type before editing the list.

— Activities tab

Figure 6.8 Use this tab to access the Activities display.

Figure 6.9 This display lists all activities for the current contact that have yet to be cleared or deleted.

— Select/Open Activity box

Figure 6.10 Use this gray box to select or open an activity.

New terms you should know...

Calendar: A graphic representation of upcoming and overdue activities. ACT! calendars correspond to real-world calendars and can be printed in a variety of commercial calendar and planner/organizer formats. Calendars are covered in detail in Chapter 8.

Viewing activities

Once created, activities can be viewed from the Contact view, any of the three Calendar views, or the Task List view. Viewing activities serves the obvious purpose of letting you know what you need to be doing, but also allows you to open up any particular activity to see or change its parameters.

Here, we'll focus on viewing activities from the regular Contact view display. The Calendar and Task List views are discussed in detail in Chapter 7, *ACT!'s Many Views*.

To view activities for a single contact

1. Locate the contact record whose activities you want to view.

2. Click on the **Activities** tab in the lower-left portion of the display (**Figure 6.8**).

    All activities associated with the contact will be shown in the bottom portion of the display (**Figure 6.9**). Use the scroll bar on the right side of the display to view additional activities for this contact.

To view or change activity parameters

1. From the list of activities (click on the Activities tab if you haven't already done so), double-click on the gray box at the far left of the activity you want to view or edit (**Figure 6.10**).

2. Change any activity parameters as desired.

3. Click the **OK** button.

Assigning new contacts to an activity

Occasionally you will need to assign a contact to an already-scheduled activity. Perhaps you assigned the activity to the wrong contact and now need to correct the mistake, or you may want to add a second contact (or a third or fourth) to an existing activity. If, for example, your boss wants to be included in a conference call with a client, or you decide to invite a couple of colleagues to join you for an already-planned lunch meeting, you'll need to assign new contacts to those activities.

To assign a new contact to an activity

1. Locate and open the activity for which you want to change or add contacts. New contacts must be assigned from within the Schedule Activity dialog box.

   See the previous section *Viewing Activities* for instructions on viewing activities.

2. Click on the **Contacts** button and select **Select Contacts** from the resulting menu (**Figure 6.11**). This will bring up a Select Contacts dialog box (**Figure 6.12**).

3. If the current contact for this activity is incorrect, select the contact from the Scheduled With list (on the right side of the dialog box) and click the **Remove** button.

4. To add contact(s), select the contact name(s) from the list in the lower-left portion of the dialog box, then click the **Add** button.

5. Click the **OK** button to return to the Schedule Activity dialog box, then click **OK** again to exit the Schedule Activity dialog box and return to the main display.

Contacts button ¬

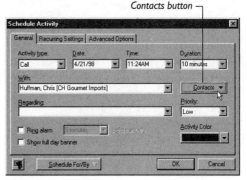

Figure 6.11 The Contacts button is really a pop-up menu.

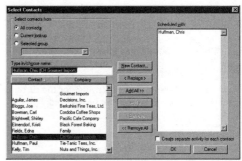

Figure 6.12 From this dialog box, you can remove existing contacts from or add new contacts to an activity.

✔ Tips

■ Remember that you can use the Ctrl-click and Shift-click combinations to select multiple names before clicking the Add button.

■ You can use the New Contact command in the pop-up Contacts menu to add a contact to your database while scheduling an activity. This is ideal if, for example, you are cold-calling and only want to have people in your database once you have them scheduled for an appointment.

Current Lookup option

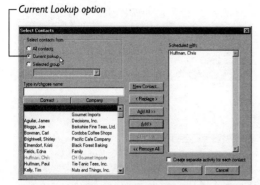

Figure 6.13 Selecting the Current Lookup option is the fastest way to add all the contacts that you are working with.

Scheduling activities for many contacts

As we have seen, you can add multiple contacts to an activity from within the Schedule Activity dialog box. There will be times, though, when adding contacts manually will be unwieldy. For large-scale activities like cold calling, introductory letters, and follow-up calls, it may be easier to use a lookup to find all of the contacts you want to work with and then add the entire lookup to the scheduled activity.

To schedule an activity for many contacts using a lookup

1. Perform a lookup (as discussed in Chapter 5) to locate the records of all contacts with whom you want to schedule the activity.

2. Click on the **Schedule Call, Schedule Meeting,** or **Schedule To-Do** button in the toolbar (depending on the type of activity to be scheduled).

3. Set all the parameters within the Schedule Activity dialog box as desired.

4. Click on the **Contacts** button and select the **Select Contacts** command.

5. In the upper-left portion of this dialog box, select the **Current Lookup** option (**Figure 6.13**).

6. Click the **Add All** button.

   This will add all contacts from the current lookup to the Scheduled With list.

7. Click the **OK** button to return to the Schedule Activity dialog box, then click **OK** again to exit the Schedule Activity dialog box and return to the main display.

Scheduling activities for groups

As mentioned in Chapter 4, *Working with Groups*, one nice feature of a group of contacts is that you can easily schedule an activity for the entire group. This process is similar to that of scheduling activities for multiple contacts.

To schedule an activity for all members of a group

1. Select the desired group from the **Group** pop-up list at the bottom of the display (**Figure 6.14**).

2. Click the **Schedule Call**, **Schedule Meeting**, or **Schedule To-Do** button in the toolbar, depending on the type of activity you want to schedule.

3. Set the desired parameters within the Schedule Activity dialog box (as discussed on page 90).

4. Click the **Contacts** button to access the Select Contacts dialog box.

5. In the upper-left portion of this dialog box, click on the **Selected Group** option (**Figure 6.15**).

6. From the drop-down list, choose the group you want to work with.

   Since you selected a group before scheduling the activity, the correct group should already be selected. If you did not select the group first, though, you can select it here.

7. Click the **Add All** button.

   This will add all contacts from the selected group to the Scheduled With list.

8. Click the **OK** button to return to the Schedule Activity dialog box, then click **OK** again to exit the Schedule Activity dialog box and return to the main display.

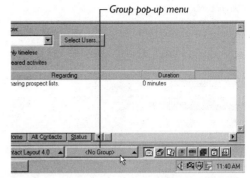

Group pop-up menu

Figure 6.14 This pop-up menu gives you access to all existing groups.

Selected Group option

Figure 6.15 By choosing Selected Group here, you can add contacts from any group in your database.

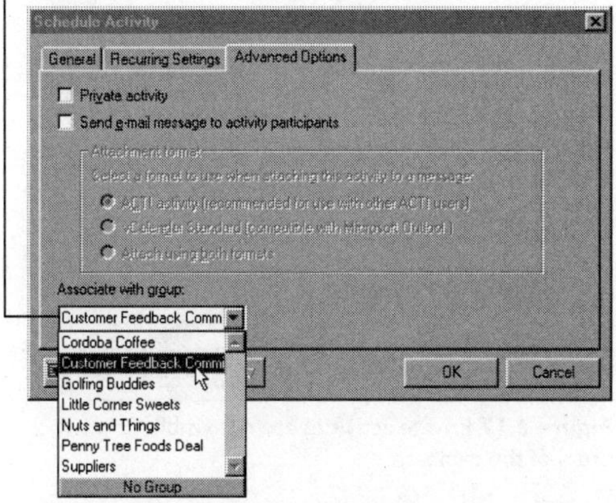

Figure 6.16 Associating an activity with a group is not the same as adding group members to the activity.

Associating an activity with a group

With this option, the activity is still scheduled for just one individual, but the activity is displayed in the Activity tab of the View Groups display, as well as in the contact's Activity tab. This makes it easy to keep track of any activities that have to do with the group, even if they do not involve all group members. For example, you might schedule a meeting with only one member of your Budget Committee (the chairperson, perhaps), but every time you view the Budget Committee group information, you want to see that you met with that one person.

To associate an activity with a group

1. Go to the record of the contact for whom you want to schedule the activity.

   The contact will usually (but not always) be a member of the group that you want to associate the activity with. You can select the group from the Group pop-up menu at the bottom of the display.

2. Click the appropriate activity-scheduling button in the toolbar.

3. Set the parameters within the Schedule Activity dialog box as desired.

4. Click on the **Advanced Options** tab at the top of the dialog box.

5. Select the group you want to associate this activity with from the Associate with Group drop-down list in the lower-left corner of the dialog box (**Figure 6.16**).

   If you selected a group prior to clicking on one of the activity-scheduling buttons, the selected group will already be displayed in the Associate with Group combo box.

6. Click the **OK** button to return to the Contact view.

Scheduling private activities

If you share a database with other users, all of your activities are visible to all users of the database. This can be invaluable when it comes to scheduling meetings, tracking account activity, etc. There will be times, though, when you will want to make some of your activities private. There is really no need, for instance, for all of your colleagues to know about your upcoming Income Tax Evaders Anonymous meeting.

Activities can easily be marked as private and, once so marked, will not show up on the calendars of other users, or even of the database administrator.

Scheduling a private activity

1. Go to the record of the contact for whom you want to schedule the activity.

   If you just need to change a public activity to a private one, skip these first three steps and instead open the activity as discussed on page 90 and go straight to step 4.

2. Click on the **Schedule Call, Schedule Meeting,** or **Schedule To-Do** button in the toolbar, depending on the type of activity you want to schedule.

3. Set the parameters within the Schedule Activity dialog box as desired.

4. Click on the **Advanced Options** tab at the top of the dialog box.

5. Click the **Private Activity** checkbox in the lower right of the dialog box (**Figure 6.17**).

6. Click the **OK** button.

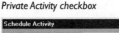
Private Activity checkbox

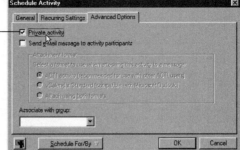

Figure 6.17 Private activities are not visible to other users of the database.

New terms you should know...

Private: Private items (activities, records, etc.) can only be viewed by their creator.

Public: Public items can be viewed by any user of the database.

Schedule For/By button

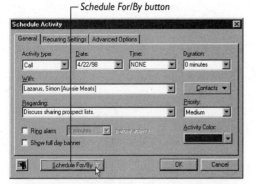

Figure 6.18 Use this button to expand the bottom section of the Schedule Activity dialog box.

Scheduled For drop-down list

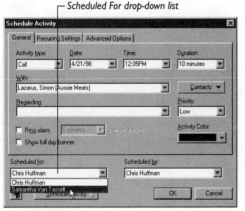

Figure 6.19 Select the person for whom you are scheduling the activity.

Scheduling activities for others

In a multiuser database, ACT! allows one user to schedule activities for other users. The most obvious application of this is that an assistant can schedule meetings, phone calls, or to-do activities for their boss without having to exit the database and log back on under their boss's name.

To schedule an activity for another user

1. Select the contact record you want to work with.

2. Click on the appropriate activity-scheduling button and set options within the Schedule Activity dialog box as desired.

3. Click on the **Schedule For/By** button (**Figure 6.18**).

   This will expand the Schedule Activity dialog box to include options for scheduling the activity for another user.

4. From the Scheduled For drop-down list, select the user for whom you are scheduling the activity (**Figure 6.19**).

5. If your name doesn't already appear in the Scheduled By drop-down list, select it now.

6. Click the **Schedule For/By** button again to collapse this section of the dialog box, if desired.

7. Click the **OK** button to exit the Schedule Activity dialog box.

Setting alarms

If you would like ACT! to remind you of imminent activities, you can set an alarm when scheduling an activity. Setting alarms is a very simple process, but there are two big caveats to keep in mind: First, your computer must be on, and second, ACT! must be up and running in order for the alarm to go off. If your computer isn't on, you will (obviously) not be able to hear or see the alarm, and if ACT! isn't running, it can't check to see if there are any alarms that need to be displayed.

Therefore, alarms are most useful for people who are at their desks most of the time with the computer on. For those of us who are on the road or in and out of the office, ACT!'s alarms are not all that useful.

To set an alarm for an activity

1. As you have done throughout this chapter, go to the desired contact record, click on the appropriate activity-scheduling button, then set the date, time, and other parameters for the activity.

2. While still in the Schedule Activity dialog box, click the **Ring Alarm** checkbox on the left side of the dialog box (**Figure 6.20**).

3. From the drop-down list immediately to the right of the Ring Alarm checkbox, choose the desired amount of lead time for the alarm.

   The lead time is the time between when the alarm goes off and when the activity is actually scheduled to occur.

4. Click the **OK** button.

✔ Tip

- The default lead times for alarms are set in the Preferences dialog box. Refer to Appendix A, *Preferences*, to change these default lead times.

Ring Alarm checkbox

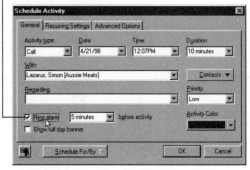

Figure 6.20 Setting an alarm for an activity will tell ACT! to alert you when the activity is imminent.

New terms you should know...

Alarm: A reminder of an imminent or over-due activity. ACT! alarms consist of a single warning beep and a floating dialog box.

SETTING ALARMS

Daily frequency option   *Activity Occurs options*

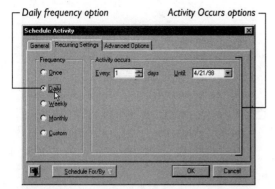

Figure 6.21 The options for daily recurring activities

Weekly frequency option   *Activity Occurs options*

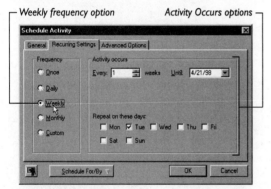

Figure 6.22 Weekly recurring activities have slightly different options.

Scheduling recurring activities

A recurring activity is any activity that occurs on a regular basis, such as weekly department meetings, monthly budget reports coming due, or regular lunches with clients or friends. ACT! lets you schedule four kinds of recurring activities: daily, weekly, monthly, or custom. Custom recurring activities are tied to specific *dates*, rather than *days* (that is, the 15th of each month, rather than the second Friday of each month).

Scheduling a recurring activity

1. Go to the record of the contact for whom you want to schedule the activity.

2. Click on the **Schedule Call, Schedule Meeting,** or **Schedule To-Do** button in the toolbar, depending on the type of activity you want to schedule.

3. Set the date, time, duration, and all other options within the Activity Information tab of the Schedule Activity dialog box.

4. Click on the **Recurring Settings** tab at the top of the dialog box.

5. From the Frequency section at the left side of the dialog box, select the **Daily, Weekly, Monthly,** or **Custom** option.

   Daily, weekly, and monthly items can be set to repeat every *x* days, weeks, or months. Custom items can be set to repeat on certain dates every *x* months.

6. If you selected the Daily option, specify how often the activity should repeat itself and when it should stop occurring (**Figure 6.21**).

   If you selected the Weekly option, specify how often the activity should repeat itself, when it should stop occurring, and what days of the week it should occur on (**Figure 6.22**).

If you selected the Monthly option, specify how often the activity should repeat itself, when it should stop occurring, which weeks during the month it should occur, and which days of the week it should occur on (**Figure 6.23**).

If you selected the Custom option, specify how often the activity should repeat itself, when it should stop occurring, and which dates of the month it should occur on (**Figure 6.24**).

✔ Tip

■ For the Custom option, you can specify the last day of the month by choosing the 31st. If a month has only 28 or 30 days, the activity will occur on the 28th or the 30th of that month.

Monthly frequency option   *Activity Occurs options*

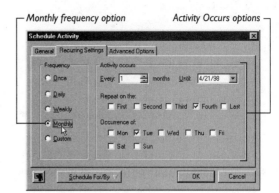

Figure 6.23 Monthly recurring activities have still more options.

Custom frequency option   *Activity Occurs options*

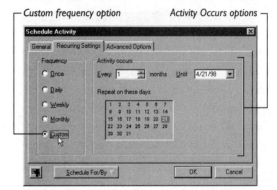

Figure 6.24 Unlike the other three types of recurring activities, custom recurring activities are date-based, rather than day-based, as shown in the options available.

Open Activity box

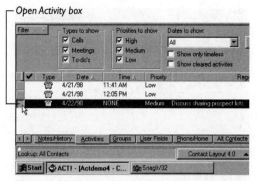

Figure 6.25. Double-click this box to open the activity.

Rescheduling activities

Any changes that you need to make to an activity can be made from the Schedule Activity dialog box. For any given activity, you can access this dialog box from the Activities tab for the contact with which the activity is associated.

To reschedule an activity

1. Locate the record for the contact with whom the activity you want to change is scheduled. If the activity is scheduled with more than one contact, it doesn't matter which record you use to access the activity.

2. Click on the **Activity** tab at the bottom of the display.

3. Double-click on the gray box at the far left of the entry for the activity that needs to be changed (**Figure 6.25**).

4. From within the Schedule Activity dialog box, make any necessary changes and click the **OK** button.

✔ Tip

- It is even easier (and much cooler) to use the mouse to reschedule activities from the calendar views. Check out Chapter 8 for all the details!

Responding to alarms

Whenever an ACT! alarm goes off, a single beep will sound (no matter how many alarms are going off) and you will be presented with a dialog box listing all upcoming or overdue activities (**Figure 6.26**). In addition to this dialog box, the ACT! button on your computer's task bar will blink until all alarms have been dealt with.

Your choices of how to deal with the alarms include snoozing the alarms (our favorite), clearing the alarms, clearing the activity, rescheduling the activity, or going to the contact record in question before deciding what to do.

In the Alarms dialog box, you have the option of dealing with your alarms one at a time, in groups, or all at once. The following steps assume that the Alarms dialog box is up on your screen (as it will be whenever an alarm goes off).

To respond to an alarm

1. Select the alarm or alarms that you want to respond to.

   If the Alarms dialog box contains multiple alarms and you want to deal with more than one of them in the same fashion, Ctrl-click or Shift-click to select the alarms you want to work with; or click the **Select All** button to select all the alarms at once.

2. If you want to view the contact record(s) of the people with whom the activities are scheduled before dealing with the alarms, click the **Go To** button.

   This creates a lookup of all records associated with the selected alarms. The Alarms dialog box will remain on-screen, but you can also view the information in the contact record(s).

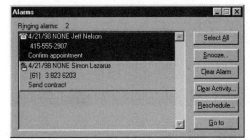

Figure 6.26 This dialog box, a single beep, and a flashing ACT! button in the toolbar are the extent of the alarm's effects.

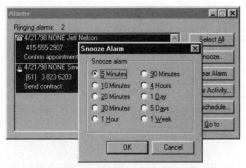

Figure 6.27 Snoozing alarms for days at a time, now there's a great idea!

3. To snooze the selected alarm(s), click the **Snooze** button, select the duration of the snooze from the Snooze Alarm dialog box (**Figure 6.27**), and click **OK**.

The default snooze duration is five minutes, which is barely enough time to curl up under your desk and fall back asleep.

To clear the alarm (which turns the alarm off but leaves the activity in the database to be dealt with later), click the **Clear Alarm** button.

4. To clear the activity (removing it from the database and creating a history entry for the result of the activity), click the **Clear Activity** button.

You will be presented with a Clear Activity dialog box. The options in this dialog box are discussed in detail in the *Clearing an activity* section on page 106.

5. To reschedule the selected activity, click the **Reschedule** button and change the date, time, and any other parameters you wish in the resulting Schedule Activity dialog box.

Clearing activities

Clearing an activity is very different from deleting an activity (which is discussed on page 107). *Deleting* an activity removes it from the database as if it had never been there. *Clearing* an activity removes it from the list of upcoming activities but creates a corresponding entry in the history database. You should clear all activities whether successfully completed or not. This allows you to accurately track all activity for your contacts.

To clear an activity

1. Locate the record for the contact with whom the activity you want to clear is scheduled.

2. Click the **Activity** tab at the bottom of the display.

3. Click (once) in the first column (it is labeled with a checkmark and is just to the right of the gray box) at the left of the entry for the desired activity (**Figure 6.28**).

   This is the Clear Activity box for the activity.

4. In the resulting Clear Activity dialog box (**Figure 6.29**), change the date or time from the drop-down lists, if they are incorrect.

5. Edit the Regarding text, if necessary.

6. If the result is anything other than "Completed," click to select the correct result.

   By the way, the Erased option lets you clear an activity without creating a history entry.

7. If you want to schedule a follow-up activity, click on the **Follow Up** button and schedule a new activity in the resulting Schedule Activity dialog box.

8. Click the **OK** button to finish clearing the activity.

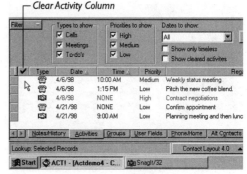

Clear Activity Column

Figure 6.28 The ambiguously labeled checkmark column is the Clear Activity column.

Figure 6.29 ACT! requires additional information on all cleared activities from you in order to create accurate history entries.

Deleting activities

You can easily delete activities from the database whenever you find it necessary. This method of deleting activities is a bit of a cheat that allows you to bypass the Clear Activity dialog box. Because this method of removing activities does not create history entries for completed activities, only use it to remove mistakes, not as a quick way to clear an activity from a calendar.

To delete an activity

1. Locate the record for the contact with whom the activity you want to change is scheduled. Again, if the activity is scheduled with more than one contact, it doesn't matter which record you use to access the activity.

2. Click the **Activity** tab at the bottom of the display.

3. Click (just once) on the gray box at the far left of the entry for the activity that you want to delete.

4. From the Edit menu, select the **Cut** command.

   By cutting the activity (and never pasting it anywhere) you bypass the Clear Activity dialog box completely.

Printing activity lists and calendars

If you are going to be away from your computer for any length of time, it will be helpful to print out a listing of all of your upcoming activities.

You have two choices when printing activities. You can print them out in either a text-based report format or a more graphical calendar format.

To print a list of activities

1. From the File menu, select the **Print Activities** command.

2. Click the **OK** button in the Print dialog box to send the data to the printer.

To print a calendar of activities

1. From the File menu, select the **Print** command.

2. In the Print dialog box, select the desired calendar type (daily, weekly, or monthly) from the Printout Type drop-down list (**Figure 6.30**).

3. From the list of available calendar formats on the left side of the dialog box, select the format that best matches your needs.

4. Click the **OK** button.

5. At the resulting Print dialog box, click the **OK** button again to send the data to the printer.

Printout Type drop-down list

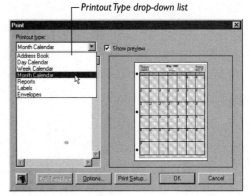

Figure 6.30 Three different types of calendar are available.

7

ACT!'s Many Views

ACT! offers you quite a few different ways to view information. In addition to the main Contacts view display, there are a Contact List window that shows you the basic data for all of your contacts in list format; a Groups window for viewing information about groups of contacts; three different calendar windows; a comprehensive Task List view; an E-mail window; and a completely separate word-processing module.

Keeping all of these different views straight can seem a daunting task, but ACT! makes things relatively easy by placing the controls for the various views into a few logical groupings.

This chapter discusses how to move from one view to another, and how to get the most out of the views. Three of the more complex topics related to views—the calendar views, e-mail, and ACT!'s word-processing module—are discussed in their own chapters.

Working in the Contacts view

The main display within ACT! is the Contacts view. It is this view that is presented to you whenever you open a database.

The Contacts view is divided into two sections. The top section contains standard fields for most of the information you will need to refer to on a regular basis, such as contact name, phone number, address, and so on. You can change the fields displayed in the top section of the Contacts view using the Layout pop-up menu (**Figure 7.1**).

The bottom section of the Contacts view can contain information from seven different categories. You can bring up a new category by clicking on any of the seven tabs in the lower-left portion of the display (**Figure 7.2**). Thus, the data displayed in the bottom section of the Contacts view will change according to your needs.

In the lower-right corner of the display is a set of eight view icons (**Figure 7.3**). These icons are used to access different views or display windows within ACT!. The Contacts view is only the first of these eight views.

✔ Tip

■ The Contacts view and Groups view windows are divided with a horizontal split bar. You can point to this split bar, then press and drag up or down to change the sizes of the top and bottom sections of your window.

■ You can also double-click on the split bar to toggle the bottom section between its two states. In one state, it takes up the full window; in the other, it uses just the allocated amount of space.

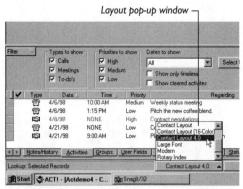

Layout pop-up window

Figure 7.1 The Layout pop-up menu determines which fields are displayed in the top section of the Contacts view.

View tabs

Figure 7.2 These tabs are used to view different kinds of data for the selected contact record.

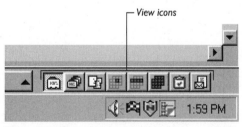

View icons

Figure 7.3 These eight icons give you access to ACT!'s different views.

WORKING IN THE CONTACTS VIEW

Figure 7.4 The Modern layout is just one of the many different layouts available.

Changing layouts

As mentioned in the previous section, the Layout pop-up menu gives you access to different sets of fields. The ten standard layouts are Alternate, Blank, Classic Contact 1, Classic Contact 2, Contact Layout, Contact Layout (16-Color), Contact Layout 4.0, Large Font, Modern, and Rotary Index. Some layouts give you access to different fields, while others just change the look of the display (**Figure 7.4**).

Any layouts that you create are also added to the Layout pop-up menu. Creating and modifying layouts are discussed in Chapter 13, *Productivity Power Tools*.

To change layouts

1. Click on the **Layout** pop-up menu at the bottom of the Contacts view window.

2. Select the layout you want from the list of available layouts.

    If the layout you are looking for is not immediately visible in the list, you can use the scroll bar to scroll up or down to see more layouts.

A plethora of terms

One common (and fairly justified) complaint about recent versions of ACT! is that all of the different windows and window elements can be very confusing. Not only are the elements themselves confusing, but the terms used to refer to these elements can seem somewhat arbitrary and more varied than is really necessary. For example, the view icons in the lower-right corner of the display are referred to as *icons*, even though they sure look like regular old *buttons* to most users. The Contacts and Groups *views* really refer to the Contacts and Groups *windows*, and the splitting of windows results in terms like the Activities tab *display* or *section* or *pane* (as in window pane), depending on who you talk to. It seems as if a thesaurus exploded in the ACT! development and user community with the release of version 3.0, with the result that different people use different terms to refer to the same things.

Arranging columns

A lot of the data you will see while using ACT! is displayed in columns (the information in the Notes/History tab, for example).

The columns can be manipulated to enable you to see and work with the information in whatever manner is easiest. Specifically, these columns can be resized to display more (or less) data, and they can be rearranged to place different columns of data next to each other.

To resize a column

1. Move the mouse to place the cursor on the right edge of the column heading (**Figure 7.5**).

   When you are in the right spot, your cursor will change to a vertical line with arrows pointing left and right. You don't actually have to be in the heading, but that is probably the easiest place to see the division between one column and the next.

2. Press and drag the right edge of the column heading to the right (for a wider column) or to the left (for a narrower column).

To move a column

1. Point to the center of the column heading for the column that you want to move.

2. Press and hold the mouse button and drag the column to its new location (**Figure 7.6**).

   As you drag the mouse, the cursor will turn into a little closed fist, indicating that you have "grabbed" the column and are taking it with you.

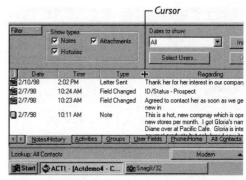

Figure 7.5 The cursor looks like this when you change column widths.

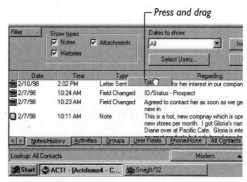

Figure 7.6. You can rearrange columns by pressing and dragging the headings around.

Figure 7.7 In this dialog box, you choose which fields you want to add as new columns.

Adding and removing columns

In addition to moving and resizing existing columns, you can also add columns to or remove columns from any of the columnar displays. These new columns can be used to show the contents of additional database fields that exist in ACT! but are not normally part of the display.

To add a column to a display

1. Point to any existing column heading or to the empty space to the right of the last column heading in the display.

2. Click the right mouse button.

3. From the shortcut menu, select the **Add Columns** command.

4. In the Add Columns dialog box (**Figure 7.7**), select a field to be displayed in the new column.

5. Click the **Add** button.

To remove a column from a display

1. Point to the column heading for the column that you want to remove.

2. Press and hold the mouse button and drag up to the space directly above the column headings.

   Your cursor will turn into a little trash can, reflecting what you are about to do with this column.

3. Let go of the mouse button. The column is deleted.

Sorting columnar data

Data listed in columnar fashion can easily be sorted based on the information in certain columns. Which columns are sortable depends on where you are. For example, you can sort by the Regarding column in the Activities tab, but not in the Notes/History tab. The column by which the data is currently sorted is indicated by an arrow in the column heading (**Figure 7.8**). Sorting by column is almost always a *one-key sort*; that is, the data is sorted based only on the information in one column. The exception to this is any chronological sort, which is always done by the Date column first, then by the Time column. Sorting is the easiest thing you will ever do in any of the tab displays.

To sort data displayed in columns

1. Click on the column heading for the column by which you want your data sorted.

✔ Tip

- By default, all sorts are in ascending alphanumeric (0-9 then A-Z) or chronological (oldest to newest) order. To reverse this, simply click again on the column heading. The data will then be sorted in reverse order, as indicated by a down arrow in the column heading, instead of an up arrow.

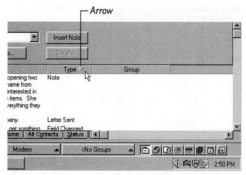

Figure 7.8 The arrow in the column heading indicates the basis for the current sort order.

Show Types checkboxes

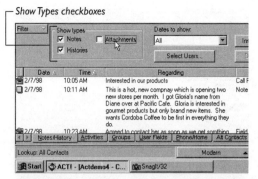

Figure 7.9 Filter by entry type using these checkboxes.

Figure 7.10 This dialog box lets you view the entries made by specific users of the database.

Show Cleared Activites checkbox

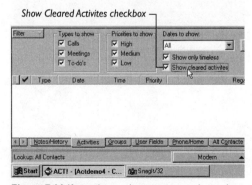

Figure 7.11 If you choose these options, only timeless or already-cleared activities will be displayed.

Filtering data

From time to time you may want to view only certain types of data in the tab displays, hiding all other types. For example, you may want to see only history entries created by one of the database's users, or you may want to see only overdue activities (i.e., those whose scheduled date or time has already passed). You might also want to review only notes that you've written before meeting with a client. As discussed in Chapter 3, the process of temporarily removing information from a display is called filtering. Information in displays can be filtered by user, date, or type of data.

To filter data in columnar lists

1. To filter out certain types of entries, click on the Notes, Histories, or Attachments checkboxes (**Figure 7.9**) to deselect those items and hide them from view.

    If you are viewing activities, you can also filter by priority (High, Medium, or Low).

2. If desired, select an entry from the Dates to Show drop-down list.

    If you select Date Range, you will be presented with a dialog box in which you can specify an arbitrary range of dates.

3. To see only entries made by a particular user of the database, click on the **Select User** button and select the desired user from the resulting dialog box (**Figure 7.10**). This only applies to multiuser databases, of course.

4. If you are viewing data from an Activities tab, you can also choose to view only timeless or already-cleared activities as well (**Figure 7.11**).

FILTERING DATA

Working in the Contact List view

The Contact List view is a way of looking at a large number of contacts all at once (**Figure 7.12**). The advantages of being able to see many contacts at once are pretty obvious (but we won't let that stop us from pointing them out anyway). For one thing, it is generally faster and easier to locate a contact from the Contact List than by flipping through your records one at a time.

✔ Tips

- From the Contact List, you can go the to main Contacts view for any contact by double-clicking on the gray selection box on the far left of the row for that contact (**Figure 7.13**).

- Columns can be resized, moved, added and deleted from the Contact Listview as described earlier in this chapter.

- You can also create new records, write notes, schedule activities, and create documents for contacts directly from the Contact List view by clicking on the appropriate button in the toolbar (**Figure 7.14**). Just make sure to select the correct contact by clicking the gray selection box before scheduling the activity or creating the note or document.

- The Contact List view is also a great way to modify lookups or create custom lookups, as discussed in Chapter 5, *Lookups and Queries*.

- If you are viewing more records than will fit on your screen, you can use the vertical scroll bar to bring more records into view. If you need to see additional columns of contact data, use the horizontal scroll bar at the bottom of the Contact List view window.

Figure 7.12 The Contact List view

Figure 7.13 The gray selection box can be used to jump between the Contact List view and the Contacts view.

Figure 7.14 The Contact List toolbar contains the exact same buttons that you see in the regular Contact view.

WORKING IN THE CONTACT LIST VIEW

Group List *Group Toolbar* *Data Area*

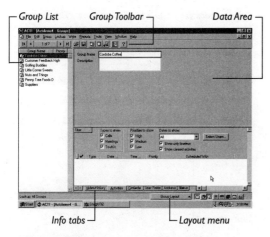

Info tabs *Layout menu*

Figure 7.15 The Groups view window

Group Layout pop-up window

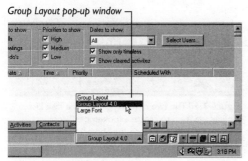

Figure 7.16. Like the Contacts view, the Groups view offers different layouts.

Working in the Groups view

The Groups view is discussed in greater detail in Chapter 4, *Working with Groups*, but there are some general features that bear mentioning here.

✔ Tips

■ The Groups view is similar to the Contacts view in that the window is divided into different parts. Unlike the Contacts view, though, the Groups view has three sections, rather than just two (**Figure 7.15**).

■ The left section of the Groups view contains a columnar listing of groups and group data. This section can be resized using the vertical split bar on its right border. Within this data area, columns can be resized, moved, added, and deleted as discussed earlier in this chapter.

■ The top section of the Groups view displays editable fields for the name and description of the selected group.

■ The bottom section is used to display various data about the selected group. At the bottom of this section is a set of tabs. These tabs work like the tabs at the bottom of the Contacts view display. The split bar separating this bottom section from the top section of the Groups view window can be moved as discussed earlier.

■ At the very bottom of the Groups view window is a pop-up Group Layout menu (**Figure 7.16**). This menu serves the same purpose that the Layout menu serves in the Contacts view window. You can select different standard and user-created group layouts from here.

Working in the Task List view

The Task List view (**Figure 7.17**) is similar to the Activities tab display in the Contacts view. The obvious difference is that the Task List view is a full-window view, with no split bar or additional data to look at. Information about upcoming activities is displayed in a columnar format, just as in the Activities tab display. The main difference is that while the Activities tab display only shows the scheduled activities for the active contact record, the Task List view shows all activities for all records in the database. This is a real "to do" list, and includes all phone calls that you need to make, meetings that you have scheduled, and miscellaneous to-do activities that you need to complete.

✔ Tips

- The Task List view also has its own toolbar, with seven buttons that you've seen before (for opening, saving, and printing data, scheduling activities, and accessing the help system). There are, however, two new buttons (**Figure 7.18**): one for creating a lookup of all the contacts listed on this screen and one for accessing the Filter dialog box.

- As with the other columnar displays in ACT!, columns can be resized, moved, added, and deleted within the Task List view as discussed earlier in this chapter.

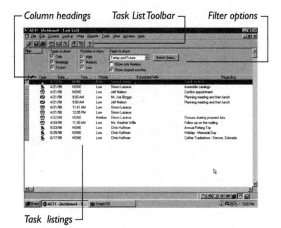

Column headings   Task List Toolbar   Filter options

Task listings

Figure 7.17 As the name suggests, the Task List view is a big list of tasks.

Create Lookup   Filter Tasks

Figure 7.18 The two new buttons on the Task List toolbar are used to create a lookup of all contacts in the Task List and to change the contacts listed here.

Filter Tasks button ⌐

Figure 7.19 Clicking the Filter button is an easy way to get to the Filter dialog box.

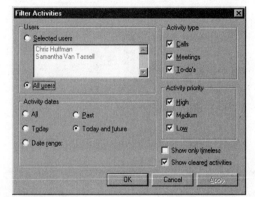

Figure 7.20 This is where you can filter out items you don't need to see.

Filtering activities in the Task List view

The Task List view displays activities for all contacts in the database, rather than for a single contact. Because you could easily have hundreds of activities scheduled for dozens of different contacts, it is likely you will need ACT!'s filtering function here.

You can filter the Task List either via the shortcut menu or with the Filter button in the toolbar (**Figure 7.19**).

To filter Task List data

1. Click on the **Filter** button in the toolbar; or, alternatively, click the right mouse button anywhere in the white data area and select the **Filter Activities** command from the shortcut menu.

   Either method will bring up the Filter Activity dialog box (**Figure 7.20**).

2. To filter by user, generating a Task List for just one or more users, click on the **Selected Users** option in the upper-left portion of the dialog box and select the users whose tasks you want to see.

3. To filter by date, click on the desired date option in the "Select Dates" portion of the dialog box.

4. To filter Notes/History entries by data type, select the desired options from the "Show" section of the dialog box.

5. To filter activities by data type, select the desired options from the "Activity Type" and "Activity Priority" sections of the dialog box.

6. To see only timeless or only cleared activities, click to select either option in the lower-right corner of the dialog box.

7. Click the **OK** button.

Modifying activities in the Task List view

There are two ways to modify activities while in the Task List view. Depending on your preference, you can either open up the Schedule Activity dialog box and use that to edit activities in the Task List, or simply change most of the activity parameters directly from the Task List itself. Activities can also be cleared directly from the Task List view.

To edit an activity in the Task List view

1. To change the Type, Date, Time, Priority, Duration, or Group for an activity, click in the appropriate column for the activity you want to change, then click on the resulting drop-down arrow and select a new choice (**Figure 7.21**).

2. To change the contact with whom an activity is scheduled, click on the current contact name. This will turn the contact name into a gray button (**Figure 7.22**). Click on this button again to get a Select Contacts dialog box, within which you can change the contact(s) for the selected activity.

3. To change what the activity is regarding, click in the Regarding column for the activity you want to change and either edit the existing text or select something from the drop-down list.

To clear an activity from the Task List view

1. Click in the first column to the right of the gray selection box for the activity that you want to clear (the column heading is a checkmark).

    Remember that the checkmark column heading indicates the Clear Activity column.

Task drop-down list

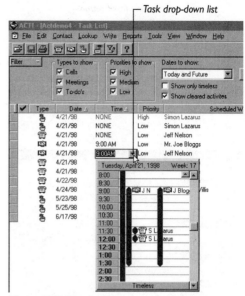

Figure 7.21 All task details except the contact name can be changed with the drop-down list.

Click on Contact Name

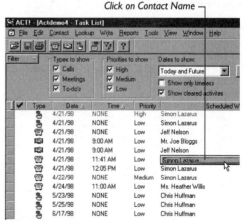

Figure 7.22 Clicking on a contact name turns it into a button for accessing the Select Contacts dialog box.

Figure 7.23 This is the same Clear Activity dialog box you will see whenever you clear an activity, no matter what view you are in.

2. In the resulting Clear Activity dialog box (**Figure 7.23**), change the date or time, if necessary.

3. Edit the Regarding text, if desired.

4. Click on one of the result option buttons to select the result of the activity..

   The Erased option lets you clear an activity without creating a history entry.

5. If you want to schedule a follow-up activity, click on the **Follow Up Activity** button and schedule a new activity in the resulting Schedule Activity dialog box.

6. Click the **OK** button to finish clearing the activity.

✔ Tip

■ If you want to open the Schedule Activity dialog box for any activity and do your editing there, simply double-click on the gray selection box at the far-left edge of the row for the activity you want to change.

CALENDARS

Whether you need to completely rearrange your appointments for an entire week or just want a quick look to see how busy a certain day is, the calendar views give you an indispensable graphic view of all of your scheduled activities.

Most of the tasks that can be accomplished from the calendar views can also be accomplished from other views; the calendars just give you a different way to view and work with your activity data.

Viewing the calendars

You can easily access any of ACT!'s three calendar views using the view icons located in the lower-right corner of the display (**Figure 8.1**).

All three of the calendar views are divided into four basic parts (**Figure 8.2**). The top of each display has a toolbar with standard buttons for opening and printing, scheduling activities, moving forward or backward (a day, week, or month at a time, depending on which calendar view you are in), creating lookups and filtering (discussed later in this chapter), and accessing SideACT! and the online help system.

Underneath the toolbar is the main display area, with all scheduled activities displayed in a daily, weekly, or monthly format.

To the right of the main display area are a mini-calendar and a data area. The mini-calendar is used to navigate within the calendar displays (see page 133) and the detail area underneath it shows much more information about the selected day's activities than can be shown in the main display area.

To view the calendars

1. Click on the view icon in the lower-right corner of the display (see **Figure 8.1**) for the type of calendar (daily, weekly, or monthly) that you want to see.

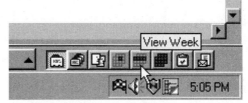

Figure 8.1 The view icons give you access to the Daily, Weekly and Month calendar views.

Figure 8.2 Each calendar view includes a toolbar, a main display area, a mini-calendar, and a data area containing a detailed listing of activities.

Mini-calendar

Figure 8.3 This mini-calendar lets you navigate to different dates within any of the calendar views.

Double-arrow buttons
Single-arrow buttons

Figure 8.4 The double-arrow buttons move you backward or forward a year at a time. The single arrows move you backward or forward a month at a time.

Navigating within calendars

When you first view any of the calendars, you are presented with the current day, week, or month (depending on which of the three calendars you chose to view). If you want to look at different dates, it is a simple matter of selecting a different date using the mini-calendar within the Calendar window (**Figure 8.3**). If you want to look at a different time within the selected date (for Daily and Weekly calendar views only) you can do so with a standard scroll bar.

To view different calendar dates or times

1. To move forward or backward a year at a time, click on the double-arrow (or double-triangle, if you prefer) buttons in the upper-left and upper-right corners of the mini-calendar (**Figure 8.4**).

   The double-arrow button in the upper left takes you back a year; the right double arrow takes you forward a year.

2. To move forward or backward a month at a time, click on the single-arrow buttons next to the double-arrow buttons in the upper corners of the mini-calendar (**Figure 8.4**).

   Again, the left button takes you back in time and the right takes you forward to the next month.

3. Once you have the correct year and month, click on any day in the mini-calendar to view it in the main display area.

✔ Tips

- You can quickly move among the Daily, Weekly, and Monthly calendar views using the mini-calendar. Double-click on any day in the mini-calendar to jump to the

NAVIGATING WITHIN CALENDARS

Daily view for that day, double-click on the day headings ("S M T W T F S") to jump to the Weekly view that includes the selected day, or double-click on the month and year at the very top of the mini-calendar to jump to the Month view for the selected day. For both the week and month shortcuts your cursor will indicate whether you are about to jump to a Weekly or Monthly view.

Figure 8.5 The mini-calendar shortcut menu

- If you overdo it a bit and find yourself looking 50 years in the future, you can quickly get back to today's date by right-clicking on either the month and year area or the day headings at the top of mini-calendar, then selecting **Today** from the shortcut menu (**Figure 8.5**).

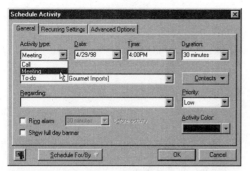

Figure 8.6 This is the same Schedule Activity dialog box you will see no matter where you schedule the activity from.

Scheduling from the calendars

While there is nothing wrong with scheduling activities using the activity-scheduling buttons (as discussed in Chapter 6, *Activities and Schedules*) it can be advantageous to schedule activities from the calendar views. The most obvious benefit of this is that you can see how busy a given day is before committing to meet with a client or make a dozen phone calls. The tradeoff is that you must take an extra step in the Schedule Activity dialog box to specify the contact with whom you want to schedule the activity. When you schedule using the toolbar buttons this is usually not necessary, since you will generally locate the correct contact record before scheduling the activity.

To schedule an activity from a calendar

1. Go to the Daily calendar view for the date for which you want to schedule the activity.

2. Double-click on the time slot for which you want to schedule the activity.

   You can only specify the starting time on the calendar. You will have to specify any duration longer than a half-hour in the Schedule Activity dialog box.

3. In the Schedule Activity dialog box (**Figure 8.6**), choose whatever options are appropriate for the activity you want to schedule by clicking on any of the drop-down menus and selecting from the choices listed. Click the **OK** button when you are done.

   Don't forget to select the activity type from the first drop-down list in this dialog box! For more information on the options in the Schedule Activity dialog box, see page 90.

New terms you should know...

Activity: An entry denoting some sort of task that needs to be performed. ACT! divides activities into three categories: phone calls, meetings, and to-dos (or to-do activities).

SCHEDULING FROM THE CALENDARS

127

Rescheduling calendar activities

In Chapter 6, we recommended that you think about rescheduling your activities from the calendar views. While this is faster than rescheduling activities within the Schedule Activity dialog box, the real advantage is that it's just so darn cool. If you want to impress a colleague with how easy ACT! can be, show them this (and if they ask about creating custom reports, try to change the subject).

To reschedule a calendar activity

1. Locate the activity you want to reschedule using the Daily, Weekly, or Monthly calendar views.

   If you need to change the time of an activity, you will have to do that from the Daily calendar view. You can use the Monthly or Weekly calendar views to change the date of an activity.

2. Position your cursor over the activity you want to change.

   Your cursor will turn into a four-headed arrow (**Figure 8.7**).

3. Press on the activity and hold the mouse button down. With the mouse button held down, drag the activity to the desired date or (in the daily calendar) time slot (**Figure 8.8**).

✔ Tip

■ You can drag an activity to a date that is outside the current week or month by dragging the activity off the calendar to the right of the main display area (to move forward in time) or to the left (to move backward). The calendar will move forward or backward an entire week or month at a time.

Figure 8.7 The four-headed arrow cursor, a distant relative of the infamous two-headed chicken cursor.

Figure 8.8 Pressing on an activity and dragging it to a new location is the fastest way to reschedule activities.

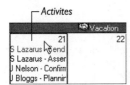

Figure 8.9 This detail area lists all activities for the selected date.

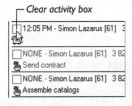

Figure 8.10 This box can be used to clear an activity.

Figure 8.11 Complete this dialog box so that your history entries will be as accurate as possible.

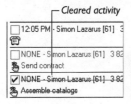

Figure 8.12 The crossed-out activities have already been cleared from the calendar.

✔ Tip

■ You can also clear an activity by selecting it on the calendar and hitting the Delete key on your keyboard. For monthly calendars, though, this isn't always an option, since the main display for monthly calendars is only capable of showing the first five activities for each day.

Clearing calendar activities

You can also clear activities directly from the calendars. Clearing an activity from a calendar produces the same Clear Activity dialog box that you'd get if you cleared the activity from any of the other views or from the Alarm dialog box.

In any of the calendar views, activities can be cleared either from the main display area or from the detail area on the right side of the window.

To clear an activity from a calendar

1. Locate the activity that you want to clear in any of the calendar views.

2. If you are using the Weekly or Monthly views, click on the date of the activity to be cleared.

   Selecting the date in the weekly or monthly calendars puts all of that day's activities in the detail area on the right side of the window (**Figure 8.9**).

3. Locate the activity to be deleted in the list of the selected day's activities (on the right side of the window).

4. Click in the Clear box at the beginning (left side) of the entry for the activity (**Figure 8.10**).

   This brings up the Clear Activity dialog box.

5. In the Clear Activity dialog box (**Figure 8.11**), select the actual date and time (if they're different from the scheduled date and time), make any necessary changes to the Regarding entry, and select the correct result of the activity. Click **OK** when you are done.

   Cleared activities remain on your calendar, but are shown with a line through all the text in both the main display and detail list areas (**Figure 8.12**).

Restoring calendar activities

If you ever accidentally clear an activity you can easily undo the clear, restoring the activity on your calendars to its original state.

To restore a cleared activity

1. Locate the incorrectly cleared activity in the detail listing on the right side of the calendar window.

   You may need to go back to your calendars and select the day of the activity if you have moved to a new date or a non-calendar view since clearing the activity.

2. Click on the checkmark in the Clear box at the beginning (left side) of the detail listing for the cleared activity (**Figure 8.13**).

3. At the resulting dialog box (**Figure 8.14**), click the **Yes** button.

   The activity is restored and is now listed as a yet-to-be-completed activity.

✔ Warning

■ Restoring a cleared activity does not remove the history entry created when the activity was originally cleared. You will need to go in and manually delete the history entry (as explained in Chapter 3, *Managing Records* on page 48). If you do not, you will have two history entries for the completion of a single activity, one of which will be false.

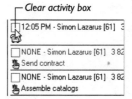

— Clear activity box

Figure 8.13 This Clear box can also be used to unclear an activity.

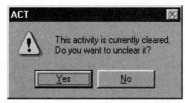

Figure 8.14 Click Yes here to unclear an activity.

Filter button

Figure 8.15 The Filter button brings up the Filter Calendar dialog box.

Figure 8.16 The Filter Calendar dialog box

Filtering calendar activities

Filtering, which was first discussed in Chapter 3, *Managing Records* (beginning on page 44), is also an option in the calendar views. Filtering lets you reduce the number of activities that appear on your calendars based on which user scheduled the activity, the type of activity, or the priority of the activity. Filtering is perfect when you want to see just meetings or just high-priority activities, for example.

To filter activities in the calendar views

1. Click on the **Filter** button (**Figure 8.15**) in the toolbar of any of the calendar views.

   This will bring up the Filter Calendar dialog box (**Figure 8.16**).

2. To see only entries made by one particular user of the database, click on the **Selected Users** option and select the desired user from the list.

   This only applies to multiuser databases, of course.

3. To filter out certain types of activities, click on the **Calls, Meetings,** or **To-do's** checkboxes to deselect those items and hide them from view.

4. To hide all entries of a specific priority, click on the **High, Medium,** or **Low** checkboxes in the Activity Priority section of the dialog box.

5. If you do not wish to see cleared activities, click on the **Show Cleared Activities** checkbox to deselect it.

6. Click the **OK** button

Creating calendar lookups

A very handy feature of ACT!'s calendar views is the ability they give you to create a lookup of all the records that appear on a calendar. This is an ideal way to send out introductory or reminder letters or faxes to all contacts that you will be interacting with during a given period of time. You can also use this lookup to print out contact reports or phone/fax directories of all of the contacts on a calendar (to take with you on business trips, for example). Once this lookup is created, you can treat it like any other lookup, modifying it or saving it as a group for future use. (For more on lookups, refer to page 66 in Chapter 5, *Lookups and Queries*).

To create a lookup based on calendar data

1. Select the calendar view (Daily, Weekly, or Monthly) you want to work with.

2. Navigate to the specific day, week, or month that contains the contacts you want to work with.

3. Filter the calendar as desired (see *Filtering calendar activities* in this chapter).

4. Click on the **Create Lookup** button in the toolbar (**Figure 8.17**).

   ACT! takes you back to the main Contacts view. The current lookup is now based on the records in the calendar view you just left, as indicated by the "Lookup: Selected Records" notation in the status bar (**Figure 8.18**).

Create Lookup button

Figure 8.17 The Create Lookup button gives you a quick and easy way to create a lookup of all contacts associated with activities on your calendar.

Figure 8.18 This lets you know that you are looking at a subset of your database.

✔ Tips

- Your lookup will be based on the entire calendar (day, week, or month). You cannot select part of a calendar. If you do not want all of the contacts on the calendar to be part of the lookup, you will have to edit the lookup manually (from the Contact List view, as discussed in Chapter 7, *ACT!'s Many Views* on page 116).

- Combining the filtering and lookup capabilities of the calendar views is a powerful technique. You can filter out everything but your meetings, then create a lookup for reminder e-mail notes or letters of introduction to just the people you will be meeting with. Or maybe you'll want to filter out everything but phone calls, then create a lookup for a report of phone numbers of just the people you need to call.

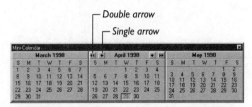

Figure 8.19 This mini-calendar is available to you even when you are not in one of the calendar views.

— Double arrow

— Single arrow

Figure 8.20 The double-arrow buttons move you backward or forward a year at a time. The single arrows move you backward or forward a month at a time.

Viewing the mini-calendar

In addition to the regular calendar views, ACT! also has a mini-calendar that can be displayed on top of any window, allowing you to refer to a calendar while you do just about anything in ACT!.

To view the mini-calendar

1. From the View menu, select the Mini-Calendar command.

   A three-month mini-calendar (**Figure 8.19**) appears on your screen, floating above whatever window you were in. The selected date is indicated by a concave block, and today's date appears in red.

2. To work in the background window, just click in it.

   The mini-calendar stays on-screen, but is not active.

3. To view different months, click on the left and right single- and double-arrow buttons at the top of the middle month (**Figure 8.20**).

4. To close the mini-calendar, click on the close box (the "X") in the upper-right corner or move the mini-calendar by dragging its title bar, just like any window.

✔ Tips

■ The F4 keyboard shortcut is great here, as it can be used to both show *and* hide the mini-calendar. This makes the mini-calendar much more convenient and, thus, much more useful.

■ You can jump to the Daily calendar view for any day by double-clicking on it, or jump to the Weekly or Monthly calendar views by selecting a date and then double-clicking the day of the week headings ("S M T W T F S") for the Weekly view or the month and year heading for the Monthly view.

VIEWING THE MINI-CALENDAR

Viewing mini-calendar activities

Because of its small size the mini-calendar cannot display much information, and is really intended more as a quick reference than as an alternative to the regular calendar views. It can, however, display some activity data to help you manage your time wisely. This is another little-known but very cool feature you can use to impress your friends and colleagues.

Figure 8.21 The activity listing for the selected date in the mini-calendar

To view activities in the mini-calendar

1. Locate the date for which you want to view activities.

   To move a year at a time, click on the double-arrow buttons in the corners of the middle month. Click on the button in the upper-left corner to go backward or click on the button in the upper-right corner to go forward.

   To move forward or backward a month at a time, click on the single-arrow buttons next to the double-arrow buttons.

2. Right-click on the desired date.

   A pop-up scrolling list of all activities scheduled for that date will appear below the mini-calendar (**Figure 8.21**).

3. Scroll through the list as necessary to view all activities.

✔ Tip

■ You can clear activities from this list by clicking on the checkbox at the beginning (left side) of each listing. This is exactly the same as clearing the activity from any of the calendar views, as discussed earlier in this chapter.

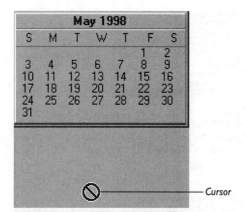

── Cursor

Figure 8.22 This cursor indicates that you can't do anything here.

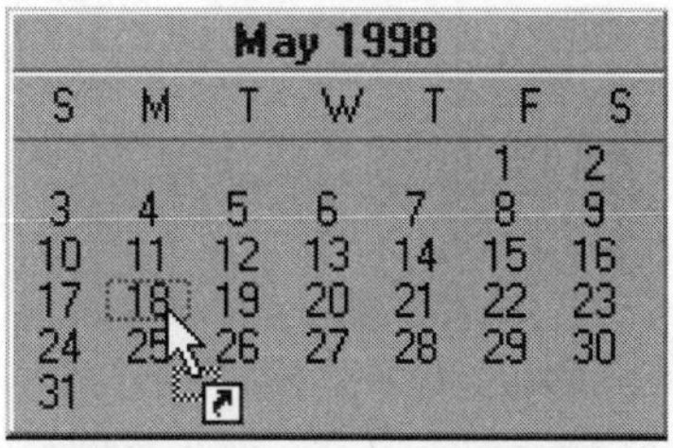

Figure 8.23 The cursor changes when you drag it over a mini-calendar date.

Scheduling activities with the mini-calendar

The last of ACT!'s incredibly cool, now-how-much-would-you-pay, but-wait-there's-more calendar features is that it enables you to schedule activities using the mini-calendar. This is the fourth possible way to schedule activities that we've discussed in this book. No one way is any better than any other. Try them all and see which one works best for you.

To schedule an activity with the mini-calendar

1. From the main Contacts view, locate the contact record for the person with whom you wish to schedule an activity.

2. Bring up the mini-calendar.

   You can select **Mini-Calendar** from the View menu or you can use the F4 shortcut.

3. Position the mouse on any gray, unused area of the contact record (not in a field or on any button, menu, etc.).

4. Press the mouse button and hold it down.

   Your cursor will turn into the universal null symbol (**Figure 8.22**).

5. Drag the cursor onto the mini-calendar and point to the desired date for this activity.

   The date will become outlined and your cursor will turn into a Windows shortcut symbol (**Figure 8.23**).

6. Release the mouse button, then select the activity type and all other options from the resulting Schedule Activity dialog box.

   For more information on the options in the Schedule Activity dialog box, see page 90 in Chapter 6, *Activities and Schedules*.

Printing Calendars

In addition to all of the useful things ACT! lets you do with your calendars on the screen, you can also print them out in dozens of different formats. Printing calendars is similar to printing other types of ACT! data, and just as easy.

To print a calendar

1. From any of the calendar views, select the Print command from the File menu.

2. From the Printout Type drop-down menu, select Day Calendar, Week Calendar, or Month Calendar (**Figure 8.24**).

3. In the list of available formats, click on the format that best suits your needs (**Figure 8.25**).

   The on-screen preview is an invaluable aid here. If you have printed calendars from an organizer or some other source that you want to match, simply compare them with the preview.

4. Click the **OK** button.

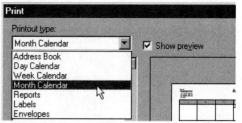

Figure 8.24 Select the type of calendar you want from this drop-down menu.

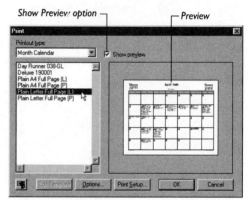

Figure 8.25 The preview is invaluable in selecting the correct calendar format.

PRINTING CALENDARS

WORD
PROCESSING IN ACT!

In the course of any business day, you will undoubtedly need to create all sorts of documents: letters, memos, faxes, reports, e-mail messages, etc. All of these documents can be created with ACT!. This chapter focuses on creating and working with standard document types. Reports are covered in their own chapter (Chapter 10) and faxes and e-mail are covered in the *Staying in Contact* chapter (Chapter 11). Once created, these documents can be saved, edited, or printed using standard word-processing skills that you probably already possess. Furthermore, ACT! can track any document printed and sent to a contact by creating an appropriate history entry in the contact's record.

Unlike most of ACT!'s other work modes, its word processor is actually a separate application. Because of this you will need to actually *exit* the word processor when you want to return to your normal ACT! window.

ACT! also allows you to use another application (either Microsoft Word or Novell's WordPerfect) as your word processor if you like. This chapter deals exclusively with ACT!'s own word processor. For help with either Word or WordPerfect, refer to your software's documentation.

Choosing a word processor

If you prefer to use either Microsoft Word or WordPerfect as your word-processing application, you can change the default word processor in the Preferences dialog box. Once you have changed the default word processor, ACT! will launch the selected application for all of your document-creation and document-editing tasks. If you select a word processor that is not installed on your system and then try to create a document, ACT! will present you with a warning dialog box (**Figure 9.1**) and then abort the task.

Inexplicably, ACT! only supports a single version of each of these word processors, version 7.x. This means that if you are using either an older or a newer version of Microsoft Word (Word 7.x is part of Office 97) or WordPerfect, you will not be able to use it as your word processor in ACT!.

To select a word-processing application

1. From the Edit menu, select the **Preferences** command.

   This will bring up the Preferences dialog box.

2. Click on the Word Processor drop-down list in the upper-left corner of the dialog box (**Figure 9.2**).

3. From the list, select **ACT! Word Processor** (the default), **Microsoft Word 7.x - Word 97**, or **WordPerfect 7.x**.

4. Click the **OK** button to exit the dialog box.

Figure 9.1 If ACT! can't find the selected word processor, this is what you'll see when you try to create a document.

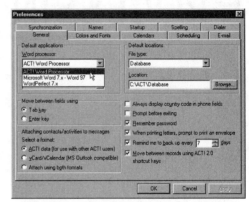

Figure 9.2 ACT! supports its own word processor, plus Word and WordPerfect.

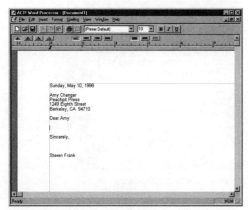

Figure 9.3 A new document based on the "Letter" template.

Creating documents

Creating documents in ACT! usually involves the use of a template of some sort. A *template* is a pre-formatted and partially completed document that is used as the basis for new documents. For example, ACT! comes with a letter template that includes placeholders for the contact's name, company, address, city, state, and ZIP code, as well as the salutation and complimentary close.

There are three different ways in which you can create a new word processing document:

♦ You can create a document from a standard template, such as a letter, memo, or fax.

♦ You can create a document using a non-standard template of your own design.

♦ You can just create a new, blank document not based on any template at all.

To create a letter, memo, or fax from a standard template.

1. Locate the record for the contact to whom you want to send the letter, memo, or fax. ACT! will automatically insert data from the current contact record into the newly created document, so you must be on the correct record *before* creating the document.

2. From the Write menu, select the **Letter**, **Memorandum**, or **Fax Cover Page** command. The ACT! word processor (or Word or WordPerfect, if you have selected either of those as your preferred word processor) is launched and a new document is created (**Figure 9.3**).

3. Edit, format, save, and print the document as you normally would.

   If you are using Word or WordPerfect, refer to your application's documentation for help with these tasks. If you are using ACT!'s word processor, the rest of this

---

New terms you should know...

Template: A document that is used as the basis for other documents. Typically, a template contains "boilerplate" text (standard text that is to appear in every new document) and field placeholders (where data from contact records will be inserted).

chapter will give you all the help you might need.

4. When you are finished, select the **Exit** command from the File menu to return to the main ACT! display.

Remember, the ACT! word processor is a separate application from ACT!, so you have to exit it when you are done.

To create a document from a custom template.

1. Locate the record of the contact to whom you will be sending the document.

2. From the Write menu, select the **Other Document** command.

3. From the resulting Open dialog box, select the document template you want to use and click the **Open** button.

ACT! creates a document based on the selected template, and includes data from the active contact record where indicated in the template.

To create a document from scratch

1. From the File menu, select the **New** command.

2. In the New dialog box (**Figure 9.4**) select **ACT! Word Processor Document** and click the **OK** button.

If you use a different word processor, you can select either "Microsoft Word 7.x - Word 97 Document" or "WordPerfect 7.x Document."

Figure 9.4 ACT!'s New dialog box.

Figure 9.5 You can easily change page margins from this dialog box.

Changing margins

Changing document margins is a very simple task in ACT!'s word processor. Just about the only times you'll need to change the margins of a document are to make the text fit on the page better or to allow for text or graphics on company stationery.

To change document margins

1. From the Format menu, select the **Page Margins** command.

2. In the Page Margins dialog box (**Figure 9.5**), change the margins as desired by either typing new values or clicking on the arrows next to each margin value.

3. Click the **OK** button to exit.

Formatting paragraphs

Formatting your paragraphs in ACT! is basically a matter of changing the alignment, indentation, or line spacing of some or all of the paragraphs in your document. You can easily do all of these in the ruler at the top of the word-processing window.

To change paragraph alignment or line spacing

1. Select the paragraph(s) that you want to change.

2. To change paragraph alignment (left, center, right, or justified), click on the desired paragraph alignment button in the ruler (**Figure 9.6**).

3. To change line spacing (single, one-and-a-half, or double), click on the desired line spacing button in the ruler (also **Figure 9.6**).

4. Click anywhere in your document to deselect the paragraphs.

To change paragraph indentation

1. Select the paragraph(s) whose indentation you want to change.

2. Press on the indent marker you want to move and drag it horizontally to its new position.

   To change the left indent, drag the left triangle indent marker (**Figure 9.7**).

   To change the first line indent, drag the "thumbtack" marker (**Figure 9.7**). Usually, this marker is partially obscured by the left indent marker, so grab it at the very bottom (the "head" of the "thumbtack").

   To change the right indent, drag the right triangle indent marker (**Figure 9.7**).

3. Click anywhere in your document to deselect the paragraphs.

Ruler buttons

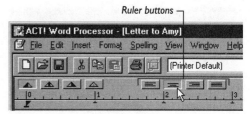

Figure 9.6 You can change paragraph alignment and line spacing with these ruler buttons.

Left indent

First line indent

Right indent

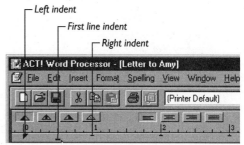

Figure 9.7 The indent markers are located at either side of the ruler.

✔ Tip

- You can easily select all paragraphs in a document by choosing the Select All command from the Edit menu. This is the fastest way to (for example) double-space or justify your entire document.

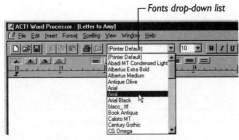

Fonts drop-down list

Figure 9.8 All the fonts on your computer are available to ACT!

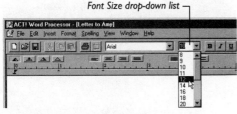

Font Size drop-down list

Figure 9.9 ACT!'s word processor has a pretty standard size-selection drop-down list.

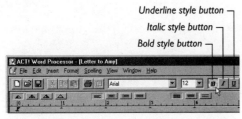

Underline style button

Italic style button

Bold style button

Figure 9.10 B for bold, I for italic, and U for underline

Formatting characters

Like paragraph formatting, character formatting just changes how your document looks. Character formatting affects the appearance of individual letters and numbers (or groups of letters and numbers) in your document Types of character formatting include boldfacing, italicizing, or underlining text and changing the font (typeface) or the size of text.

To change character formatting

1. Select the text that you want to change.

2. Change the font, size, or style of emphasis by using the Font and Size drop-down lists or the style buttons in the toolbar.

   To change the font, click on the Font button in the toolbar and select a new font from the drop-down list (**Figure 9.8**).

   To change the text size, click on the Size button (the arrow) and select a new size from the drop-down list (**Figure 9.9**), or click in the Size text box itself and type in a new value (from 2 to 500).

   To change the style (or emphasis) of your text, click on the Bold, Italic, or Underline buttons in the toolbar (**Figure 9.10**).

3. Deselect the text by clicking anywhere in your document.

New terms you should know...

Formatting: The process of changing the appearance of data in a document. You can format text by making it bold or italicized, format paragraphs by centering or double-spacing them, and format graphic elements by changing the color or line width, to name just a few examples.

FORMATTING CHARACTERS

Working with tabs and tab stops

Using tabs and tab stops is one of the most frustrating aspects of any word processor. This is unfortunate, since two simple rules of thumb can prevent most of the problems you might otherwise encounter.

First of all, there is a big difference between a tab and a tab stop. A *tab* is a character that you type in your document. It pushes any text following it to the next tab stop. A *tab stop* is a ruler setting that tells a tab where to stop (makes sense, doesn't it?). Because each tab takes you to the next tab stop, it is critical that you *use only one tab to separate items* when you are typing. (That is, if you are creating a list, type Item A, then a tab, then Item B, then a tab, then Item C. Do not use multiple tabs to make things line up!)

Second, before you even think about setting, moving, or removing tab stops, make sure that you select precisely the paragraphs that you want to work with. Each paragraph has its own tab stop settings, so *you must select the correct paragraphs before you start messing with those tab stops.*

To set a tab stop

1. Select the paragraph(s) for which you want to change the tab stops.

2. Click on the appropriate button for the type of tab stop you want to set (**Figure 9.11**).

3. Click in the ruler at the desired location for the new tab stop (**Figure 9.12**).

4. Deselect your text by clicking anywhere in the document.

To move a tab stop

1. Select the paragraph(s) that contain the tab stops to be moved.

Tab Stop buttons

Figure 9.11 The four tab stop buttons.

Figure 9.12 Tab stops are placed on the ruler.

2. Press on the desired tab stop and drag it horizontally to a new location on the ruler.

3. Deselect your text by clicking anywhere in the document.

To delete a tab stop

1. Select the paragraph(s) that contain the unwanted tab stop.

2. Press on the desired tab stop and drag it vertically down off of the ruler.

The tab stop marker on the ruler will turn gray when you have dragged it down far enough. Usually an inch or so is all that is required.

3. Deselect your text by clicking anywhere in the document.

New terms you should know...

Tab: An invisible text character that pushes all text that follows it to the right to the next tab stop set in the ruler.

Tab stop: A ruler setting that tells a tab where to stop. Tab stops are part of a paragraph's formatting instructions.

Headers and footers

Even if you aren't familiar with the terms "header" and "footer," you are familiar with headers and footers. A header is anything (such as a title) that appears at the top of each page in a document and a footer is anything (such as a page number) that appears at the bottom of each page in a document.

Headers and footers allow you to add page numbers, date and time stamps, your name and phone number, or anything else that you can think of to each page of your document.

To create a header or footer

1. From the Format menu, select the **Header and Footer** command.

2. Click on the header and/or footer check-box(es) in the Header and Footer dialog box (**Figure 9.13**) to create a header or footer (or both) for your document.

   Once you have turned on headers or footers, you can also change the distance between the header or footer and the edge of the paper. It's sometimes necessary to increase this distance to allow for borders or other elements on company stationery. We don't recommend reducing this distance from the default setting of .5", since most laser printers cannot print much closer to the edge of the page than .5" and your header or footer text may not print completely.

3. If you do not want the header and footer to show up on the first page of your document, click on the "Exclude header and footer from first page" checkbox.

4. Click the **OK** button to exit the dialog box.

5. Click in the newly created header or footer areas of your document (**Figure 9.14**) and type in whatever text you want.

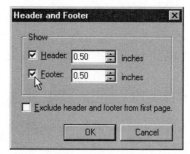

Figure 9.13 The Header and Footer dialog box.

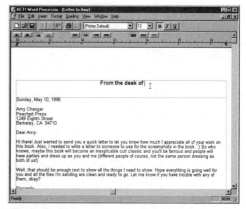

Figure 9.14 After creating the header or footer, just click in it and start typing.

✔ Tip

■ Headers and footers are the ideal places to put page numbers. Make sure you check out the "Working with pages" section on page 147.

HEADERS AND FOOTERS

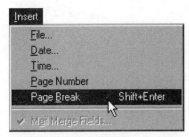

Figure 9.15 One command is all it takes to create a page break.

Working with pages

There are two page-specific tasks that you will need to perform in ACT!'s word processor from time to time: adding or removing page breaks and adding or removing page numbers.

Page breaks let you start a new page wherever you want, rather than having to wait until the page you are on fills up with text. If up to this point in your word-processing career you've been using 20 or 30 (or more) carriage returns to push text onto another page, you'll love this.

Page numbers let you (hold onto your hats) number your pages. Page numbers are generally placed in a header or footer. Once created, page numbers can be formatted or deleted like any regular block of text.

To add a page break

1. Position your insertion point just before the text that you want to appear on the next page.

2. From the Insert menu, select the **Page Break** command (**Figure 9.15**).

To remove a page break

1. Position your insertion point at the very beginning of the page after the page break. That is, if you want to remove the page break currently at the end of page one, position your insertion point at the very beginning of page two.

2. Hit the **Backspace** key on the keyboard. This will backspace over the invisible page break character, removing it.

To add page numbers

1. If your document does not already have headers or footers, create them (as discussed on page 146 of this chapter).

New terms you should know...

Header: Anything (text, placeholder fields, or graphics) that appears at the top of each printed page in a document.

Footer: Like a header, but appearing at the bottom of each printed page in a document.

2. Position your insertion point within the header or footer (depending on where you want the page numbers to appear).

3. From the Insert menu, select the **Page Number** command.

The correct page number now appears in the header or footer of every page of your document (**Figure 9.16**).

4. Format your page number as desired.

Page number

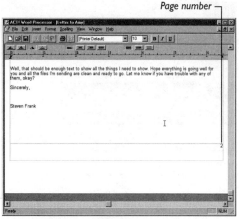

Figure 9.16 A page number placed in the header or footer changes from page to page.

WORKING WITH PAGES

Figure 9.17 Inserting a file is as easy as opening a file.

Inserting text files and placeholders

In addition to page breaks and page numbers, the Insert menu also lets you insert text files and date or time placeholders into your documents.

By inserting files you can add lengthy blocks of text or tables of data to your document, even if the text or table is several pages long, as long as you already have a file with the necessary data on disk somewhere. Think of inserting a file as a copy and paste on steroids.

Inserting date and time placeholders is a great way to make sure that your documents always have the correct date or time on them, since the placeholder text is updated with the current date or time whenever you open or print the document. You can also use insert plain date and time text (not placeholders) into your documents, but it's faster to just type it in (unless you don't know the correct date or time).

To insert a text file

1. Position your insertion point where you want the new text to appear.

2. From the Insert menu, select the **File** command.

3. In the Insert dialog box (**Figure 9.17**), select the file you want to insert and click the **OK** button.

   The entire contents of the file will be inserted into your document at the insertion point.

To insert date and time text or placeholders

1. Position your insertion point where you want the date or time to appear.

2. From the Insert menu, select either the **Date** command or the **Time** command.

3. Select the "Always update in document" option (**Figure 9.18**) to create a placeholder for the current date or time, or the "Never update in document" option to insert the date or time as text.

If you are inserting a date, you also have the option of inserting the date in either long or short format (**Figure 9.19**).

4. Click the **OK** button to insert the date or time into your document.

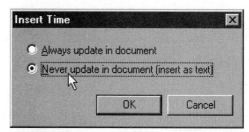

Figure 9.18 The "Always update in document option" creates a placeholder and is the only way to go.

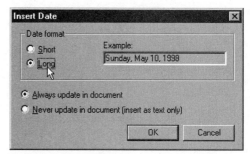

Figure 9.19 Inserted dates come in two varieties.

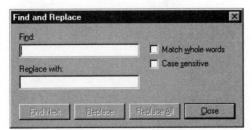

Figure 9.20 You can find and replace text form this dialog box.

Finding and replacing text

If you need to find a particular word or phrase in a long document, you can locate it quickly and easily using the word processor's Find and Replace command. If you need to change the word or phrase after locating it, the Find and Replace command will let you do that, too. Replacing text is especially useful if you have consistently misspelleda word, called someone by the wrong name, or quoted the wrong price.

To find text

1. From the Edit menu, select the **Find and Replace** command.

2. In the Find and Replace dialog box (**Figure 9.20**), type the text you want to find in the Find text box.

3. Click on the "Match whole words" or "Case sensitive" options if you want them on.

   If "Match whole words" is on ACT! won't find the specified text unless it is a whole word of its own (for example, it would not find "bill" when it is part of "billing" or "bills").

   If "Case sensitive" is on ACT! won't find the specified text unless its case matches the search text exactly (if it's looking for "bill" it will ignore "Bill").

4. Click the **Find Next** button.

   ACT! will highlight the first instance of the specified text in your document. If this is not the instance that you are looking for, continue clicking the Find Next button until you get to the instance that you want.

5. Click the **Close** button when you are done.

To replace text

1. From the Edit menu, select the **Find and Replace** command.

2. In the Find and Replace dialog box, type the text that you are looking for in the Find text box and type the text that you want to replace it with in the text box labeled "Replace with."

3. Click in the "Match whole words" or "Case sensitive" checkboxes to turn those options on, if desired.

4. To replace all instances of the search text, click on the **Replace All** button.

5. To replace selected instances of the search text, click on the **Find Next** button until you locate an instance you want to change, then click on the **Replace** button. Repeat this Find Next/Replace combination to replace additional instances.

6. Click the **Close** button when you are finished.

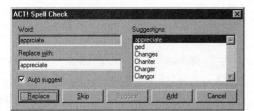

Figure 9.21 Each time ACT! finds an unrecognized word, you'll be presented with this dialog box.

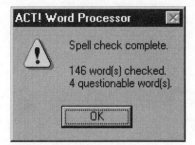

Figure 9.22 A brief summary of your spelling prowess.

Checking your spelling

Like all word processors, ACT!'s word processor has a spell checker built into it. The spell checker will quickly locate most misspellings and let you change them. Keep in mind, though, that ACT's word processor doesn't really know how to spell. It just checks to see if it recognizes each word in your document. This means that it might flag correctly spelled words that it hasn't seen before (like technical terms and proper names) and that it might miss incorrectly spelled words if the incorrect spelling happens to match that of another word (for example, if you type "the" as "thee").

To spell-check a document

1. From the Spelling menu, select the **Check Document** command.

   ACT! will begin checking your document for words that it doesn't recognize. When it finds the first unknown word, it will display the Spell Check dialog box (**Figure 9.21**).

2. Click on the **Replace, Skip,** or **Add** button to replace the selected word, skip it, or add it to your user dictionary.

   ACT! will display a list of possible replacement words on the right side of the dialog box, highlighting its best guess as to the correct spelling.. If this is not the correct word, you can click on any other word in the list or simply type in the correct spelling before clicking on the Change button.

   Adding a word to your user dictionary with the Add button will cause ACT! to ignore the word in all future spell checks.

3. Continue replacing, skipping, or adding words until ACT! finishes the spell check and presents you with a Spell Check Summary dialog box (**Figure 9.22**).

4. Click the **OK** button to continue working on your document.

✔ Tip

- You can spell-check a portion of a document (rather than the entire document) by selecting the desired block of text first, then choosing the Check Selection command from the Spelling menu.

Working with dictionaries

As you perform spell-checks of your documents, you can add words that ACT! doesn't recognize to your user dictionary. This will prevent ACT! from flagging the word the next time you run a spell-check. You can also create multiple dictionaries (one for medical terms and one for legal terms, for example). We do not recommend this, as you may then have to run a spell-check, switch dictionaries, and then run the spell-check again.

Note that you do not have to create your first user dictionary. ACT! does that for you automatically.

To create a dictionary

1. From the Spelling menu, select the **Create User Dictionary** command.

   ACT! presents you with a New User Dictionary dialog box, which is almost identical to a standard Open or Save dialog box.

2. Type a name for your new dictionary and click the **Open** button.

To switch dictionaries

1. From the Spelling menu, select the **Select Dictionaries** command.

   This opens the Preferences dialog box and activates the Spelling tab within it.

2. Click on the build button to the right of the current "Main dictionary" or the current "User dictionary" listing (**Figure 9.23**).

   You should only change your main dictionary if you are writing in another language. You will usually only change which user dictionary you are using.

3. In the Choose Dictionary dialog box (**Figure 9.24**), select the desired dictionary and click the **Open** button.

Figure 9.23 All dictionary changes are made from this screen, which is actually just one page of the Preferences dialog box.

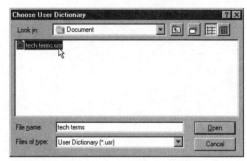

Figure 9.24 You can choose from any dictionaries that you have created or acquired.

WORKING WITH DICTIONARIES

Figure 9.25 You can modify the contents of any user dictionary from here.

4. Click the **OK** button to return to the word-processor window.

To edit a dictionary

1. From the Spelling menu, select the **Modify User Dictionary** command.

   ACT! displays a User Dictionary dialog box (**Figure 9.25**).

2. To add a word, click on the **Add** button, type the word in the Add Word dialog box, and click **OK**.

3. To remove a word, click on the word you want to remove and click the **Remove** button. At the warning dialog box, click the **Yes** button.

4. To modify a word, click on the word you want to modify, click on the **Modify** button, and type in the new version of the word. Click on the **OK** button.

5. When you are done editing, click the **OK** button at the bottom of the User Dictionary dialog box to return to the word processor.

Managing documents

Document management in ACT!'s word processor is much like it is in most applications you're familiar with. Saving and opening files is a snap, especially since ACT! automatically defaults to the correct folder (the Documents folder) each time you save or open files. The only real difference is in printing files, since ACT! prompts you to print envelopes for documents (a nice touch, we think) and to create a history entry. This history entry is then added to the contact record's Notes/History tab for later viewing and use in reports.

To save a document

1. From the File menu, select the **Save As** command.

If you just want to save changes to an already existing file, choose Save from the File menu and you're done.

2. In the Save As dialog box, type in the name you want for the file and click the **Save** button.

ACT! saves all word-processing documents into its Documents folder automatically, so there is no need to specify a location for your file. If you have lots of documents and want to organize them, you can create additional folders within the Documents folder, but we don't recommend saving files outside of the Documents folder. (Nothing bad will happen, it's just a pain to have to constantly switch out of the default documents folder every time you want to open or save a file.)

To open a document

1. From the File menu, select the **Open** command.

2. Select the file you want to open and click the **Open** button.

MANAGING DOCUMENTS

Figure 9.26 You can open word-processing files even if you aren't in the word processor.

Figure 9.27 Printing is usually just a matter of clicking OK.

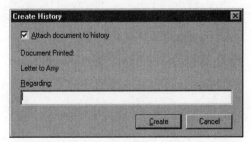

Figure 9.28 After any document is printed, you will have the option of creating a history entry.

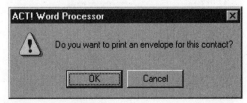

Figure 9.29 ACT! thinks envelopes go nicely with all documents.

If you want to open a word-processing document directly from the main ACT! program, use the Open command, but then change the file type at the bottom of the Open dialog box to "ACT! Word Processor Document (*.wpa)" (**Figure 9.26**). This will switch ACT! over to the Documents folder.

To print a document

1. From the File menu, select the **Print** command.

2. Change any desired settings as you would in any standard Print dialog box (**Figure 9.27**).

   You can switch printers from the Printer Name drop-down list, specify page ranges in the Print Range section, or indicate the number of copies to be printed in the Copies section.

3. Click the **OK** button to start printing.

4. In the Create History dialog box that appears after you print (**Figure 9.28**), type in what the document was regarding in the Regarding text box and click the **Create** button.

   If you do not want a history entry for this document, just click on the "Attach document to history" checkbox to turn it off.

5. After printing is complete, ACT! will ask if you want to print an envelope as well (**Figure 9.29**).

   Click **OK** to print an envelope to go with the document or **Cancel** if you do not want an envelope.

MANAGING DOCUMENTS

Printing envelopes and labels

Printing envelopes or labels for mass mailings (newsletters, flyers, and so on) in ACT! is easy and extremely useful. Unlike most of the tasks discussed in this chapter, the creation of envelopes and labels is accomplished from ACT! itself, not from the word processor.

To print envelopes

1. Make sure that you are in the main ACT! program and locate the contact or contacts for whom you want to print envelopes.

   For multiple contacts, perform a lookup or select a group, as discussed in Chapter 4, *Working with Groups* (page 56) or Chapter 5, *Lookups and Queries* (page 71).

2. From the File menu, select the **Print** command.

3. In the Print dialog box, select **Envelopes** from the Printout Type drop-down list (**Figure 9.30**).

4. Select the type of envelope you want from the list on the left-hand side and click the **OK** button.

5. In the Run Envelope dialog box, click on the desired set of contacts in the "Create report for" section on the left side of the dialog box (**Figure 9.31**) and click the **OK** button.

6. Choose the feed method that matches your printer's requirements (left, center, or right feed and face up or face down) in the Envelope Feed dialog box (**Figure 9.32**) and click **OK** one last time.

To print labels

1. Make sure that you are in the main ACT! program (not the word processor) and locate the contact or contacts for whom

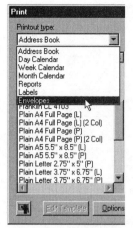

Figure 9.30 Envelopes are one of many options in ACT!'s Print dialog box.

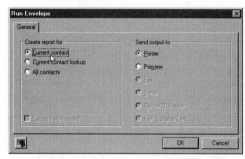

Figure 9.31 ACT! considers envelopes a type of report.

Figure 9.32 Because there are different feed methods for printing envelopes, you need to let ACT! know how your envelopes will go into your printer.

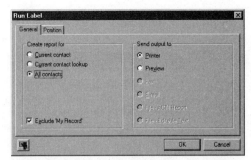

Figure 9.33 Like envelopes, labels are considered a type of report.

you want to print labels (using a lookup or group, if necessary).

2. From the File menu, select the **Print** command.

3. In the Print dialog box, select **Labels** from the Printout Type drop-down list.

4. Select the type of label you want from the list on the left-hand side and click the **OK** button.

Just find the number on the front of your Avery label box. If you are not using Avery labels, you can use the Custom label option, but you may need to edit the template to match your labels. Editing report templates is covered on page 165 in Chapter 10, *Reports*.

5. In the Run Label dialog box (**Figure 9.33**), click on the desired set of contacts in the "Create report for" section on the left side of the dialog box and click the **OK** button.

6. A standard Print dialog box appears. Make sure that the labels are ready in your printer and click the **OK** button.

Creating and customizing document templates

As we have seen, using templates as the basis for your documents can save a lot of time and effort. Once you have used any of the standard templates a few times, you will undoubtedly think of new ideas for templates or see ways in which existing templates could be improved.

Some ideas for new templates might include personal (informal) letters, thank-you notes, meeting reminders, name tags, and seating placards.

Existing templates can be modified to fit better on company stationery, include more or less contact data, use a different font or other formatting, or just have a different complimentary closing.

Templates can also be edited to include body text, so that a letter of introduction (for example), could be completely written, including all sorts of information and strategic placement of field placeholders ("Thanks again, << first name>> for this opportunity to serve you and all the fine folks at <<company name>>.") . It is these templates that will be used when you want to create form letters for mass mailings.

To create a new template

1. From the File menu, select the **New** command.

2. In the New dialog box. select the **ACT! Word Processor Template** option and click the **OK** button.

   ACT! will open a blank word-processing document, just as if you were creating a new regular document, but will also display the Mail Merge Fields dialog box (**Figure 9.34**).

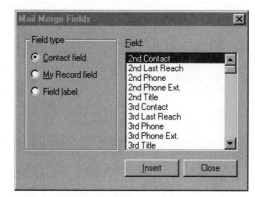

Figure 9.34 Creating a template is like creating a regular document, but you also have the option to add fields.

Figure 9.35 When modifying an existing template you start with a whole bunch of fields already in your document.

3. Type any text that you will want to appear on every document created from this template; for example, the "Dear" in the salutation and the "Sincerely" in the complimentary closing.

4. Whenever you get to a point in your typing where you want to insert a field placeholder, simply scroll through the list of fields in the Mail Merge Fields dialog box and double-click on the desired field.

   For example, after the "Dear" in the salutation you would probably want to insert the First Name field or the Salutation and Last Name fields.

5. Format your document as desired (changing margins, paragraph alignment, and character formatting, as discussed earlier in this chapter) and save normally.

To modify a template

1. From the Write menu, select the **Edit Document Template** command.

2. Select the template you want to work with in the standard Open dialog box and click the **Open** button.

   ACT! opens the template in the word processor and displays the Mail Merge Fields dialog box (just as it does when you create a new template) (**Figure 9.35**).

3. Edit and reformat the template as you would any word-processing document.

4. Delete fields manually and replace them (when desired) by scrolling through the list of fields in the Mail Merge Fields dialog box and double-clicking on the desired field.

5. Unless you are sure that you want to change the original template, select the **Save As** command from the File menu and save the file under a different name.

Modifying the Write menu

The Write menu includes commands for opening three standard document templates (Letter, Memorandum, and Fax Cover Page). If you find yourself using a particular template of your own on a regular basis, you may want to add that template to the Write menu as well. You can easily add templates to the menu or remove them with the Modify Menu command (at the bottom of the Write menu).

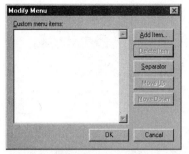

Figure 9.36 The Modify Menu dialog box

To add a template to the Write menu

1. From the Write menu, select the **Modify Menu** command.

2. In the Modify Menu dialog box (**Figure 9.36**), click on the **Add Item** button.

3. In the Add Custom Menu Item dialog box, click on the **Build** button (the one with three dots on it) (**Figure 9.37**).

4. Select the template you want to add and click the **Open** button.

5. Enter a name for this template in the "Command name to display in menu" text entry box.

6. Click the **OK** button to exit the Add Custom Menu Item dialog box, and click **OK** again to exit the Modify Menu dialog box.

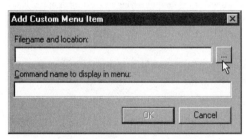

Figure 9.37 Use the Build button to select a template file.

To remove a template from the Write menu

1. From the Write menu, select the **Modify Menu** command.

2. In the Modify Menu dialog box, select the template that you want to remove.

3. Click the **Delete Item** button.

4. Click the **OK** button.

✔ Tip

- You can also rearrange menu items by using the Move Up and Move Down buttons in the Modify Menu dialog box. The Separator button will add a separator line to your menu, allowing you to group customized menu items.

MODIFYING THE WRITE MENU

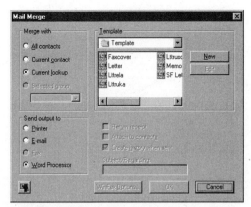

Figure 9.38 Choices, choices, choices! Never a dull moment in the Mail Merge dialog box.

Generating form letters

You'll usually create form letters when you want to send out mass mailings (printed or e-mail) or broadcast faxes. The process of generating form letters is a fairly simple one, considering all the work that goes into them. (Fortunately, ACT! is going to be doing all the work for you.) In ACT! a form letter is basically a document created from a template, but created repeatedly for an entire set of contact records.

To create a form letter

1. Select a group or create a lookup of all the contacts to whom you want to send your letter.

2. From the Write menu, select the **Mail Merge** command.

   The Mail Merge dialog box (**Figure 9.38**) appears, with all sorts of interesting options.

3. In the "Merge with" section (in the upper-left corner), select the set of contacts whose information will be merged with the form letter.

4. In the "Template" section, select the document template that you want to use as the basis for your form letter.

   The New and Edit buttons in this section allow you to create new templates or edit existing templates during the merge process. To avoid confusion, we highly recommend preparing your templates beforehand.

5. In the "Send output to" section (in the lower-left corner), select Printer, E-mail, Fax, or Word Processor.

   Depending on what you select, different options will become active in the area immediately to the right of this section. If you selected the printer as your output option, you can have a history entry

created. For e-mail, you can also request
a return receipt and attach it to the contact
record. For faxes (only available if you have
WinFax software installed and configured
on your computer) you can change the
WinFax options (usually not necessary if
WinFax has been correctly configured to
begin with).

6. After selecting all desired options, click
the **OK** button.

10

REPORTS

Ah, reports! If you have been conscientious about entering contact data accurately and completely, if you've faithfully created ACT! activities for all of the work you've been doing, if you have added notes and history entries whenever you came across pertinent contact data, then it's time for all of your hard work to pay off.

The capability to generate a wide variety of useful reports is one of the nicest and most powerful features of ACT!. These reports can be as simple (and as indispensable) as a phone list, or as thorough as a complete printout of all contact data or of all activities and time spent for days, weeks, months, or even years.

ACT! comes with several standard reports ready for you to use. You can also edit existing reports to better suit your needs or even create custom reports from scratch. This chapter discusses generating reports and making simple modifications to report templates. Because some of the facets of creating and editing report templates are so complex, an entire chapter (Chapter 16, *Advanced Reports*) has been set aside for the discussion of the more advanced aspects of working with report templates.

Understanding ACT! reports

An ACT! report is sort of the opposite of a form letter in that a form letter takes a single document and creates multiple copies for all of your contacts, while a report takes different information from all of your contacts and transforms that information into a single document.

All reports are based on templates, which are much like the templates used in creating standard documents and form letters (see Chapter 9, *Word Processing in ACT!* on page 137 for more info). A report template contains "boilerplate" text such as a title and column headings. It also contains fields placeholders. These field placeholders tell ACT! what fields to go to (in each contact or group record) to get the data that will make up the report.

When generating a report, you will usually want to perform a lookup or select a group to work with.

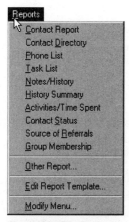

Figure 10.1 The Reports menu contains the ten standard reports.

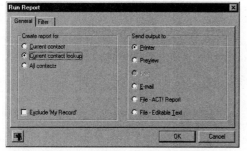

Figure 10.2 When running a report, you need to specify which records it's for and what output you want.

Generating standard reports

ACT! ships with ten standard reports, all of which are shown in the Reports menu (**Figure 10.1**). The inclusion of these standard reports in the menu makes generating your reports quick and easy, with a minimum of dialog boxes to work through.

To generate a standard report

1. Create a lookup or select a group to define the subset of records that this report will include.

   If you want to create the report for all of your records, you can obviously skip this step.

2. From the Reports menu, select the type of report that you want to create (any of the first 10 items in the Reports menu).

3. In the Run Report dialog box (**Figure 10.2**), select which subset of records you want to create the report for (in the "Create report for" section on the left side of the dialog box).

4. If you do not want your own information included in the report, click on the "Exclude 'My Record'" checkbox.

5. Select the desired output type from the list of options on the right side of the dialog box and click the **OK** button.

✔ Tip

- We highly recommend always outputting to Preview rather than the other options, especially the first time you run a report. There are few things worse than printing 200 pages worth of the wrong report. By selecting the Preview option, you will be able to review the report in ACT!'s word processor *before* printing or e-mailing it.

Generating nonstandard reports

Nonstandard reports are any reports that use a template other than the ten listed in the Reports menu. These templates may be slightly modified versions of the standard reports, custom reports of your own creation, or reports that you have been given by your database administrator.

To generate a report using a nonstandard template

1. As with standard reports, create a lookup or select a group to define the subset of records that this report will include, unless you are creating the report for all records.

2. From the Reports menu, select the **Other Report** command (**Figure 10.3**).

3. In the standard Open dialog box, select the report template that you want to use and click the **Open** button.

4. In the Run Report dialog box, select which records you want to create the report for (in the "Create report for" section on the left side of the dialog box).

5. If you do not want your own information included in the report, click on the "Exclude 'My Record'" checkbox (**Figure 10.4**).

6. Select the desired output type from the list of options on the right side of the dialog box and click the **OK** button.

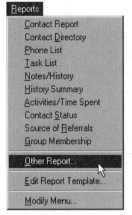

Figure 10.3 The Other Report command lets you choose from among all of your report templates.

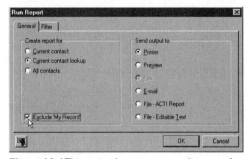

Figure 10.4 This option keeps your own data out of the reports you create.

✔ Tip

■ If you find yourself using a nonstandard report template on a regular basis, you will probably want to add that template to the Reports menu. Doing so will make the nonstandard report as easy to access as the standard reports. Modifying the Reports menu is discussed on page 183, later in this chapter.

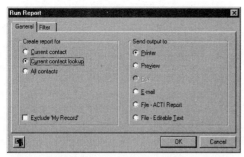

Figure 10.5 Set your regular Run Report dialog box options before filtering.

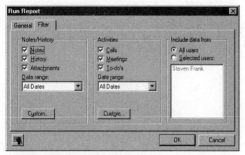

Figure 10.6 Set your Filter options from the second screen of this dialog box.

Filtering reports

One option that many ACT! users are not aware of (or don't take advantage of if they are aware of it) is that you can filter your reports during the creation process. Filtering lets you specify a date range for the report, exclude types of activities, or omit contact data such as notes or history entries.

For example, you might want to filter out notes for a report so that your personal contact notes don't become part of a widely distributed report.

All filtering is done from within the Run Report dialog box, which you see as part of the normal report-generation process.

To filter a report

1. Create the report as you normally would (creating a lookup or selecting a group, then selecting the desired report from the Reports menu).

2. Set inclusion and output options as you normally would in the Run Report dialog box (**Figure 10.5**).

   In the "Create report for" section, select the set of contacts who will be included in the report. You can also exclude your own record in this section.

   In the "Send output to" section, select the output that you want generated. (We highly recommend the "Preview" option.)

3. In the Run Report dialog box, click on the **Filter** tab (in the upper-left corner of the dialog box).

   This will activate the Filter screen of the Run Report dialog box (**Figure 10.6**), which contains all of the filtering options for reports.

4. Select the desired filtering options from the "Notes/History," "Activities," and "Include data from" sections.

In the "Notes/History" section you can exclude notes, history entries, or attachments by clicking on the appropriate checkboxes. You can also specify the dates from which you want to include notes or history entries using the Date Range pop-up list or the Custom button (to choose a custom range of dates).

The "Activities" section works exactly like the "Notes/History" section, but lets you exclude calls, meetings, and to-do activities.

The "Include data from" section lets you specify which database users you want to use in the report (this applies to a multi-user database only, of course). You can include "all users" or choose the "Selected users" option and pick from a list of users.

5. Click the **OK** button to generate your report.

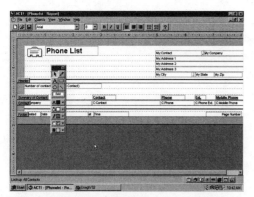

Figure 10.7 The Report Editor window is unlike anything you've seen so far in ACT!

Understanding the report template environment

All ACT! reports are based on templates. These templates contain text, graphics, and field placeholders to tell ACT! where to put the data it pulls from contact records when it generates a report . Report templates are created and edited in the Report Editor, a working environment unlike anything else in ACT! If you worked with document templates in Chapter 9, you'll have a head start on the *concept* of report templates, but the actual *construction* (or destruction, as the case may be) of report templates is going to be completely different.

The Report Editor is an object-oriented graphic editing environment, similar in concept to many drawing programs. (If you missed working with document templates, they are edited in a standard word processor, which is why knowing how to do one type of editing doesn't necessarily help you to do the other.). Everything in a report template is a separate object that can be edited, moved, formatted, or deleted without affecting any other objects. In the sample template shown in **Figure 10.7**, the rolodex graphic, report title ("Phone List"), column headings (the bold, underlined text), and field placeholders ("C:Contact," "C:Phone," etc.) are all separate objects.

Because report templates are object-oriented, you use tools that are provided for selecting and manipulating these objects. The floating palette (near the left edge of the figure) contains buttons for selecting, manipulating, and adding objects.

The concept that will probably seem the most unusual to many ACT! users is that of *report sections*. These sections are used to organize the data presented in a report. For example, anything placed in a Header section appears at the top of each page of a report, anything in the Contact section is repeated for each contact record, and anything in the Footer section appears at the bottom of each page of the report. (The "Summary of Contact" section shown in the example is used to summarize any data for all contacts—in this case, the total number of contacts in the report.) You can resize these sections as needed by simply dragging the section labels up or down.

Along the left and top borders of the editing window are rulers, which can be used to help you precisely position objects, and at the very top of the window is a toolbar, which contains fairly standard buttons for file management and text formatting. The only two unique buttons are the two object-alignment buttons (at the far right on the toolbar), which are explained in detail in the *Aligning Objects* (page 181) section, later in this chapter.

Like document templates, report templates are opened, closed, saved, and renamed using standard document-management techniques (that is, the Open, Close, Save, and Save As commands in the File menu).

New terms you should know...

Object-oriented: Any software that allows you to work with a block of data independently. A drawing program is object-oriented, since a shape can be deleted without affecting other shapes. A word processor is not object-oriented, because deleting a word at the beginning of a document affects the location of every other word in the document.

Viewing report templates

You can easily view (and edit) report templates in the Report Editor, one of ACT!'s many modules. Unlike document templates, report templates are edited within the ACT! program itself. No other application (such as the word processor used for documents) is opened.

To open a report template

1. From the Reports menu, select the **Edit Report Template** command.

2. In the resulting Open dialog box, select the template you want to view and click the **Open** button.

To close a report template

1. From within the Report Editor, select the **Close** command from the File menu.

Don't use File>Exit (as you do when you are done editing documents or document templates) or you will exit ACT!.

✔ Note

■ All of the following sections (except for the last two, *Modifying the Reports menu* and *Customizing envelope and label templates*) assume that you have already opened the report template that you want to work with.

Modifying template text

The easiest changes to make to a report template are those involving text editing, since most users are already familiar with this process. In your report templates, you can add text, edit existing text, or change the appearance of existing text.

To add text to a report template

1. Click on the Text button in the floating tool palette (**Figure 10.8**).

2. Position the crosshair cursor at the point in the template where you want the new text block to appear.

3. Press the mouse button and drag to the right to create a rectangular text block, then release the mouse button (**Figure 10.9**).

4. Type your text.

   You text will wrap to fit within the text block that you defined in step 3 (**Figure 10.10**). If you don't like the position of your text block, you can move it or resize it as discussed in the *Moving and resizing objects* section, later in this chapter.

To edit text in a report template

1. Locate the text block that contains the text you want to change.

2. Click on the Text button in the tool palette.

3. Click on the text block.

   This "opens" the text block, allowing you to edit the text within it.

4. Edit the text as you would in any text editing environment.

To format text in a report template

1. Select the text or text block that you want to format.

Figure 10.8 The Text tool button looks like a big "A."

Figure 10.9 You should define the size of a text block before typing text.

Figure 10.10 You text will wrap within the text block you create.

Figure 10.11 The Selection Arrow button looks like an arrow (almost as if there were a plan).

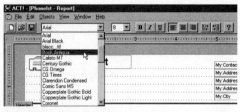

Figure 10.12 The Report Editor toolbar functions like many word-processing toolbars when it comes to formatting text.

To select an entire block, click on the Selection Arrow button in the tool palette (**Figure 10.11**), then click on the desired text block.

To select text within a text block, click on the Text button in the tool palette, click on the desired text block, then press and drag across the desired text.

2. Change the font, size, emphasis, or alignment of the selected text by clicking on the appropriate drop-down menu or button in the toolbar at the top of the window (**Figure 10.12**).

To delete text blocks from a report template

1. Click on the Selection Arrow button in the tool palette.

2. Click on the text block you no longer want.

3. Hit the Delete key on your keyboard.

Adding and removing fields

One common reason to edit a report is that it doesn't display exactly the information that you need, or it displays information that you really don't care about.

Adding and removing fields is a fairly painless procedure, at least in its basics. In Chapter 16, *Advanced Reports* (on page XX), we'll discuss additional (and more complex) options for adding fields.

To add a field to a report template

1. Click on the **Field** button in the tool palette.

2. Position the cursor where you want the new field to appear and press and drag the mouse to the right to define the size of the field object.

    When you release the mouse button, the Field List dialog box will appear (**Figure 10.13**).

    If you are replacing one field with another, you will probably want to delete the old field first, as discussed below.

3. Select the desired field from the list of available fields at the left side of the dialog box, then click the **Add** button.

4. Click the **Close** button to exit the dialog box.

    By default a label will be inserted along with the field itself. If you do not want the label, you can just select and delete it.

To remove a field from a report template

1. Click on the **Selection Arrow** button in the tool palette.

2. Click on the field you no longer want.

3. Hit the Delete key on your keyboard.

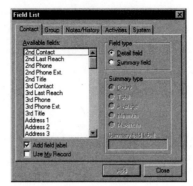

Figure 10.13 Select the field you want from this dialog box.

> ### New terms you should know...
>
> **Label**: A block of text that is used to identify the contents of a field. Labels are standard text blocks and can be edited or deleted without affecting the field that they identify.

ADDING AND REMOVING FIELDS

Figure 10.14 The Object Properties dialog box

Changing field properties

In addition to the regular formatting that you can do to the text in fields (boldfacing, changing the font or size, etc.), fields have certain properties that you can change. These properties reflect the fact that fields (unlike regular text blocks) get their data from contact records, and so might duplicate one another, be blank, or contain more text than will fit in the allotted space on the report. If you want to hide duplicate field entries, remove blank space, or wrap text on a report, you will need to change field properties.

To change the properties of a field

1. Locate the field that whose properties you want to change.

2. Make sure that you have the selection arrow active (click on it in the tool palette if necessary) and double-click on the field whose properties you need to change.

   This brings up the Object Properties dialog box (**Figure 10.14**).

3. Select the desired options by clicking on the **Don't print if duplicated, Close up blank space**, or **Wrap text** checkboxes.

4. Click the **OK** button to exit the dialog box.

Adding graphic objects to templates

Nothing spices up a report more than a nice border or some well-placed shading to highlight important information. It's very easy to add these graphic niceties.

To add a border, box, or other graphic object to a report template

1. Click on the **Rectangle, Ellipse** (oval), or **Line** button in the tool palette (**Figure 10.15**), depending on the type of object you want to create.

   The line tool is best for separating sections and the rectangle tool is best for borders and shading. The ellipse tool really isn't used all that much.

2. Position your cursor at the place in the template where you want the object to begin, then press the mouse button down and drag to where you want the object to end. Release the mouse button.

   If you make a mistake, just hit the **Delete** key and do it again.

   Once you've created the object, you will undoubtedly want to format it, which is described in the next section.

✔ Tips

■ To create a perfect square or circle or to draw a line on an exact 45° angle, hold down the Shift key while you draw the object.

■ To create a border around something, draw a rectangle that completely covers the area you want bordered, then format the rectangle so that it has no fill.

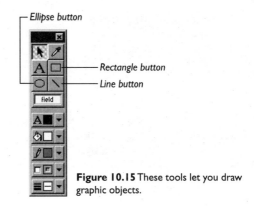

Ellipse button

Rectangle button

Line button

Figure 10.15 These tools let you draw graphic objects.

Figure 10.16 The bottom half of the tool palette contains all of the object-formatting menus.

Figure 10.17 The two wire squares indicate a clear fill or invisible line or text.

Formatting objects

Formatting objects in a report enables you to change the way an object looks without changing the actual data within the object. The majority of the formatting that you do will involve formatting text, but you will undoubtedly be formatting some graphics as well, changing the color, line thickness, or style of any graphic objects you create.

To format an object in a report template

1. Select the object by clicking on it with the selection arrow.

2. Press on any of the drop-down arrows in the bottom half of the tool palette to change (from top to bottom) the text color, fill color, line color, border style, or line thickness (**Figure 10.16**).

   Each arrow provides a different palette of choices. The first square in most of the palettes represents a clear/invisible color (**Figure 10.17**).

✔ Tips

■ You can do quick formatting on an object by double-clicking it with the selection arrow. This will bring up the Object Properties dialog box, within which you can change the color, line style, font and font size, and more.

■ You can also use the Objects menu to move items forward or backward, which lets you place one object behind another object. By doing this, you could create a colored rectangle and place it behind some text to shade the text, for example.

FORMATTING OBJECTS

Moving and resizing objects

If you are at all familiar with object-oriented graphics software (such as drawing or page layout programs), then you already know how to move and resize objects in ACT! report templates. If you aren't familiar with these types of programs, you are about to learn something that you will use for the rest of your computing life, as all object-oriented graphics programs move and resize objects in more or less the same way.

To move an object in a report template

1. If you don't already have the selection arrow cursor, click the **Selection Arrow** button in the tool palette.

    You can only move and resize objects with the selection arrow.

2. Press anywhere on the object you want to move other than its borders, and drag it to the desired location.

    That's all there is to it!

To resize an object in a report template

1. Click the **Selection Arrow**.

2. Click on the object you want to resize.

    This selects the object, as indicated by the "selection handles" around the perimeter of the object (**Figure 10.18**).

3. Position the tip of the selection arrow inside one of the selection handles.

    Your cursor will change shape to indicate the directions in which the handle can be moved (**Figure 10.19**).

4. Press on the handle and drag it in any legal direction (as indicated by the cursor) until the object is the desired size and shape.

Figure 10.18 A selected object has these selection handles.

Figure 10.19 You can drag the handle left or right.

New terms you should know...

Selection handles: Small squares which appear around the perimeter of selected objects. These small squares both indicate that an object is selected, and provide the means by which the selected object can be resized.

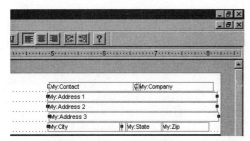

Figure 10.20 All objects you want to align must first be selected.

Figure 10.21 The Align Left and Align Right buttons.

Aligning objects

Aside from including the correct data, the single biggest factor in creating a professional-looking report is attention to detail, especially small graphic details like making sure that all of your columns line up, or that your borders are even.

Even for the meticulously patient and precise user, it is not always possible to align objects precisely. This is usually because your monitor's resolution is very crude compared to that of a laser printer, so what might look perfect on-screen is revealed to be slightly off when printed.

Fortunately, ACT! provides a fast and painless way to exactly align objects.

To align objects in report templates

1. Select all of the objects that you want to align.

   Make sure that you don't select objects that don't need to be aligned. In this example (**Figure 10.20**) we are aligning along the left edge, so the Company, State, and Zip fields are not selected. If they were selected, they would move all the way over to the left, which we do not want.

2. Click on the **Align Left** or **Align Right** buttons in the toolbar (**Figure 10.21**).

   All objects are moved horizontally to line up with the first item selected.

Adding external graphics to report templates

It's a nice touch on any report to add a little graphic enhancement such as a company logo or a bit of professional clip art. Unfortunately, ACT! does not have a feature that enables you to import or place graphics. This doesn't mean that you can't add graphics to report templates, though. You just have to use the old, reliable copy-and-paste method.

Figure 10.22 Graphics can make your reports more appealing. Hmmm, this guy looks familiar.

To add a picture or outside graphic to a report template

1. Open the document that contains the graphic you want to add to your report, in whatever application is appropriate.

2. Select the graphic.
   How you select the graphic will depend on the program that you are in.

3. From the Edit menu of your graphics program, select the **Copy** command.

4. Switch back to ACT! using the Windows task bar.

5. From the Edit menu in ACT!, select the **Paste** command.
   Your graphic will be added to your report template as an independent object (**Figure 10.22**). You can move, resize, or delete the graphic, but not format it.

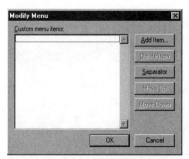

Figure 10.23 The Modify Menu dialog box

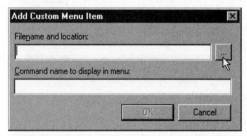

Figure 10.24 Use the Build button to select a report template file.

Modifying the Reports menu

You can quickly create any of the ten standard reports using the Reports menu. If you find yourself using a particular report template of your own on a regular basis, you may want to add that template to the Reports menu as well. Templates can be easily added to and removed from the menu with the Modify Menu command.

To add a template to the Reports menu

1. From the Reports menu, select the **Modify Menu** command.

2. In the Modify Menu dialog box (**Figure 10.23**), click on the **Add Item** button.

3. In the Add Custom Menu Item dialog box, click on the **Build** button (the one with three dots on it) (**Figure 10.24**).
   This will give you a standard Open dialog box displaying the contents of the Report folder.

4. Select the report template you want to add to the menu and click the **Open** button.

5. Enter a name for this template in the "Command name to display in menu" text entry box.

6. Click the **OK** button to exit the Add Custom Menu Item dialog box, and click **OK** again to exit the Modify Menu dialog box.

To remove a template from the Reports menu

1. From the Reports menu, select the **Modify Menu** command.

2. In the Modify Menu dialog box, select the template that you no longer want.

3. Click on the **Delete Item** button.

✔ Tip

- You can also rearrange menu items by using the Move Up and Move Down buttons in the Modify Menu dialog box. The Separator button will add a separator line to your menu, allowing you to group customized menu items.

MODIFYING THE REPORTS MENU

Customizing envelope and label templates

Envelope and label templates, while used mainly when working with documents, not reports, are edited in the exact same fashion as reports are. That is, even though you use envelopes and labels more when creating documents, they are actually reports and are edited as such.

To customize an envelope or label template

1. From the File menu, select the **Print** command.

   This brings up ACT!'s Print dialog box.

2. From the Printout Type drop-down list, select either Envelopes or Labels (**Figure 10.25**).

3. On the left side of the Print dialog box, click on the type of envelope or label whose template you want to edit.

4. Click on the **Edit Template** button.

   ACT! opens the template for you to edit (**Figures 10.26** and **10.27**).

5. Edit the template as you would any report template.

6. Save the template and close the window when you are done.

   Use the Save As command to create a new template file, or use the Save command to make changes to the existing template. (We highly recommend not altering the standard templates!)

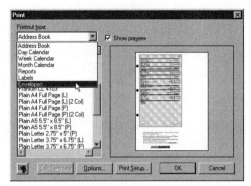

Figure 10.25 Select either Envelopes or Labels to edit a template.

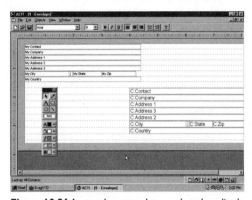

Figure 10.26 An envelope template, ready to be edited.

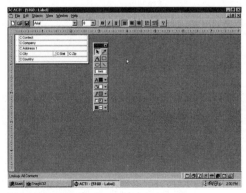

Figure 10.27 A label template, also awaiting your editing pleasure.

CUSTOMIZING ENVELOPE AND LABEL TEMPLATES

STAYING
IN CONTACT

As any successful businessperson knows, keeping in touch with your clients is the most important aspect of any business. With ACT!, you can call, fax, or e-mail them more easily and efficiently than ever.

ACT! can dial the phone for you, time and log all calls, send faxes to single or multiple contacts, check your e-mail, and send messages and files (or even contact or group records from your database) over your local e-mail system or the Internet.

Configuring the ACT! dialer

To be able to use any of ACT!'s dialer features, you must first configure the dialer. If the dialer is not configured and you click on the Dial Phone button, ACT! will force you to configure the dialer or abort the dialing attempt.

Configuring the dialer is a matter of setting options within the Dialer screen of the Preferences dialog box. These options include the type of modem you are using, where you are calling from, and a few other miscellaneous options. There isn't much to setting up the dialer, but you will need to know your modem type and which port it's plugged into (you can just look at the back of your computer to find that out).

To configure the dialer

1. Either click on the **Dial Phone** button in the toolbar and click the **Yes** button in the dialog box that appears (**Figure 11.1**), or select the **Preferences** command from the Edit menu and click on the **Dialer** tab.

   Either method will take you to the Dialer screen of the Preferences dialog box (**Figure 11.2**).

2. Click on the **Use dialer** checkbox to activate the rest of the options on this screen.

3. If you only have one modem or phone line connected to your computer, click the **OK** button at the dialog box that informs you of this. If you have multiple modems or phone lines connected to your computer, select the modem or phone line you want to use from the Modem or Line drop-down list.

   You can also change the setup for any of your modems by clicking the Setup button. This will take you to Windows' Properties dialog box for the selected

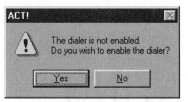

Figure 11.1 You must configure the dialer before ACT! can dial the phone for you.

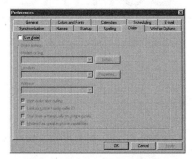

Figure 11.2 This is where you set your Dialer preferences.

CONFIGURING THE ACT! DIALER

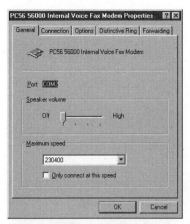

Figure 11.3 Any changes made here affect all programs that use this modem.

Figure 11.4 Creating or changing locations is usually necessary only on laptop computers.

modem (**Figure 11.3**). From here you can change any settings that your modem may support. These changes are made in Windows, not in ACT!, so they will be in effect whenever you use your modem.

4. Select a location from the Location drop-down list.

   For many users, the Default Location option is all they need. If you travel, you may want to set up additional locations by clicking the Properties button. This will bring up the Dialing Properties dialog box (**Figure 11.4**), within which you can change the settings for the current location or create new locations (by clicking the New button). This is ideal if you have a laptop computer and need to dial out from both work and home, or from regular client sites.

5. If you dial out from work and the phone line you use supports multiple extensions, you will need to select the correct line address from the Address drop-down list. Talk to your IS or phone administrator to find out which line address you should use.

6. Click on any of the four checkboxes at the bottom of the screen to select or deselect them as desired, then click the **OK** button.

   "Hide dialer after dialing" will hide the Dialer dialog box after ACT! dials the phone for you.

   "Lookup contacts for incoming calls using caller ID" will locate the correct contact(s) for incoming calls whenever possible, using the incoming Caller ID information.

   "Start timer automatically on outgoing calls" will start a timer for you so that you can track the amount of time spent on calls you make. This is ideal for lawyers, consultants, or anyone else who charges clients by the hour.

CONFIGURING THE ACT! DIALER

Lastly, "Modem has speakerphone capabilities" just lets ACT! know that your modem has speaker-phone capabilities.

✔ Tip

■ If your modem does have speaker-phone capabilities, don't hide the Dialer dialog box. You will need it to hang up the phone!

The wonders (and limitations) of Caller ID and ACT!

ACT!'s support of Caller ID is one of its really cool features. If you enable the "Lookup contact using Caller ID" checkbox in the Dialer preferences, ACT! will "listen" for the Caller ID information on all incoming calls. Whenever a call comes in with this information, ACT! will create a lookup of all contacts with the incoming phone number. Usually, this will bring up the record for the person who is calling you, and you will have all of their information and activities, as well as all of your notes, ready to go!

All of this sounds great, but there are some caveats to keep in mind:

♦ You must be using Windows 95. Caller ID doesn't work with Windows NT.

♦ Obviously, you must subscribe to Caller ID through your phone company.

♦ Your modem must support Caller ID.

♦ You must have the Unimodem V driver installed on a version of Windows 95 that supports this driver (not all versions do).

If you are unsure of whether or not your modem supports Caller ID, refer to the ACT 4.0 user manual (pages 259-262) or contact Symantec technical support.

Figure 11.5 One click away from a phone call...

Figure 11.6 The Dialer dialog box.

Calling contacts

One sure way to impress your colleagues is to have ACT! make your calls for you. (Actually it just dials the phone; you still have to do all the talking.) It's entirely possible that this will be a nice time-saving feature as well, but we all agree that getting an "ooh-ahh" from someone you work with beats saving a few minutes any day.

Before you use the dialer features of ACT! your hardware configuration (modem and phone line) must be properly set up, so make sure you complete the *Configuring the ACT! dialer* section (previous pages) first.

To have ACT! dial the phone

1. Go to the record for the contact that you want to call.

2. Click on the Dial Phone button (**Figure 11.5**).
    The Dialer dialog box (**Figure 11.6**) appears.

3. If you need to change the contact, click on the Build button (the one with the three dots on it) to the right of the contact name.

4. Select the desired phone number from the list of available numbers.

5. If you are not calling from your usual location, select a location from the Dialing from drop-down list.

6. If necessary, edit the "Number to dial" text to match the correct number.
    This is usually only necessary if either the contact is at a number that is not in the list, or you are calling from a location that requires an 8 or 9 to access an outside line.

7. Select the "Dial as a toll call" option if you are calling a number that is within your area code but still requires you to dial a 1 before the number.

CALLING CONTACTS

8. Click the **Dial** button.

Depending on your Dialer preferences settings, you may see a Timer dialog box, and the Dialer dialog box may change to include Hang Up, Speaker and Mute buttons (**Figure 11.7**).

9. When the person you are calling answers the phone, pick up your phone handset or (if your modem has speaker-phone capabilities) click on the **Speaker** button.

10. When you are done with your call, click the **Hang Up** button in the dialog box, or just hang up the phone

After you hang up, ACT! will present you with a Record History dialog box so that you can record the results of this phone call.

11. Complete the Record History dialog box to reflect the results of your call and click the **OK** button.

✔ Tip

■ You can place calls from the Task List, as well as from the Contacts view. In the Task List, select the call that needs to be made, then select the Phone Contact command at the bottom of the Contact menu. This will bring up the Dialer dialog box. After you complete a call in this fashion, ACT! will present you with a Clear Activity dialog box rather than a Record History dialog box, since making the call should clear the scheduled activity.

Figure 11.7 During a call, a Timer dialog may appear and your dialer buttons will change.

Figure 11.8 The Timer dialog box.

Logging phone calls

It pays to keep track of the work that you do, and that includes the calls that you make. If you bill on an hourly basis, it *really* pays to keep track of your calls. ACT! enables you to log all incoming and outgoing calls, which creates history entries in the appropriate contact records. ACT! also has a handy timer that lets you track just how long you are spending on each call.

To create a call history entry

1. Go to the contact record for the person whom you are calling or who has just called you.

    Again, if this person does not exist in your database yet, skip this step for now (later you can use the New Contact button in the Record History dialog box to create one for them).

2. From the Contact menu, select the **Record History** command.

    The Record History dialog box appears.

3. Complete the Record History dialog box to reflect the results of your call and click the **OK** button.

To create a timed call history entry

1. Go to the contact record for the person whom you are calling or who has just called you.

    If this person does not exist in your database yet, skip this step for now.

2. From the Tools menu, select the **Timer** command.

    The Timer dialog box appears in the upper-left corner of your screen (**Figure 11.8**).

3. Click on the **Start** button.

    During the call you can use the Pause and Reset buttons to pause or reset the timer.

4. When the call is complete, click on the **Stop** button.

The Timer dialog box disappears and the Record History dialog box appears.

5. Complete the Record History dialog box to reflect the results of your call and click the **OK** button.

If the person you just spoke with doesn't have a record in your database, click the New Contact button in the Record History dialog box (**Figure 11.9**) and create a record for them.

New Contact button

Figure 11.9 You can add new contacts to your database with this New Contact button.

✔ Tip

■ Both the Timer and Record History commands have keyboard shortcuts that you can use to save time. The keyboard shortcut for the Timer command is Shift-F4 and the keyboard shortcut for the Record History command is the easy-to-remember Ctrl-H.

Fax Software drop-down list

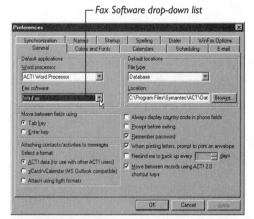

Figure 11.10 You select your fax software from the General preferences screen.

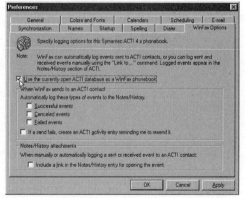

Figure 11.11 This WinFax Options screen is available only if you are using WinFax as your fax software. (Makes sense, doesn't it?)

Configuring ACT! to send faxes

Symantec has designed its excellent faxing software, WinFax Pro, to integrate with ACT! in as seamless a fashion as possible. If you use WinFax Pro as your faxing software, you can use ACT! databases as WinFax phonebooks, have WinFax create history entries and activities in your ACT! database, and even attach faxes to your contact records as files.

If you don't have WinFax Pro, you can use Microsoft Fax, the faxing software that is included as part of Windows 95.

To configure ACT! for faxing

1. From the Edit menu, select the **Preferences** command.

2. In the General screen of the Preferences dialog box, select either **Microsoft Fax** or **WinFax** from the Fax Software drop-down list (**Figure 11.10**).

   If you are using Microsoft Fax, the rest of these steps don't apply.

3. Click on the **WinFax Options** tab at the top of the dialog box.

4. In the WinFax Options screen, click on the "Use the currently open ACT! database as a WinFax phonebook" checkbox to turn this option on (this activates all of the other options) (**Figure 11.11**).

5. In the "When WinFax sends to an ACT! contact" section, set options for when ACT! should log fax events and whether or not ACT! should create a resend reminder when a fax attempt is unsuccessful.

6. If you want to be able to open faxes from the Notes/History tab, click on the "Include a link in the Notes/History entry for opening the event" checkbox.

7. Click the **OK** button.

Faxing Write menu documents to single contacts

It is very easy to send faxes from ACT!, as long as you have either Microsoft Fax or Symantec's WinFax Pro installed on your computer.

For the most part, sending a fax is like printing a document. The difference, of course, is that when sending a fax, you must tell ACT! to whom you want it sent. This results in a couple of extra dialog boxes, but for the most part, sending a fax from ACT! is faster and simpler than printing the document and then manually faxing it with a fax machine.

Because of the way documents are created with the Write menu (i.e., data from the active contact record is generally inserted into the document), Write menu documents can only be sent to a single contact. If you want to fax another type of document, or if you want to fax a Write menu document to multiple contacts, you must first either create the document manually, or save the Write menu document to disk. You can then fax it using the steps outlined in *Faxing documents to multiple contacts* on page 196.

To fax a Write menu document to a single contact

1. Go to the record of the contact to whom you want to send the fax.

2. From the Write menu, select the type of document that you want to create.

3. Edit the document as desired.

4. From the File menu, select the Send submenu and the **Fax** command (**Figure 11.12**); or click on the **Send Fax** button in the toolbar.

   If you are using a word processor other than ACT!'s, select the **Send Fax using ACT!**

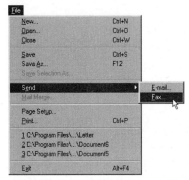

Figure 11.12 Faxes are sent from the Send submenu.

FAXING WRITE MENU DOCUMENTS TO SINGLE CONTACTS

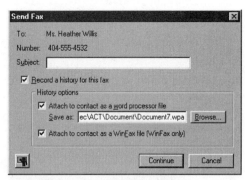

Figure 11.13 The Send Fax dialog box.

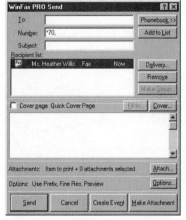

Figure 11.14 Depending on what fax software you're using, this dialog box may look different. (This screenshot is of the WinFax Pro dialog box.)

Quick Fax button

Figure 11.15 This Quick Fax button gives you one-click access to your fax software.

command from your word processor's File menu.

ACT! will present you with the Send Fax dialog box (**Figure 11.13**).

5. Enter a subject for this fax in the Subject text box.

6. Change any of the options in the dialog box, if desired, then click the **Continue** button.

These options include recording a history entry for this fax and attaching the fax to the contact record as either a word-processing or WinFax file.

7. In the dialog for your fax software (WinFax Pro or Microsoft Fax) (**Figure 11.14**), set the options for how you want the fax sent and click the **Send** button.

Refer to the documentation for your fax software for explanations of the options in this dialog box and any others that may appear during the actual faxing process.

✔ Tips

■ You can use the Quick Fax button (**Figure 11.15**) to access your fax software (either WinFax or Microsoft Fax) directly from ACT!. Clicking this button brings up the Send dialog box for your fax software, from which you can create and send a quick fax. If you do not have either of these fax software programs installed, this button is unavailable.

■ The Fax Cover Page command in the Write menu is designed to create a printed fax cover page for you to use with a traditional fax machine, but you can also use it to send a nice one-page fax memo by creating a cover page, typing your text, then sending it as a fax as discussed above.

FAXING WRITE MENU DOCUMENTS TO SINGLE CONTACTS

Faxing any document to single or multiple contacts

The major difference between faxing a Write menu document to a single contact and faxing any document to any number of contacts is that if a document is going to be faxed to multiple contacts (or a non-Write menu document is going to be created), the New or Open commands from the File menu must be used to open or create the document. This means that if you want to send a letter, memo, or other document from the Write menu to multiple contacts, you must first save it to disk and then reopen it.

In addition, when you fax to multiple contacts, ACT! will present you with a dialog box in which you specify the contacts to whom you want the fax sent.

To fax a document to single or multiple contacts

1. Use the **New** or **Open** commands from the File menu to create or open a word-processing document.

2. From the File menu, select the Send sub-menu and the **Fax** command; or click on the **Send Fax** tool in the toolbar.

   If you are using a word processor other than ACT!'s, select the **Send Fax using ACT!** command from your word processor's File menu.

   ACT! will present you with a Send Fax dialog box (**Figure 11.16**).

3. Enter a subject for this fax in the Subject text box.

4. In the "Fax recipients" section, select which set of contacts you want to select fax recipients from.

   Your selection here determines which names show up in the list of available contacts.

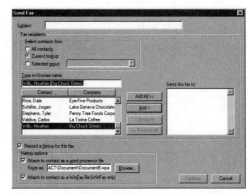

Figure 11.16 When you're faxing to multiple contacts, the Send Fax dialog box has more options.

Sort by Contact button

Sort by Company button

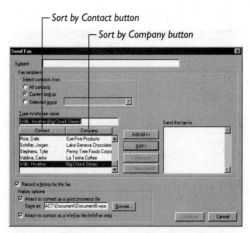

Figure 11.17 Click on these two headings to sort your contacts by name or company.

5. From the list of contacts on the left side of the dialog box, select contacts and click on the **Add** button to add them to the "Send this fax to" list. (You can also use the Add All button to add all contacts to the list.)

To make it easier to locate contacts, you can click on the "Contact" and "Company" headings to sort your contacts by either heading (**Figure 11.17**).

6. Select the history options for this fax (recording a history entry and/or attaching the fax to the contact record as a file) and click on the **Continue** button.

7. At the dialog for your fax software (WinFax Pro or Microsoft Fax), set the options for how you want the fax sent and click the **Send** button.

Again, refer to your fax software documentation for more information on this dialog box.

FAXING ANY DOCUMENT TO SINGLE OR MULTIPLE CONTACTS

Faxing reports

Quite often you may create a report containing all sorts of great information, and colleagues or clients in remote locations will want to see it. You can always print the report and fax it to them using a fax machine, but you also have the more elegant option of faxing it directly from ACT!

One advantage of this is that you don't have to reprint the report every time you make a change to its design or to the data included in it. Because faxing a report is just a different way of outputting the report, you can change the contacts or filtering options the way you normally would for any report, and then fax it directly to one or more contacts without ever going to paper. This saves time, money, and trees!

To fax a report

1. Create a lookup of the contacts you want to include in the report.

2. From the Reports menu, select the report that you want to create.

3. In the Run Report dialog box (**Figure 11.18**), select the desired options in the "Create report for" section of the General screen and in the Filter screen.

4. In the "Send output to" section of the General screen, select **Fax** and click the **OK** button.

Output options ⌐

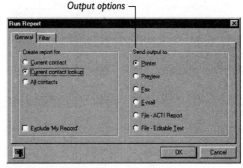

Figure 11.18 The only thing you have to do to fax a report (instead of printing it) is select the Fax option in this dialog box.

FAXING REPORTS

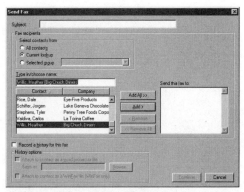

Figure 11.19 The Send Fax dialog box for reports is the same as that for faxing to multiple contacts.

5. ACT! presents you with the same Send Fax dialog box you get when you fax documents to multiple contacts (**Figure 11.19**).

6. Add the contacts who should receive this faxed report by selecting their names from the list on the left and clicking the **Add** button to add them to the "Send this fax to" list on the right.

7. If desired, select the "Record a history for this fax" option and any desired attachment options in the lower-left corner of the dialog box.

   By default, history entries are not recorded when you fax reports.

8. Click the **Continue** button.

9. Set options for your fax software in the dialog that appears and click the **Send** button to send the faxes.

Sending mail-merge faxes

Mail-merge faxes are also referred to as "form letter" faxes and "broadcast" faxes. They are simply faxes that are sent to multiple contacts, with the data from each contact's record used to tailor the fax to that particular contact.

Some examples of mail-merge faxes would include introductory letters/offers, coupons, brochures, or any other items that you want to fax to a lot of people while having them appear personalized for each recipient.

A mail-merge fax is really just another output option for any mail merge. For more information on creating mail-merge documents or templates, refer to Chapter 9, *Word Processing in ACT!*.

To send a mail-merge fax

1. If you want to send the fax to a specific group of contacts, create a lookup of those contacts.

2. From the Write menu, select the **Mail Merge** command.

   This will bring up the Mail Merge dialog box (**Figure 11.20**).

3. In the "Merge with" section of the dialog box, select the set of contacts (all contacts, the current contact, the current lookup or a group that you specify) to whom you want to send the fax.

4. In the "Template" section, select the template file that you want to use as the basis for the faxed document.

   If none of the templates listed suits your needs, you can use the New and Edit buttons to create a new template file or to edit an existing template.

5. In the "Send output to" section, click on the **Fax** option to select it.

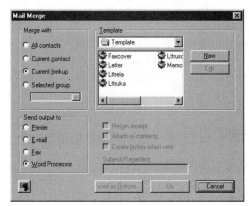

Figure 11.20 You start a mail-merge fax the same way you start any mail merge.

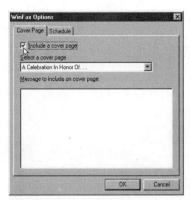

Figure 11.21 Set sending options for WinFax from here.

Figure 11.22 The WinFax Mail Merge dialog box (ACT! really likes WinFax)

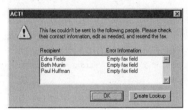

Figure 11.23 Missing fax numbers is the most common problem you'll run into.

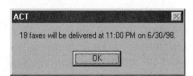

Figure 11.24 This little dialog lets you know the results of your mail-merge fax attempt.

6. If desired, select the "Create history when sent" option to create history entries for all contacts to whom you are sending this fax.

7. Type a subject for the fax in the Subject text box.

8. If WinFax is your fax software and you want to take advantage of special WinFax options, click on the **WinFax Options** button to access the WinFax Options dialog box (**Figure 11.21**).

   In this dialog box, you can specify a cover page and schedule a time to send this mail-merge fax.

9. Click the **OK** button to exit the Mail Merge dialog box.

10. If WinFax is your fax software, the WinFax Mail Merge dialog box (**Figure 11.22**) will appear.

    Select a time and date for your computer to send these faxes from the WinFax Mail Merge dialog box and click the **Continue** button.

    ACT! will prepare the mail-merge document(s) for faxing at the specified time and date. If there are any problems preparing the faxes, ACT! will present you with a dialog box describing the problem (**Figure 11.23**). Clicking the **OK** button will exit this dialog box.

11. At the Summary dialog box (**Figure 11.24**), click the **OK** button and you are done!

Configuring ACT! for e-mail

In order to use ACT! to send and receive e-mail, you must first configure ACT! and your e-mail system. This process requires a little bit of time and some very specific data, but once you do it it never has to be done again (unless you switch to a different e-mail system or a different way of accessing your e-mail). To complete this task, you will need to have all of the information about how you access your e-mail or connect to the Internet. You may want to go through the process once and write down the requested information, then talk to your IS administrator or Internet service provider. Or you can just get them on the phone before you start.

To configure ACT! for e-mail

1. From the Edit menu, select the **Preferences** command.

2. Click on the E-mail tab of the Preferences dialog box to bring up the E-mail preferences screen (**Figure 11.25**).

3. From the "Send e-mail to contacts using" drop-down list, select the e-mail system you want to use.

4. Click on the **E-mail System Setup** button to launch the E-mail Setup Wizard (**Figure 11.26**).

5. Complete the E-Mail Setup Wizard by answering the questions as they are presented to you and clicking the **Next** or **Finish** button after completing each screen of the wizard.

   Refer to the ACT! 4.0 user's manual (pages 298-305) for detailed instructions on setting up each of the six available e-mail systems.

   Once you have completed the E-mail Setup Wizard, you will return to the E-mail preferences screen.

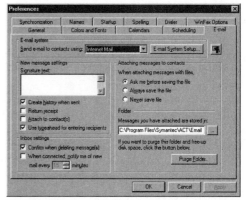

Figure 11.25 You should set e-mail preferences before you do any e-mailing.

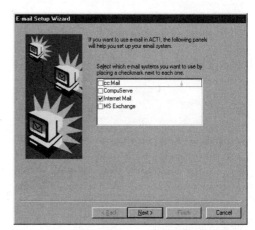

Figure 11.26 You *must* set up your e-mail system or ACT! will not be able to send or receive your e-mail.

Build button ─┐

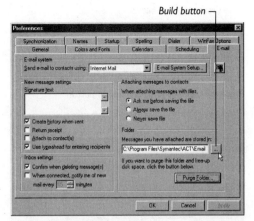

Figure 11.27 Remember, Build buttons have the three dots on them and are used to access Open dialog boxes.

Figure 11.28 Purging old files frees up valuable disk space, but don't get over-zealous or you may purge files you need.

6. In the "New message settings" section, enter any signature text that you want to use and select or deselect any new message options.

   "Signature text" is text that appears at the end of all of your e-mail messages (like your name and contact information). "Create history when sent" will create a history entry every time you send an e-mail message to a contact; "Return receipt" will send a message back to you when the recipient actually opens your message; and "Attach to contact(s)" will attach a copy of every sent message to the contact's record. If you select the "Use typeahead for entering recipients" option, you can type the first few letters of a contact's name when addressing a message and ACT! will locate the correct contact and add his or her name to the message.

7. In the "Inbox settings" section, select whether you want ACT! to confirm message deletions and specify how often to check for new messages.

8. In the "Attach messages to contacts" section, click on an option button to select how you want ACT! to handle any files attached to an e-mail message that you attach to a contact record.

9. If desired, click on the Build button (**Figure 11.27**) to set a folder for storing messages that you have attached to contact records.

10. Also if desired, click on the Purge Folder button to delete old files in this message storage folder, freeing up disk space.

    When you click the Purge Folder button, ACT! will display the Purge Folder dialog box (**Figure 11.28**), within which you can specify a cutoff date or choose to purge all files.

11. Click the **OK** button.

Creating and sending e-mail messages

The process of creating and sending an e-mail message involves addressing the message, setting message options, writing the message, and (finally) sending the message. If you have set your E-mail preferences, you may be able to skip the setting of options entirely and if you are sending the message to a single contact, you may not even need to address it (as long as you are viewing that contact's record when you create the message). If this is the case, the process is much faster, as all you have to do is type your message and click a button to send it!

To create an e-mail message

1. From the Contacts view, go to the contact record for the person to whom you want to send the e-mail message, then select the **E-mail Message** command from the Write menu. If the message is to be sent to multiple contacts, go to the record for any of them.

   A blank e-mail message appears, already addressed to the selected contact.

2. From within the E-mail view, simply click on the **Create Message** button in the toolbar (**Figure 11.29**) or select the **Create Message** command from the E-Mail menu.

3. If desired, select a different address book from the Address Book drop-down list.

   If you are using Internet Mail as your e-mail system, your only choice will be ACT! Contacts. If you are using another e-mail system, you can also choose to use the address book or directory from your e-mail program.

4. If you want to narrow the scope of your address book, select an option in the Select from drop-down list (**Figure 11.30**).

Figure 11.29 The Create Message button

Figure 11.30 This list lets you narrow the choices when you're using an address list.

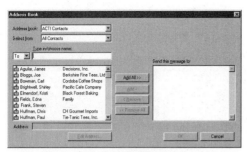

Figure 11.31 Different e-mail systems have different Address Book dialog boxes, but they all allow you to add addresses to an e-mail message.

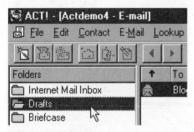

Figure 11.32 Unsent messages are stored in the Drafts folder.

✔ Tip

■ You do not have to send a message immediately after creating it. If you want to send the message at a later time (when the phone line is free or after you've edited the message), click on the Send Later button in the toolbar. Your message will be stored in the Drafts folder. You can access this message at any time by going to the E-Mail view, double-clicking on the Drafts folder, then double-clicking on the message (**Figure 11.32**). The message can then be edited and sent normally.

These options will vary depending on your e-mail system and your choice in step 3. For ACT! Contacts, your choices are All Contacts, Current Lookup, and Groups.

5. Click on the **Open Address Book** button. The Address Book dialog box will open (**Figure 11.31**).

6. In the Address Book dialog box, select name(s) from the list on the left side of the dialog box and click on the **Add** button to add them to the "Send this message to" list on the right.

You can click on the To drop-down list (above the list of available names in ACT!'s Address Book dialog box) and select either "cc" (carbon copy) or "bcc" (blind carbon copy) to change how a person is added to the list of recipients.

7. Click the **OK** button to exit the Address Book dialog box.

The names of the recipients have been added to your message and the cursor is waiting in the Subject text box.

8. Type a subject for your message in the Subject text box.

9. Select a priority from the Priority drop-down list.

10. If you want to send the message using a system other than your primary e-mail system, select that system from the Send Using drop-down list.

11. Click on the checkboxes to turn on or off the "Create history," "Return receipt," and "Attach to contact(s)" options.

12. Type your message and click the **Send** button (next to the Subject text box) or the **Send Now** button (in the toolbar) and it's on its way!

If you are not already connected to your e-mail system, you will be prompted to log on at this point.

Attaching files and records

One of the nicer features of e-mail is that it provides a convenient way to send files to other computer users. ACT! lets you attach to your messages both regular files saved to disk (as will any other e-mail system) and contact or group records from your ACT! database.

To attach a file or record to an e-mail message

1. Prepare your message normally (as described on page 204 of this chapter).

2. From the E-Mail menu, select the **Attach to Message** submenu and the **Contact**, **Group**, or **File** command (depending on what you want to attach).

   You can also just use the **Attach Contact**, **Attach Group**, or **Attach File** buttons in the toolbar (**Figure 11.33**).

   ACT! will present you with a dialog box where you can select contact or group records or a file from disk (**Figures 11.34–11.36**).

3. If you are attaching contact or group records, add the desired contacts or groups to the "Attach these contacts/groups" list (by selecting the contacts or groups and clicking the Add button). Select the format (for contacts) and whether you want to include notes/history entries and/or activity entries, and click the **OK** button.

   If you are attaching files from disk, navigate in the standard Open dialog box to locate the desired file, then select it and click the **Attach** button.

   The Attachments section of the message now lists all attached files and indicates whether you have ACT! contacts or groups attached.

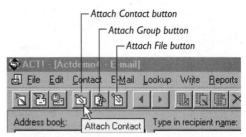

Figure 11.33 The Attach Contact, Attach Group, and Attach File buttons

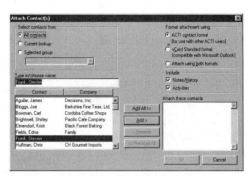

Figure 11.34 The Attach Contact dialog box.

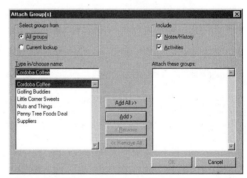

Figure 11.35 The Attach Group dialog box.

Figure 11.36 The Attach File dialog box.

✔ Tip

- You can view files attached to incoming messages by double-clicking on them and save them to disk by selecting them and choosing the Save command from the File menu. You can merge attached contact or group records with your database by double-clicking on the attached record and following the dialog box prompts. (For more information on the merging options that you'll see, refer to Chapter 15, *Exchanging Data.*)

ATTACHING FILES AND RECORDS

Reading messages

The easiest of the e-mail-based tasks, reading new messages is simply a matter of double-clicking on your inbox and double-clicking on a message.

To check for new messages, ACT! will need to check with your e-mail system, but that is easy, too.

To read new e-mail messages

1. Go to the E-mail view by clicking the **View E-mail** icon (**Figure 11.37**) or selecting the **E-mail** command from the View menu.

2. Select the Inbox folder for the e-mail system that you want to view (such as "Internet Mail Inbox").

3. To check for new messages, select the **Get/Send Mail** command from the E-Mail menu (**Figure 11.38**).

If you have not already logged onto your e-mail system, you will be prompted to do so. After you log onto your e-mail system, ACT! will retrieve and display all new messages.

4. Double-click the Inbox folder for your e-mail system.

All messages (old and new) are displayed in the list on the right side of the window (**Figure 11.39**).

5. Double-click on any message to read it.

Figure 11.37 Remember the viewing icons from Chapter 1?

Figure 11.38 This command will hook ACT! up with your e-mail system.

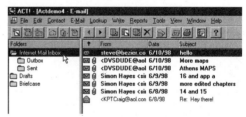

Figure 11.39 So many messages, so little time (actually, not too many messages)

Reply button ⌐

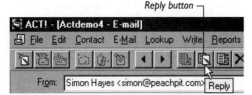

Figure 11.40 The Reply button.

Figure 11.41 This dialog box contains options for both replying to and forwarding messages.

Replying to and forwarding messages

After you've read a message, you may want to respond in some way. You might want to send a reply back to the original author of the message or to everyone who got the message ("Sounds like a plan. When should we meet?"), or you might want to forward the message on to someone else ("Thought you might be interested in seeing this."). As with many of the basic e-mail tasks, responding to messages is fast and simple.

To reply to a message

1. Open the message you want to reply to (if you are not already reading it).

2. From the E-Mail menu, select the **Reply to Message** command.

   You can also just click the **Reply** button on the toolbar (**Figure 11.40**).

3. In the Reply/Forward Options dialog box that appears (**Figure 11.41**), select the desired options then click the **OK** button.

   "Include message body" and "Include attachments" repeat the body of the original message in your reply and include any attachments to the message in your reply, respectively. "Reply to all" will send your reply to all recipients of the original message, not just to the person who sent the message.

4. Type your reply in the body area of the new message and click the **Send** button.

To forward a message

1. Open the message you want to forward, if necessary.

   From the E-Mail menu, select the **Forward** command; or click on the **Forward** button on the toolbar (**Figure 11.42**).

2. In the Reply/Forward Options dialog box that appears, select the desired options and click the **OK** button.

3. Click the Open Address book button and address the message as explained in the *Creating and sending e-mail messages* section on page 204.

4. Type any introductory or explanatory text in the body area of the new message and click the **Send** button.

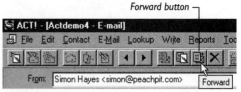

Forward button

Figure 11.42 The Forward button.

Delete Message button ⌐

Figure 11.43 X marks the spot for the Delete Message button.

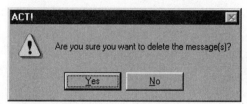

Figure 11.44 ACT! checks to be sure you *really* want the message deleted.

Deleting messages

Once you have read, pondered, acted on, replied to, or forwarded a message, there will probably be no reason to keep looking at it. Unwanted messages can easily be deleted with a button-click or two.

To delete a message

1. Double-click on the folder that contains the unwanted message.

2. Select the message that you want to delete.

3. From the E-mail menu, select the **Delete Message** command; or click on the **Delete Message** button in the toolbar (**Figure 11.43**).

4. In the confirmation dialog box (**Figure 11.44**), click the **Yes** button to confirm the deletion.

✔ Tip

■ Remember, you can Shift-click and Ctrl-click to select multiple messages, enabling you to delete dozens of unwanted messages with a single click of the Delete Messages button (and another click of the Yes button in the confirmation dialog box).

DELETING MESSAGES

12

SIDEACT!

With version 4.0, Symantec has introduced a supplementary program to ACT! called SideACT! SideACT! is not in any way a miniature version of ACT!, but rather a "to-do list" utility for storing and recording activities quickly and easily.

Some of the advantages of SideACT! are that it is small, fast, and easily accessible. The big disadvantage, though, is that it is a one-trick pony (even if that one trick is rather useful). All it really does is let you record to-do activities and then transfer them to your ACT! database. Hopefully, with version 5.0 of ACT!, Symantec will expand SideACT! to include a directory of contact phone numbers, at the very least (hint, hint).

Understanding SideACT!

During the installation of ACT! 4.0, a SideACT! icon is added to your Windows task bar (**Figure 12.1**). This icon can has two purposes. If you point to the icon a label will appear (**Figure 12.2**) with a brief summary of your list items. If you double-click on the icon, SideACT! will open, displaying your to-do list.

The SideACT! window (**Figure 12.3**) is a fairly simple affair. Across the top are a menu bar and toolbar for saving, printing, copying, pasting, and other standard activities. In addition to the usual buttons in the toolbar, there are buttons for entering an activity, changing activity type, moving or copying an item to ACT!, or even launching ACT! from SideACT!

Below the toolbar is a text area where you type in your activity descriptions. Once you have typed a description, you can add it to the list by simply hitting the Enter key.

The bottom of the window is the to-do list itself. Each item is listed in the order in which it was entered, along with the description, date, and type. At the far left of each entry is a selection symbol and a Completed checkbox.

SideACT! icon ⌐

Figure 12.1 The SideACT! icon in the task bar.

Figure 12.2 The SideACT icon with a label summarizing list content.

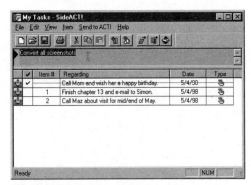

Figure 12.3 As befits a small utility application, the SideACT! window is very simple.

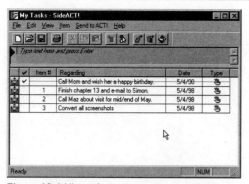

Figure 12.4 All text for new activities is typed in this area.

Entering activities in SideACT!

Entering new activities couldn't be easier. Because you use the Enter key to create an activity item in SideACT!, you can create your entire to-do list without ever taking your hands off the keyboard.

To create a SideACT! activity entry

1. In the SideACT! window, position the insertion point in the colored text area, if necessary (**Figure 12.4**).

   It will probably be there already, as that is the default state for SideACT!.

2. Type a description for your activity.

   Your description's length is limited to 70 characters of text.

3. Hit the Enter key.

✔ Tip

- To create a new paragraph within a description, use the Ctrl-Enter keyboard combination.

Editing list entries

You can easily edit to-do activities in SideACT! directly in the list. It is a simple matter of locating the entry, clicking in the appropriate box, and making the change.

To edit a SideACT! entry

1. Locate the entry you wish to edit.

2. Click in the **Regarding** box for the desired item and edit the text as you would in any text box (**Figure 12.5**).

3. Click in the **Date** box for the desired item, delete the existing date, and type in a new date.

4. Click in the **Type** box for the desired item and select a new type from the drop-down list.

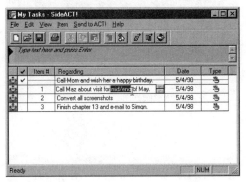

Figure 12.5 You can edit text for existing activities from the list itself.

EDITING LIST ENTRIES

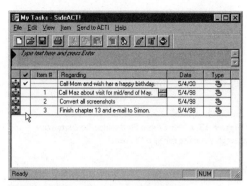

Figure 12.6 The Clear Activity checkbox.

Clearing activities in SideACT!

Clearing items from your to-do lists is even easier than creating them in the first place. Each entry contains a Clear box which can be used to clear activities in much the same fashion as in ACT! calendars (as discussed on page 130 in Chapter 8, *Calendars*).

Clearing an activity is different from deleting it. Deleting an activity deletes it from the list (no surprise there). If you clear the activity, though, it remains on the list and can be transferred to ACT! along with all your other activities. It just transfers as an already completed activity, and becomes a history entry rather than an activity that still needs to be done.

To clear a list item

1. Locate the list item you want to clear.

2. Click in the Clear box, which is the empty box at the far left of the entry line (**Figure 12.6**).
   This crosses out the item, marking it as completed, but leaves it on the list.

✔ Tip

■ The Edit menu contains two useful commands for working with already completed items: The Delete Completed Items command lets you permanently remove all completed items, and the Move Completed Items to End command takes all the completed items and moves them to the bottom of your list.

New terms you should know...

Clearing: Changes the status of an activity from pending to complete. Clearing has little effect in SideACT!, but in ACT! changes the item from a yet-to-be completed activity to a completed history entry.

FINDING ITEMS IN SIDEACT!

Finding items in SideACT!

If your to-do list is so long that you cannot quickly find an activity, you can have SideACT! locate the activity for you. (Of course, another option would be to to get some work done so your to-do list isn't so long.)

To find a list entry

1. From the Edit menu, select the **Find** command.

2. In the Find dialog box (**Figure 12.7**), type a text string to search for.

3. Click the **Find Next** button.

   SideACT! will highlight the first entry line that contains the specified text. If this is not the entry you are looking for, continue clicking the **Find Next** button until you get to the desired entry.

4. Click the **Close** button when you are done.

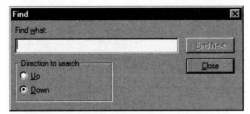

Figure 12.7 This simple Find dialog box lets you search your list for specific text.

Managing SideACT! lists

The to-do list that SideACT! opens by default is called "My Tasks." For most people, this one list will be enough. If desired, however, you can create additional lists. For example, you may want to separate your business and personal activities, or create several different lists for people who share the same computer.

Once you have multiple lists, though, you will need to take care that you are entering activities into the correct list. (Activity entries can be moved from list to list, but it is easier to just enter them into the correct list to begin with.)

To create a new SideACT! list

1. From the File menu, select the New command.

   A new, blank SideACT! File opens, replacing the previous file.

2. From the File menu, select the Save As command.

3. Type a file name in the standard Save As dialog box and click the OK button.

To open a SideACT! list

1. From the File menu, select the Open command.

2. Select the desired SideACT! file from the resulting Open dialog box and click the OK button.

Managing SideACT! entries

Individual entries within a SideACT! list can be deleted, moved, or copied to another list (using the Cut, Copy, and Paste commands), or even copied and pasted into another application entirely.

To delete SideACT! entries

1. Click on the selection icon at the far left (**Figure 12.8**) to select the desired entry or entries.

   Remember, you can always use Ctrl-click and Shift-click to select multiple entries. Ctrl-click to select additional nonadjacent items and Shift-click to select additional adjacent items.

2. Press the **Delete** key.

3. In the warning dialog box (**Figure 12.9**), click the **Yes** button to confirm that you want to delete the entry or entries.

To move or copy SideACT! entries

1. Click on the selection icon at the far left to select the desired entry or entries.

2. From the Edit menu, select the **Cut** or **Copy** command.

   Use Cut if you want to remove the entries from this list or Copy if you want them to remain.

3. Open the destination list or other document.

   You can access other SideACT! lists with the Open command in the File menu. You will need to open other types of documents using the application that they were created in.

4. Select the destination and choose the **Paste** command from the Edit menu.

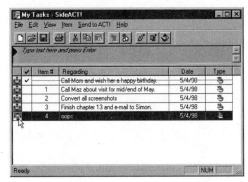

Figure 12.8 This symbol is used (like the gray boxes in ACT!) to select an entire line item.

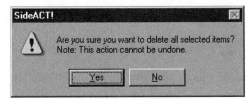

Figure 12.9 Deleted items cannot be restored.

MANAGING SIDEACT! ENTRIES

Reordering lists

As mentioned earlier in this chapter, your to-do items are listed in the order in which they were created. You can change this order in one of three ways: manually (by pressing and dragging), by editing the item numbers themselves, or via commands in the Item menu.

To reorder list entries

1. Select the desired entry or entries in the list.

2. Do one of the following: Drag the selected item(s) up or down to the desired position, select the Move Item Up or Move Item Down commands from the Item menu, or edit the "Item #" entry for the desired item.

✔ Tip

- The keyboard shortcuts for the commands Move Item Up (Ctrl-up arrow) and Move Item Down (Ctrl-down arrow) provide the fastest and easiest way to move items.

Printing lists

As amazing as it seems, there are still some things that you can't do with a computer, phone, or fax machine while sitting at your desk. For those times when you need a "real" to-do list, SideACT! can send your data to the printer with just a few mouse clicks.

To print a SideACT! list

1. If you do not want to print the entire list, select just the entries that you want printed.

2. From the File menu, select the **Print** command.

3. To print just the entries that you selected in step 1, click on the Selection option in the Print Range portion of the Print dialog box (**Figure 12.10**).

4. Click the **OK** button.

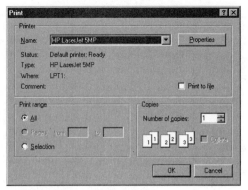

Figure 12.10 SideACT!'s Print dialog box is as simple as SideACT! itself.

PRINTING LISTS

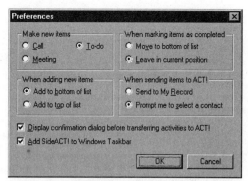

Figure 12.11 The options here are simple and fairly obvious.

Setting SideACT! preferences

Unlike ACT!, SideACT! has a limited number of options when it comes to setting program preferences. These options include the type and location of new items, a couple of SideACT!-to-ACT! transfer options, and the option of having the SideACT! icon in the Windows task bar. What SideACT! does have in common with ACT! as far as preferences are concerned is how they are accessed, via the Edit menu.

Most of the items in the Preferences dialog box are fairly self-explanatory. For those options that may not be obvious, explanations have been provided.

To set SideACT! preferences

1. From the Edit menu, select the **Preferences** command.

2. Make any desired changes to the existing selections in the Preferences dialog box (**Figure 12.11**).

   In the "When sending items to ACT!" section, choose the Send to My Record option only if these are personal activity items. Once transferred to ACT!, these activities cannot be associated with contacts other than "My Record." The default option is the safest, as it prompts you to associate the activities with a contact during the transfer process.

   If you want an uninterrupted transfer of data from SideACT! to ACT!, click on the checkbox to turn off the "Display confirmation dialog before transferring activities to ACT!" option.

   If, for some reason, you do not want a SideACT! icon in your Windows task bar, click to turn off that option as well.

3. Click the **OK** button.

Transferring list items to ACT!

As we have seen in this chapter, SideACT! is a valuable tool for creating and maintaining to-do lists. As such, it is a valuable program in and of itself. There may be times, though, when you really need to get your activities into ACT! for any of a number of reasons (assigning them to contacts, transferring them to other users, or including them in calendars and reports, to name just a few). Transferring your activities to ACT! is the most complex of SideACT!'s tasks, but is still a relatively simple matter.

To transfer list items to ACT!

1. If you use more than one SideACT! list, open the list from which you want to transfer items.

2. Select the list items that you want to move or copy to ACT!.

   If no items are selected, a dialog box will appear after step 3, asking if you want to transfer all list items (**Figure 12.12**).

3. If you need to change destination databases, choose the **Select Database** command from the Send to ACT! menu.

   This will bring up a Select Database dialog box (**Figure 12.13**). From here, you can type in the name of the desired database, or click on the Browse button and select the database from a standard Windows Open File dialog box.

4. From the Send to ACT! menu, select either **Move to Database** or **Copy to Database**.

   Move to Database will remove the items from the SideACT! list, while Copy to Database will result in the items appearing in both locations.

   Selecting either command will bring up a confirmation dialog box (**Figure 12.14**).

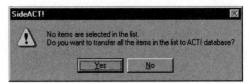

Figure 12.12 There is no need to select items if you want to transfer the whole list to ACT!

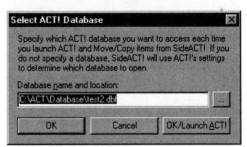

Figure 12.13 To look for another database, use the Build button (the three dots).

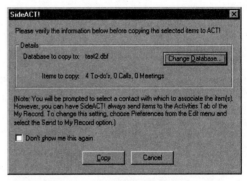

Figure 12.14 This confirmation dialog box lets you double-check everything before continuing with the transfer.

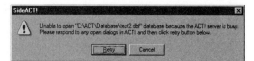

Figure 12.15 You must deal with the destination database before SideACT! can continue.

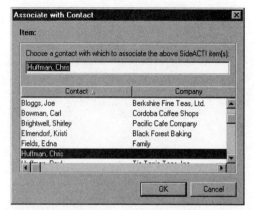

Figure 12.16 Select the contact with which you want to associate the transferred items from here.

5. Click on the **Copy/Move** button (it will match the command you selected from SideACT!'s Move to ACT! menu) at the bottom of the dialog box.

   SideACT! will launch ACT! and begin the transfer process. If the destination database requires a password or presents you with a backup reminder, you will have to deal with those dialog boxes before completing the transfer (**Figure 12.15**). Deal with the dialog boxes, then click on the Retry button in this dialog box to continue the transfer. (Remember, you an switch between applications using the Windows task bar at the bottom of your screen.)

6. In the Associate with Contact dialog box (**Figure 12.16**), select a contact from the list and click on the **OK** button.

   All selected SideACT! items are transferred to the ACT! database and associated with the selected contact. Uncompleted list items become normal activities, and completed list items become history entries.

✔ Tips

- All transferred list items will be associated with a single contact, so if you want to associate different items with different contacts, you will need to do multiple transfers. (But don't bother. The tip below will make your life much easier, especially for multiple transfers.)

- If you have an ACT! database open, you can just open SideACT!, select the list items you want to move, and drag them directly from SideACT! into ACT!. From the Contacts view you just drag them onto the active record; from the Contact List you can drag them to any contact you want; and from a calendar you drop them on a date and the Associate with Contact dialog box will appear, from which you can select the contact you want.

New terms you should know...

Transfer: To move or copy a SideACT! item to an ACT! database. This is similar in effect to copying and pasting or cutting and pasting, except that incoming SideACT! items are converted to ACT! activities or history entries. No link exists between transferred items, so marking an item complete in one program has no effect on an already transferred item in the other program.

PRODUCTIVITY POWER TOOLS

This chapter is for everyone who has ever scratched their head and wondered why certain things in ACT! are they way they are. (You won't necessarily get any answers, but at least you can change things so that they're the way you want them to be.) This chapter deals with the myriad ways in which you can customize ACT! to suit your personal tastes or business needs. You can create or customize layouts; add, modify, or delete menus, toolbars, and keyboard shortcuts; and create macros to automate even the most onerous tasks.

Creating layouts

In addition to the many layouts that ACT! ships with, you also can also use layouts that you create yourself. These layouts might be modified versions of existing layouts, customized to meet your specific needs, or you might want to create completely unique layouts that bear no resemblance to anything any other ACT! user has ever seen.

To create a new layout

1. Go to the view for which you want to create a new layout (i.e., the Contacts or Groups view).

2. From the Tools menu, select the **Design Layouts** command.

   This opens the Layout Designer window (**Figure 13.1**).

3. From the File menu, select the **New** command.

   A completely blank layout appears (**Figure 13.2**).

   Initially at least (and possibly always) you will want to create your new layouts by modifying existing ones rather than starting from scratch. In that case, skip step 2 above. Instead, select the layout you want to use as the basis for your new layout from the Layout pop-up list (**Figure 13.3**) and then do step 3 to save it with a different name. This will save you the bulk of the work of creating a new layout. From the File menu, select the **Save As** command.

4. In the Save As dialog box, type a name for the layout and click the **Save** button.

5. Add fields and other objects as explained on the following pages, using the Save command periodically to save your changes.

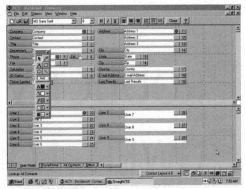

Figure 13.1 The Layout Designer window.

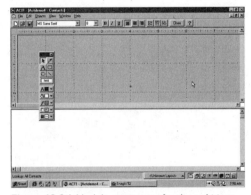

Figure 13.2 A blank layout is great for the ambitious, but many users prefer to modify existing layouts.

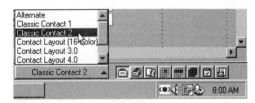

Figure 13.3 This list includes all layouts, including both default and user-created layouts.

✔ Tips

- You can return to ACT!'s normal viewing mode from the Layout Designer by selecting the Records command from the View menu.

Sharing Layouts

In a business situation, the benefits of having everyone using the same layout for data entry are fairly obvious but profound. It helps to ensure that everyone enters data into the correct fields, making reports accurate and useful. Consistent and cooperative data entry also is extremely helpful when you synchronize databases from two or more users. Furthermore, shared layouts are easy to update.

The easiest way to share layouts is to simply create a folder on a network drive that all users can access and make sure that everyone's copy of ACT! is pointing to that shared folder. The default location for layout files can be set from the General screen of the Preferences dialog box. If you put all new layouts in that folder, they will appear automatically on the users' screens the next time they open their databases.

New terms you should know...

Layout: An arrangement of fields and text for data entry and editing in either the Contacts or Groups view. All layouts (default and user-created) are available from the Layouts pop-up menu at the bottom of both of these views.

Moving and resizing fields and objects in the Layout Designer

When you're in the layout design mode, you can move and resize fields, field labels, and other objects just as you can when designing a report template. Basically, it's just a matter of selecting, then pressing and dragging.

To move a field or other object

1. Make sure that the selection arrow tool (**Figure 13.4**) is selected in the tool palette. (Click on it if necessary.)

2. Point to the middle of the field that you want to move.

3. Press on the field and drag it to the desired location.

To resize a field or other object

1. Make sure that the selection arrow tool is selected in the tool palette.

2. Click on the field that you want to resize.

3. Position the mouse cursor over any of the handles around the perimeter of the field.

   The handles look like empty boxes. When you position the cursor over one, the cursor changes shape. It becomes a two-headed arrow, indicating that you are on a handle and showing the directions in which the handle can be moved (**Figure 13.5**).

4. Press on the handle and drag in either indicated direction to stretch or shrink the field.

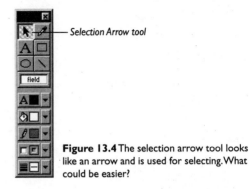

Selection Arrow tool

Figure 13.4 The selection arrow tool looks like an arrow and is used for selecting. What could be easier?

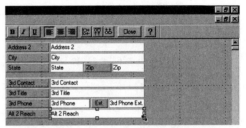

Figure 13.5 If the cursor changes shape to one of these two-headed arrows, you are on the right spot.

MOVING AND RESIZING FIELDS AND OBJECTS

Figure 13.6 The very clearly labeled Field button.

Figure 13.7 Select the field you want to add from this list.

Adding and removing fields

Quite often when customizing an existing layout, and always when creating new layouts from scratch, you will need to add fields. Adding fields in the Layout Designer is identical to adding fields in the Report Designer. Removing fields is also the same.

To add a field to a layout

1. Click on the Field button in the tool palette (**Figure 13.6**).

   If you are replacing one field with another, you will probably want to delete the old field first, as discussed below.

2. Position the cursor where you want the new field to appear and press and drag to the right to define the size of the field object.

   When you release the mouse button, the Fields dialog box will appear (**Figure 13.7**).

3. Select the desired field from the list of available fields at the left side of the dialog box, then click the **Add** button.

4. Click the **Close** button to exit the dialog box.

   By default a label will be inserted along with the field itself. If you do not want the label, you can just select and delete it. (You can also turn off the Add Label option in the Fields dialog box to keep it from being inserted in the first place.)

To remove a field from a layout

1. Click on the selection arrow tool in the tool palette.

2. Click on the field you no longer want.

3. Hit the **Delete** key on your keyboard.

Changing field properties

All fields (as well as other objects) have properties that determine how they look and function. Changing field properties allows you to change the color and font used in the field, as well as the name of the field itself.

To change the properties of a field

1. Make sure the selection arrow tool is active in the tool palette.

2. Double-click on the field whose properties you want to change.

   This will bring up the Object Properties dialog box for that field (**Figure 13.8**).

3. In the Style screen of this dialog box, select the desired fill color, frame style, frame color, and frame width for this field. Refer to the sample in the lower-left corner as you make your selections.

4. Click on the **Font** tab and select the desired font, style, size, effect, and color (**Figure 13.9**)

   Colors are selected from the pop-up menu in the lower-left corner of the Font screen.

5. Click on the **Format** tab and change the field name, if desired.

6. Click the **OK** button to exit the Object Properties dialog box.

✔ Tip

■ You can also use the pop-up menus in the bottom half of the tool palette to make graphical changes to your fields (fill color, border width, etc.).

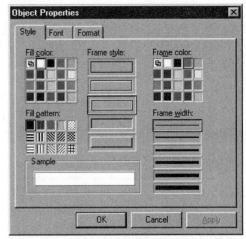

Figure 13.8 The Object Properties dialog box is where you can change most "physical" aspects of your field.

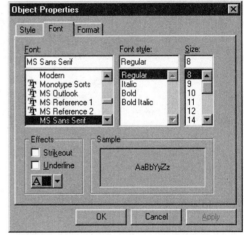

Figure 13.9 All font formatting is available to you from here.

CHANGING FIELD PROPERTIES

Group Stop box —— ┌— Field Order box

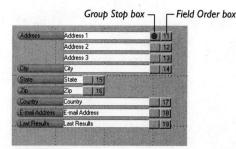

Figure 13.10 The first box is the group stop box and the second is the field order box.

Changing field entry order

One very handy "power tool" available to the ACT! layout designer is the ability to change the order in which data gets entered into fields. This order is determined by two boxes that appear at the right side of each field in the layout (**Figure 13.10**). The first box is the group stop box, and the second is the field order box.

Group stop boxes are either empty or contain a red stop sign. The red stop signs determine which field the cursor jumps to when you hit the Enter key. Field order boxes contain numbers that determine the order in which the cursor travels from box to box when you hit the Tab key. (Reverse this if you have switched your preferences so that the Enter key is used to move between fields.) Setting and removing group stops is useful for enabling the user to jump from one block of fields to the next. Field order is (obviously) critical to making data entry as easy as possible.

One minor, but very popular, change is to switch the order of the first two fields, so that the contact's name is entered first, and then his or her company.

To swap field entry order

1. Click on the field order box of one of the two fields whose order you want to swap.

2. Click on the field order box of the second field.

3. The order numbers are swapped, changing the data entry order.

To create a new field entry order

1. From the Edit menu, select the **Field Entry Order** submenu and the **Clear** command.

   If the field order boxes were not already visible, selecting this command will also make them visible.

New terms you should know...

Group stop: A field property that marks the field as a destination when the user hits the Enter button (when Tab is used to go through the fields in order).

---

2. Click on the field order boxes (the right-hand boxes) in the order in which you want data to be entered into the fields (**Figure 13.11**).

✔ Tips

■ If you make a mistake and want to reset the field entry order back to the default, you can select the Reset command from the Field Entry Order submenu of the Edit menu.

■ You can set or remove group stops (which normally determine where the cursor goes when you hit the Enter key, as opposed to the Tab key) by clicking on the group stop box (the left-hand box) for the desired field.

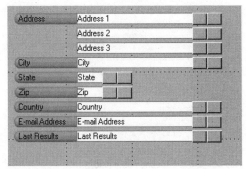

Figure 13.11 Creating the field order is a simple matter of clicking on boxes in the desired sequence.

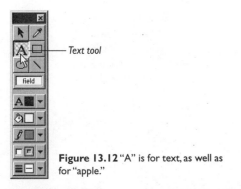

— Text tool

Figure 13.12 "A" is for text, as well as for "apple."

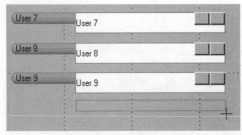

Figure 13.13 The size of this text block determines how your text will wrap as you type.

Adding text to layouts

You may want to add text to a layout for any number of reasons. The most obvious reason is to identify the layout to the user. Other common reasons for adding text to a layout are to include company name and information and to make sure that the user always has the numbers of his or her IS support team or even Symantec's technical support number.

Text can also be used to explain the purpose of any customized user fields.

To add text to a layout

1. Click on the **Text** button in the tool palette (**Figure 13.12**).

2. Position the crosshair cursor over the place in the template where you want the new text block to appear.

3. Press the mouse button down and drag to the right to create a rectangular text block, then release the mouse button (**Figure 13.13**).

4. Type your text.

   Your text will wrap to fit within the text block that you defined in step 3. If you don't like the position of your text block, you can move it or resize it as described earlier in this chapter.

Adding graphics to layouts

Most ACT! layouts contain very few graphic objects, if any. But that is no reason for you not to add graphics to your layouts. Simple graphic objects can make a layout easier to read and use by dividing and emphasizing different layout areas. They can also, unfortunately, have the opposite effect, so consider carefully before adding extra lines and borders to your layouts.

To add graphic objects to a layout

1. Click on the rectangle, ellipse (oval), or line tools in the tool palette (**Figure 13.14**), depending on the type of object you want to create.

   The line tool is best for separating sections and the rectangle tool is best for borders and shading.

2. Position your cursor over the place in the template where you want the object to begin, then press the mouse button down and drag to where you want the object to end (**Figure 13.15**). Release the mouse button.

   If you make a mistake, either hit the Delete key and do it again or use the selection arrow tool to move or resize it.

✔ Tips

- To create a perfect square or circle, or to draw a line on an exact 45° angle, hold down the Shift key while you draw the object.

- You can format objects either by double-clicking them and making changes in the Object Properties dialog box, or by making selections from the pop-up menus at in the bottom half of the tool palette (**Figure 13.16**).

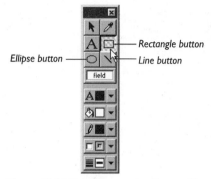

Ellipse button — Rectangle button
Line button

Figure 13.14 Use the rectangle, ellipse and line buttons to draw shapes on your layout.

Figure 13.15 Press and drag with any of the shape tools to create your shape.

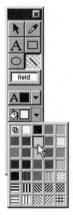

Figure 13.16 The bottom half of the tool palette contains menus for formatting your objects.

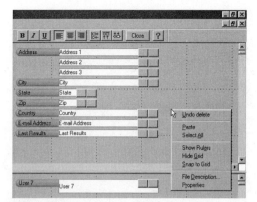

Figure 13.17 The Background shortcut menu.

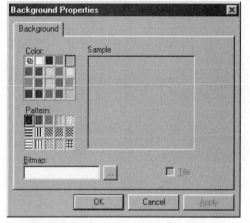

Figure 13.18 The Background Properties dialog box.

Formatting layout backgrounds

In addition to adding graphic objects to a layout, you can also make changes to the background of the layout. These changes include different colors (very nice) and patterns (kind of annoying and hard on the eyes). But the best thing about formatting a layout background is that you can use a picture as the background. This is how the Modern layout was created.

Good examples of background graphics would include company logos and pictures of corporate headquarters or outdoor scenes. Avoid any graphics that are garish, busy, or distracting.

To format the background of a layout

1. Position the cursor over any empty space on your layout. (That is, not over a field, label, or other object.)

2. Click the right mouse button to access the shortcut menu for the background (**Figure 13.17**).

3. Select the **Properties** command from this menu.

4. In the Background Properties dialog box (**Figure 13.18**), select the desired color or pattern for your background. Refer to the sample area as you make your selections.

To add a background graphic to a layout

1. Position the cursor over any empty space on your layout.

2. Click the right mouse button and select the **Properties** command from the shortcut menu.

3. In the Background Properties dialog box, click on the Build button to the right of the Bitmap text box (**Figure 13.19**).

4. Navigate in the resulting standard Open dialog box to locate the bitmap (.bmp) file that you want to use.

5. Select the desired file and click the **Open** button.

6. Click the **OK** button to exit the Background Properties dialog box.

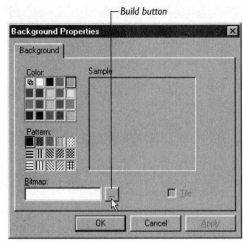

Figure 13.19 Use this Build button to locate and select a background picture.

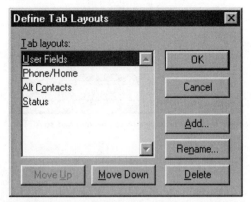

Figure 13.20 This dialog box lists all tabs and lets you add, delete, or modify tabs.

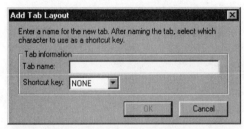

Figure 13.21 The Add Tab Layout dialog box is used to either add a tab layout or send e-mail, I can never remember which.

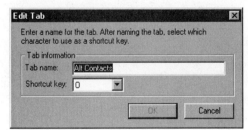

Figure 13.22 Renaming tabs and assigning shortcuts is the name of the game here.

Modifying layout tabs

Most ACT! users have no idea that the tabs at the bottom of the Contacts and Groups windows can be customized to suit their particular needs. New tabs can be added, unwanted tabs can be deleted, and tabs can be renamed.

If you create a new tab, you then add fields to it to display whatever information is desired.

To add a layout tab

1. From the Edit menu, select the **Tabs** command.

2. In the Define Tab Layouts dialog box (**Figure 13.20**), click on the **Add** button.

3. In the Add Tab Layout dialog box (**Figure 13.21**), type in a name for your new tab.

4. If you want a shortcut key for this new tab, select one from the Shortcut Key drop-down list of available letters.

5. Click the **OK** button to exit the Add Tab Layout dialog box and click **OK** again to exit the Define Tab Layouts dialog box.

To rename a tab

1. From the Edit menu, select the **Tabs** command.

2. In the Define Tab Layouts dialog box, select the layout you want to rename from the list of existing layouts and click on the **Rename** button.

3. In the Edit Tab dialog box that appears (**Figure 13.22**), change the existing tab name.

4. If desired, select a new shortcut key from the Shortcut Key drop-down list.

5. Click the **OK** button (twice) to exit both the Edit Tab and Define Tab Layouts dialog boxes.

To reorder tabs

1. From the Edit menu, select the **Tabs** command.

2. In the Define Tab Layouts dialog box, select the tab you want to move from the Tab Layouts list.

3. Click on the **Move Up** or **Move Down** buttons to move the tab to the desired position.

4. Click the **OK** button.

To delete a tab

1. From the Edit menu, select the **Tabs** command.

2. In the Define Tab Layouts dialog box, select the tab you want to delete from the Tab Layouts list.

3. Click on the **Delete** button.

4. In the confirmation dialog box (**Figure 13.23**), click the **Yes** button.

5. Click the **OK** button to exit the Define Tab Layouts dialog box.

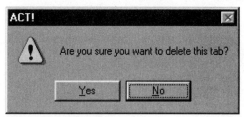

Figure 13.23 Deleting tabs can be very bad, so ACT! double-checks.

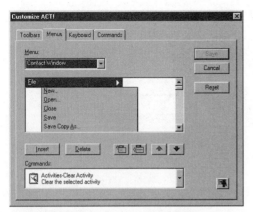

Figure 13.24 The Customize ACT! dialog box is where most of your customization takes place.

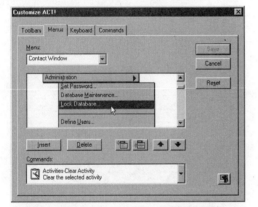

Figure 13.25 The new command goes under the selected command.

Figure 13.26 This is a list of ACT! commands, one of which will be linked to your new menu command.

Customizing menus

ACT! is an extraordinarily customizable program. Virtually anything in ACT! can be customized, including all of its menus. You can customize menus (as well as toolbars and keyboard shortcuts) in the Customize ACT! dialog box, which is accessed form the Tools menu.

In this dialog box you can add or remove menu commands, rearrange existing commands, and even add separator lines and submenus.

To add a menu command

1. From the Tools menu, select the **Customize** command.

2. In the Customize ACT! dialog box (**Figure 13.24**), click on the **Menus** tab.

3. From the Menu drop-down list, select the ACT! window that contains the menu you want to work with.

   Although labeled "Menu," this drop-down list is actually a list of ACT! windows. Go figure.

4. Scroll through the graphic list of menus and menu commands and click on the command or separator line below which you would like to add your new command (**Figure 13.25**).

   New commands are always inserted just under the selected menu item.

5. From the drop-down list of ACT! commands at the bottom of the dialog box, select the command that you want to insert into the menu (**Figure 13.26**).

6. Click on the **Insert** button.

7. Click on the **Save** button.

8. Click on the **Close** button.

To reorder menu commands

1. From the Tools menu, select the **Customize** command, then click on the **Menus** tab of the Customize ACT! dialog box.

2. From the Menu drop-down list, select the ACT! window that contains the menu you want to work with.

3. Select the menu item that you want to move from the graphic list of menus.

4. Click on the Up or Down Arrow buttons to move the menu item up or down (**Figure 13.27**).

5. Click the Save button, then the **Close** button.

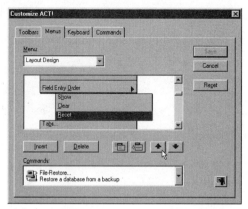

Figure 13.27 The up and down arrows (no hints as to which is which)

To remove a menu command

1. From the Tools menu, select the **Customize** command, then click on the Menus tab of the Customize ACT! dialog box.

2. From the Menu drop-down list, select the ACT! window that contains the menu you want to work with.

3. Select the menu item that you want to remove from the graphic list of menus.

4. Click on the **Delete** button.

5. Click on the **Save** button, then the **Close** button.

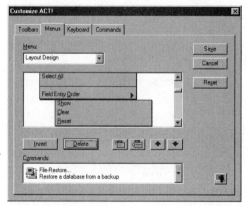

Figure 13.28 The Submenu button looks like a little menu, and the Separator button has a separator line.

✔ Tips

■ You can add separator lines and submenus by selecting the menu item below which you want the separator line or submenu to go, then clicking on the Submenu or Separator buttons (**Figure 13.28**).

■ You can be quickly rearrange menu items by simply selecting the menu item you want to move and then pressing and dragging it to a new position.

■ If you completely ruin your menus, just click the Reset button to reset all menus back to their default settings. You'll lose all the good changes you made, but you'll also get rid of the bad.

CUSTOMIZING MENUS

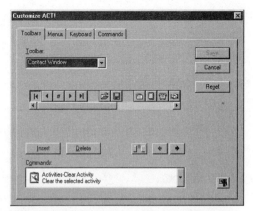

Figure 13.29 The Toolbars screen of the Customize ACT! dialog box.

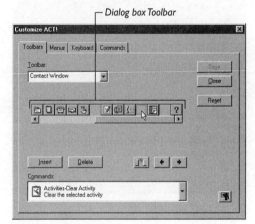

Figure 13.30 Click the toolbar in the dialog box, not the real toolbar.

Customizing toolbars

Toolbars are another aspect of ACT! that can be fully customized. You can add or remove buttons or change the order in which they appear in the toolbar. The procedures for customizing toolbars are very similar to those for customizing menus, as you will see.

To add a toolbar button

1. From the Tools menu, select the **Customize** command.

2. The Customize ACT! dialog box opens.
   If the Toolbars screen is not the active screen (**Figure 13.29**), click the Toolbars tab.

3. Select the window that contains the toolbar you want to modify from the Toolbar drop-down list.

4. Click on a location in the sample toolbar near the top of the Toolbars screen to specify where you want the new button to appear (**Figure 13.30**).
   The new button will be inserted immediately to the left of the specified location.

5. From the list of commands at the bottom of the dialog box, select the command that you want linked to the new button.

6. Click the **Insert** button, then the **Save** button, then the **Close** button.

To reorder toolbar buttons

1. Select the **Customize** command from the Tools menu and click the Toolbars tab, if necessary, to bring it to the front.

2. Select the window that contains the toolbar you want to modify from the Toolbar drop-down list.

3. Click on the toolbar button that you want to move.

CUSTOMIZING TOOLBARS

4. Click on the Left or Right Arrow buttons to move the selected toolbar button (**Figure 13.31**).

5. Click on the **Save** button, then the **Close** button.

To remove a toolbar button

1. Select the **Customize** command from the Tools menu and click the Toolbars tab, if necessary, to bring it to the front.

2. Select the window that contains the toolbar you want to modify from the Toolbar drop-down list.

3. Click on the toolbar button that you want to remove.

4. Click on the **Delete** button.

5. Click on the **Save** button, then the **Close** button.

✔ Tips

■ As with menu items, you can move toolbar buttons by selecting the desired button, then pressing and dragging it to a new position.

■ You can easily add a spacer between any two existing buttons by selecting a toolbar button and then clicking on the Spacer button (**Figure 13.32**). The spacer will appear to the left of the selected button.

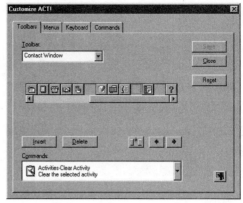

Figure 13.31 It's easy to move the selected button.

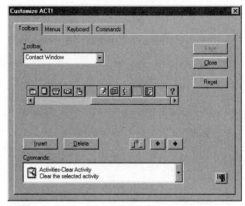

Figure 13.32 The Spacer button looks like what it does.

CUSTOMIZING TOOLBARS

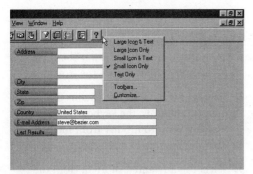

Figure 13.33 This is the shortcut menu for all ACT! toolbars.

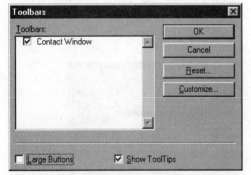

Figure 13.34 The Toolbars dialog box is the only place where you can turn tooltips on and off.

Changing toolbar properties

Most objects in ACT! have properties, as we saw when working in the Report Designer and Layout Designer. ACT!'s toolbars also have properties that can be changed to suit your preferences. These properties are relatively simple, and focus primarily on the sizes of the buttons and the amount of labeling that the buttons have.

In order to change a toolbar's properties, you must make it visible (which is generally a matter of just going to the proper view or window) and then right-click on it.

To change the look of a toolbar

1. Go to the window whose toolbar you want to change.

   Position the mouse cursor over any empty space in the toolbar and click the right mouse button, which brings up the shortcut menu for the toolbar (**Figure 13.33**).

2. From the shortcut menu, select the desired options.

   The first five commands let you choose between large and small icons, with or without text. We feel that the default setting of "Small Icon Only" is best, but experiment to see what works best for you.

   Selecting the Toolbars command brings up the Toolbars dialog box (**Figure 13.34**). Within this dialog box you can select which available toolbars you want to see (most views have only one), and whether you want to see large icons and/or the pop-up tooltips. You can also reset a toolbar or go to the Toolbars screen of the Customize ACT! dialog box from here.

Customizing keyboard shortcuts

Keyboard shortcuts, like menus and toolbars, can be fully customized. Because they are not visible, you do not have the option (nor the need, for that matter) to rearrange or reorder keyboard shortcuts. You can, though, add shortcuts of your own and delete existing shortcuts (which doesn't delete the command, just the shortcut for the command).

To add a keyboard shortcut

1. From the Tools menu, select the **Customize** command.
   The Customize ACT! dialog box opens.

2. Click the **Keyboard** tab to activate the Keyboard screen (**Figure 13.35**).

3. Select the window that contains the menus (and thus, the keyboard shortcuts) that you want to modify from the Shortcut Keys drop-down list.

4. From the list of commands at the bottom of the dialog box, select the command for which you want to create a keyboard shortcut.

5. Click in the Shortcut Key text box and enter the keyboard combination that you want to use for the selected command (**Figure 13.36**).
   If the keyboard combination you choose is already in use, the Insert button changes to the Replace button, indicating that you will be replacing an existing shortcut.

6. Click on the **Insert** or **Replace** button, then the **Save** button.

7. Click the **Close** button to exit the dialog box.

To delete a keyboard shortcut

1. Select the **Customize** command from the Tools menu and click the Keyboard tab, if necessary, to bring it to the front.

2. Select the window that contains the menus (and thus, the keyboard shortcuts) that you want to modify from the Shortcut Keys drop-down list.

3. Select the unwanted shortcut from the scrolling list.

4. Click on the **Delete** button.

5. Click on the **Save** button, then the **Close** button.

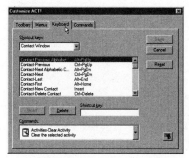

Figure 13.35 Keyboard shortcuts can be customized in much the same way that menus and toolbars are.

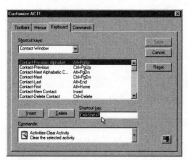

Figure 13.36 If you choose a keyboard shortcut that is already in use, you will have the option to replace the existing shortcut.

CUSTOMIZING KEYBOARD SHORTCUTS

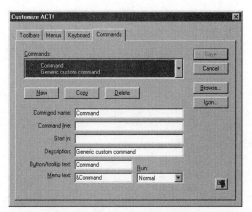

Figure 13.37 Creating commands is very different from customizing menu, toolbars, and shortcuts, as this screen indicates.

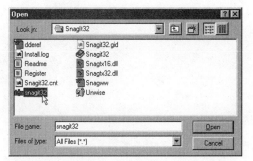

Figure 13.38 User-created commands always link to external files, such as programs, ACT! macros or word processing documents.

Creating commands

ACT! uses the term "command" both for the menu items that cause action (this is the normal use of the term) and for the actions themselves. Thus, you can create an ACT! menu command to perform an ACT! command. New keyboard shortcuts and toolbar buttons that you create are also linked to the commands that are performed when the keyboard shortcut is entered or the toolbar button is clicked on.

ACT! has a long list of default commands that a user can use for his or her buttons, menus, and shortcuts, but new commands can also be created. These commands generally open a document or launch another application, but they can also be used to perform all sorts of internal actions by linking the command to a macro file, instead of a document or program file. (Macros are discussed on page 249.)

To create a new ACT! command

1. From the Tools menu, select the **Customize** command.

2. Click on the **Commands** tab to access the Commands screen (**Figure 13.37**).

3. Click the **New** button.

4. Enter a name for the command in the Command Name text box.

5. Click the **Browse** button and, using the standard Open dialog box, locate and open the application, document, or ACT! macro file that you want to be linked to the new command (**Figure 13.38**).

6. If desired, in the Start In text box, enter the folder name that contains the files used by the application you selected.

7. Enter a description of the command in the Description text box.

8. If you will be attaching the command to a button, enter button or tooltip text in the Button/tooltip Text text box.

9. If this command will be added to a menu, enter the menu text in the Menu Text text box.

10. If the command launches an application, select the desired run state (normal, minimized, or maximized) for the application (**Figure 13.39**).

11. Click the **Save** button and the **Close** button.

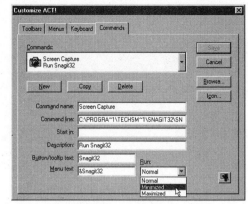

Figure 13.39 This drop-down list determines in what state the launched program will run.

Figure 13.40 The Record Macro dialog box.

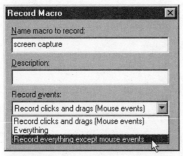

Figure 13.41 "Record Everything Except Mouse Events" is the best option here, unless you absolutely have to use the mouse.

New terms you should know...

Macro: A list of actions performed by the user and recorded by ACT!. When instructed, ACT! can repeat the recorded actions, freeing the user from repetitive tasks.

Sneakernet: "Sneakernet" is a term for the old-fashioned process of printing a document or saving a file to disk and then walking over to someone's office or cubicle and handing it to them yourself.

Recording macros

Simply put, a macro is just a list of actions that your computer can be called upon to perform any time you want. Macros can be used to perform simple tasks such as printing a document or creating a lookup, but the real power of the macro is that the computer can run lengthy, complex macros as easily as short, simple ones. You can save yourself huge amounts of time (and frustration) by creating macros for your time-consuming, pain-in-the-neck tasks, especially those that you have to perform on a regular basis.

For example, if every Monday you have to create several different lookups of different groups, generate two or three reports for each lookup, and send those reports to a large group of people (some by e-mail, some by fax, and some via good old Sneakernet), you can create a macro that performs all of those tasks for you. Then each Monday morning you can start the macro running and get in a cup of coffee and half of the Sunday comics while the macro runs.

To record a macro

1. From the Tools menu, select the **Record Macro** command.

2. In the Record Macro dialog box (**Figure 13.40**), enter a name and description for the macro in the Name Macro to Record and Description text entry boxes.

3. In the Record Events drop-down list, select what you want ACT! to record (**Figure 13.41**).

   Choose "Everything" to record keystrokes, mouse movements, and mouse actions. Choose "Record clicks and drags..." to record only keystrokes and mouse actions (and location, of course), but not the actual mouse movement. Choose "Record Everything Except Mouse Events" to record only keystrokes.

4. Click the **Record** button.

5. Do everything that you want ACT! to record. Be careful, because if you make a mistake here, it will be repeated every time you run the macro.

6. Press Alt-F5 to stop recording. (You could also choose the **Stop Recording** command from the Tools menu, but using the keyboard shortcut prevents your last click on the Tools menu from being recorded.)

✔ Tips

■ Whenever possible, choose the "Record Everything Except Mouse Events" option and use keyboard shortcuts to perform all of your tasks. Macros that do not include mouse movement or actions are by far the most reliable macros you can make.

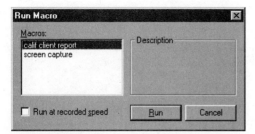

Figure 13.42 All existing macros are listed here.

Figure 13.43 Macros are saved into the Macros folder.

Running macros

Any macro that you create is available to you from the Run Macro dialog box, which is found in the Tools menu. By simply selecting the desired macro and telling ACT! to run it, you can accomplish the equivalent of dozens or even hundreds of commands with a few simple mouse clicks. Consider attaching the macros that you use most often to toolbar buttons or menu commands for easy access.

To run a macro

1. From the Tools menu, select the **Run Macro** command.

2. In the Run Macro dialog box, select the macro that you want to run from the list of available macros (**Figure 13.42**).

3. If desired, click on the "Run at recorded speed" checkbox to select this option.

    This is really only necessary if the macro includes time-critical events, such as a pause of a certain length while your computer logs onto the Internet.

4. Click the **Run** button.

✔ Tip

- A faster (and much cooler) way to run a macro is to assign it to a menu command, toolbar button, or keyboard shortcut. Just follow the steps for creating a new ACT! command (as explained on page 247) but select a macro file instead of a regular program or document file (**Figure 13.43**). Macro files are in the Macro folder inside the Act folder (which is in the Symantec folder, which is in the Program Files folder, which is on your hard drive). Once the command is created, it can then be attached to a menu command or toolbar button like any other ACT! command.

SECURITY AND BACKUP

It has been said (in this book and in many other places) that the key to being successful in business is to be successful in developing relationships. That is what ACT! is all about. And if the key to business success is in your ACT! database, it makes sense to protect your database carefully. This chapter deals with two different types of protection: security and backup.

ACT!'s security features consist primarily of its abilities to create multiple users of the same database (for privacy and to compartmentalize data), to set the security levels of those users, and to password-protect the database against unauthorized access. The security features are meant to prevent malicious or misguided mischief.

The backup features of ACT! are generally for protection against inanimate or unintentional disasters such as hard-drive failure, fire, theft, or plain old human stupidity:

> **Are you sure you want to erase the contents of your entire hard drive?**
>
> **[OK] [Cancel] [Just shoot me now]**

Backing up is a concept that is (or should be) familiar to everyone who uses a computer. ACT! has a nice little backup feature that is quick and very easy to use.

Understanding multiuser databases

When first created, all ACT! databases are single-user databases. (But, human nature being what it is, people inevitably want to settle down and raise a family. These people then need married-user databases. No, wait a minute....) A database is a single-user database until you or your database administrator add additional users.

The only reason to add users to a database is that two or more people need access to the *same* contact data. A good example of this is a secretary or assistant who needs to be able to set appointments or locate information for his or her boss. Both the secretary/assistant and the boss need to access the exact same contact records, calendars, and notes.

The other common business situation doesn't involve a multiuser database, but rather, several copies of the same single-user database. For example, a group of salespeople might each have their own copy of a customized database. Everyone would have the same database, with the same fields, layouts, and report and letter templates, but each person would enter their own contacts into their own database.

When a user opens a multiuser database, they are prompted to enter their name and password. Once they do this, ACT! will only display their own private data and public data entered by other users. A user cannot see private data created by another user unless he or she logs on as that user. Furthermore, each user has his or her own "My Record" record, so documents and reports will include the information for just the current user.

UNDERSTANDING MULTIUSER DATABASES

New terms you should know...

Private: Any record or activity that is only visible to the user who originally created it. A contact can be made private from the Status tab display and activities can be made private from the Advanced Options tab of the Schedule Activity dialog box.

Public: A record or activity that is visible to all users of the database.

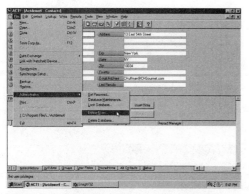

Figure 14.1 All of the security features are in the Administration submenu.

Figure 14.2 This dialog box lets you create, modify, and delete users.

Creating new users

New users can be added to an existing database as needed. Creating a new user does not affect the database records or the other users of the database in any way. In fact, the only thing that happens (for the most part) is that a new "My Record" record is created for the new user. Since this record is not visible to any other users, however, it has no effect on them or their use of the database.

During the creation of a new user, you can also set a password and security level for the new user.

To create a new user

1. From the File menu, select the Administration submenu and the **Define Users** command (**Figure 14.1**).

   The Define Users dialog box appears (**Figure 14.2**).

2. Click on the **Add User** button.

3. Type in the new user's name in the User Name text box.

4. Type a password for the new user in the Password text box.

5. Select a security level from the Security Level drop-down list.

   Administrator gives the user full access to all ACT! features, including database modifications, adding and deleting fields, etc.

   Standard lets the user see, edit, add, and delete records and perform database synchronization. (See *Synchronizing data* Chapter 17.)

   Browse allows the user only to view database records.

6. If this user is being created to receive synchronizations only (and not to actually access this database), click on the "Enable logon" option to turn it off.

CREATING NEW USERS

255

7. If you are going to synchronize data with this user, click on the checkbox labeled "Enable synchronization" to turn it on.

Note: If you do enable synchronization, you will not be allowed to leave the dialog box without setting up synchronization data (**Figure 14.3**). Because the discussion of these options is lengthy and doesn't apply to most users, we are skipping it here. Steps 6 and 7 are discussed fully in Chapter 17, *Synchronizing Data*.

8. Click the **OK** button to exit the dialog box.

You will be prompted to assign "My Record" records to all new users (**Figure 14.4**).

9. If you want to fill in their "My Record" data now, select the desired users and click on the **Assign Now** button. To let each user fill in his or her own "My Record" data when they first log on, click on the **Assign Later** button.

✔ Tips

■ As always with passwords, make sure that the password is easy to remember but hard to figure out (if possible), and keep a written record of your password somewhere. If you forget your password, chances are slim that anyone (including Tech Support) will be able to help you.

■ If you aren't sure whether you want to synchronize data with a user, leave the "Enable synchronization" option off. It's faster and a whole lot easier to skip it for now. You can always go back and turn this option on when you need it.

■ You can also use the Define Users dialog box any time you need to change a user's security level or assign a new password to a user.

Figure 14.3 Synchronization adds a lot of work to creating new users, and ACT! won't let you skip any of it.

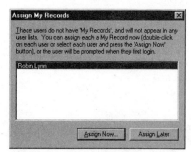

Figure 14.4 Each user will have his or her own "My Record" record; you can create it yourself or you can let them create it later.

New terms you should know...

User: A person with "official" access to the database. Users can have different security levels, granting them different levels of access, from simply browsing the database to altering records, layouts, templates, and more.

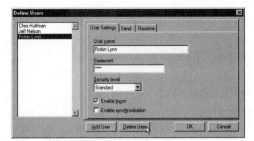

Figure 14.5 Later, loser! (er... user, that is)

Figure 14.6 All records that belonged to the recently departed user must be reassigned or deleted.

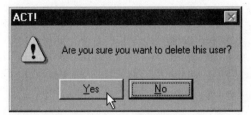

Figure 14.7 Again, ACT! double-checks before deleting stuff.

Deleting users

During the natural evolution of any business, people will leave the company, move on to other positions, or merely be assigned new duties. Any of these changes can make it necessary to delete users from an ACT! database.

Deleting a user from the database is a fairly simple process, but does raise one important question: What happens to all the records that belonged to that user? ACT! gives you two choices: Delete the records or assign them to another user. You select which option you want.

To delete a user from a database

1. From the File menu, select the Administration submenu and the **Define Users** command.

    This brings up the Define Users dialog box.

2. From the list on the left side of the dialog box, click on the name of the user that you want to delete and then click the **Delete User** button (**Figure 14.5**).

    ACT! will present you with a dialog box (**Figure 14.6**) asking you what you want to do with the records that belonged to the deleted user.

3. Select the "Reassign to another user" option, if necessary (it should already be selected).

4. Select the desired user from the list of existing users and click the **OK** button.

    If you want to delete all of the records for the unwanted user, you can click the "Delete records" option, instead. We just hesitate to ever recommend deleting potentially large numbers of records without first at least looking at them.

5. In the warning dialog box (**Figure 14.7**), click the **Yes** button to confirm that you want to delete the selected user.

Setting passwords

In a multiuser database, only users with Administration-level security privileges can change the passwords of other users, but anyone can change their own password using the Set Password command (in the Administration submenu of the File menu). In a single-user database, passwords are optional; the owner can use the Set Password command to add password protection where there was none previously, or to change an existing password to a new one.

To set or change a password

1. From the File menu, select the Administration submenu and the **Set Password** command.

2. In the Set Password dialog box (**Figure 14.8**), enter the old password (if any) in the Old Password text box.

   This prevents unauthorized users (that is, anyone who doesn't know the old password) from creating a new password. If the you don't enter the correct old password, ACT! will not allow you to create a new password (**Figure 14.9**).

3. Enter the new password twice (to ensure accuracy) in the New Password and Retype New Password text boxes.

4. Click the **OK** button.

Figure 14.8 Enter the old password once and the new password twice.

Figure 14.9 If you don't know the old password, you can't create a new password.

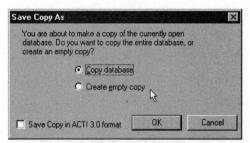

Figure 14.10 You can copy everything, or just the framework of the database.

Copying databases

Copying your ACT! database is both the simplest way to create a backup copy of your database and the only way to create a "template" of your database for others to use.

Saving a copy of a database provides a quick and easy backup for when you want to try something and are not completely confident in your ability to avoid destroying your database (such as when you're importing data from another source or editing database layouts). Because copies are saved in the same location as the original database, this is not the best way to back up your data. If, however, you have a removable cartridge drive or access to a networked hard drive, saving a copy of your database might be just the ticket for a simple backup strategy.

You can also save an empty copy of your database, which includes all database settings and layouts, but none of your contact records. This is how you would distribute a customized database setup to colleagues or other database users.

To copy a database

1. From the File menu, select the **Save Copy As** command.

2. In the Save Copy As dialog box (**Figure 14.10**) select either "Copy database" or "Create empty copy", depending on what kind of copy you want to create.

   You can also select the "Save Copy in ACT! 3.0 format" option if you are going to give this copy to a user of version 3.0 of ACT!

3. Click the **OK** button.

   A standard Save As dialog box appears.

4. Name the file and click the **Save** button to save the copy of the database.

✔ Tip

■ If you are using the Save Copy As command as your primary backup, make sure you switch to a removable drive (in the Save As dialog box) before saving. Backing up to your hard drive defeats the whole purpose of backing up, which is to have copies of important data in case your hard drive crashes (which is by far the biggest cause of lost data).

COPYING DATABASES

Backing up databases

The more you use ACT!, the more valuable the data in it will be, and the more important it will be to back up your database on a regular basis. ACT!'s backup feature is the best way to back up your ACT! data. Not only is it easy to use, it has a helpful reminder feature that alerts you when it's time to back up your data again.

The only reason not to use ACT!'s backup feature is if you have another backup strategy already in place (such as an automated backup of your hard drive to a tape, removable cartridge, or network drive using a backup utility program).

✔ Warning

- If you do use another backup strategy, be sure to back up *all* of the files that are associated with your database. There are 15 or so of them. They have different extensions, but the root of each file name is the name of your database (**Figure 14.11**).

To back up a database

1. From the File menu, select the **Backup** command.

2. Click on the Options tab at the top of the dialog box to bring up the Options panel.

3. If you don't want to include envelopes, labels, layouts, or reports in the backup, deselect the appropriate options (**Figure 14.12**).

4. If desired, change the number of days for the reminder option.

   You can also turn off the reminder altogether, but we don't recommend it (not that we don't trust you to remember to back up on your own).

5. Click on the General tab to switch back to the original General panel (**Figure 14.13**).

Figure 14.11 The database and all related files share the same name, but have different file extensions.

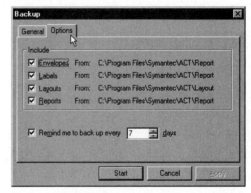

Figure 14.12 By default, everything gets backed up.

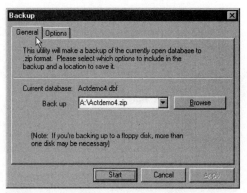

Figure 14.13 The General panel is where you set the location of the backup file.

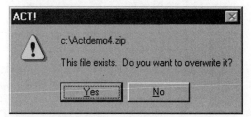

Figure 14.14 You can back up right over an older backup, if you want.

6. Unless you will be backing up to floppy disks, change the backup location by typing the new location in the Back Up combo box or by using the Browse button to specify a new location.

7. Click the **Start** button.

ACT! will create a compressed .zip file containing all of your database information. If you are overwriting an older backup, ACT! will warn you of this (**Figure 14.14**). If your backup will not fit on a single floppy (or other removable disk), ACT! will prompt you to insert the next disk in the set.

BACKING UP DATABASES

Restoring databases

Suppose that, whether through your own innate lameness or due to circumstances beyond your control, one or all of your database files are missing or damaged, or the data within the files has been deleted or otherwise ruined. Now you need to make use of that backup you created (you have been backing up regularly, right?). Fortunately for you, restoring a backup is just as easy as creating the backup to begin with.

To restore a database

1. From the File menu, select the **Restore** command.

   The Restore dialog box appears (**Figure 14.15**). Listed in the dialog box are both the location of the last backup created and the location of the database that was last backed up. Unless you have been performing multiple backups of separate databases, you will not need to change this information.

2. If necessary (which is not likely), change the "File to restore" and "To folder" locations using either the drop-down lists or the Browse buttons.

3. Click on the **Start** button.

4. If you already have the database that you want to restore open, ACT! will inform you of this fact (**Figure 14.16**). Click the **Yes** button to continue.

5. If any of the files in the backup already exist in the destination folder (which will occur if the database or one of its related files is damaged but not completely deleted or otherwise lost), ACT! will inform you of this as well (**Figure 14.17**). Click the **Yes to All** button to restore all files from the backup.

   All files are replaced by the clean backup copies, and you are ready to work!

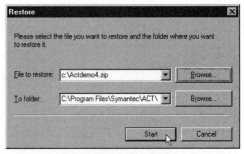

Figure 14.15 Basically, all ACT! needs to know is the location of the backup file and the location of the damaged or missing database.

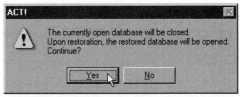

Figure 14.16 You can restore an already open database.

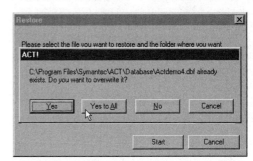

Figure 14.17 If any of the files being restored already exist, you have to tell ACT! that it's okay to over-write them.

RESTORING DATABASES

15

EXCHANGING DATA

Whether you need to bring in thousands of contact records from a Microsoft Access database, transfer a dozen records from a handheld electronic organizer, or export a selected ACT! lookup to Microsoft Word for some sophisticated mail merging, getting records into and out of ACT! is relatively simple. ACT! can handle a number of different file formats and has some handy features for making sure that the right information goes into the desired fields.

If you are exchanging data with another software program, you don't need anything but ACT! and your data. If you are importing or exporting data to or from a palmtop computer or electronic organizer, you will need the appropriate ACT! software on your palmtop or organizer.

✔ Tip

- If you use a PalmPilot organizer, you can download the ACT! PalmPilot Link software from Symantec's Web site free of charge! (Go to **www.symantec.com** and check out the software downloads.)

Understanding import and export file formats

All applications store data on disk in certain file formats. Many of these file formats can be read by other applications. (For example, most word processors can read other word processors' file formats, and many can read spreadsheet file formats.) Some common file formats include .txt, .xls, .wks, and .dbf. .txt files are text file, .xls files are Microsoft Excel files, .wks files are Lotus 1-2-3 files and .dbf files are database files. ACT! can read .dbf and .txt file formats, as well as files from the two most popular families of databases, dBASE and Q&A. ACT! can't read other file formats, even though they may contain all of the necessary data, because of the way the data is arranged or because they contain extra information that confuses ACT!.

If you are working in another software program and want a file to be readable to ACT!, make sure you save the file in one of the above formats. (To do this, select the Save As command from the program's File menu, enter a name for the file, and at the bottom of the Save As dialog box, select .txt, .xls, or .dbf from the File Type drop-down list.)

✔ Tips

- If you can, try to use the .dbf file format as your first choice, followed by the .txt format. ACT!, being a database, likes .dbf files best since ACT! stores it's own databases in this standard database file format.

- If you need to use the .txt format, make sure that the text is delimited (separated) by either tabs or commas. Most programs will give you the option to save as delimited text, but if not, you will need to edit the data manually to separate data with tabs or commas (a huge pain, but fortunately not often necessary).

Figure 15.1 This "wizard" will walk you through the process of importing data.

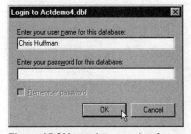

Figure 15.2 You can't import data from a database to which you don't have access.

Figure 15.3 Select the type(s) of records you want to import.

Importing records from ACT! databases

Not surprisingly, the easiest files to import into an ACT! database are other ACT! databases. The most common reason people merge two ACT! databases is that they have created multiple databases (as many new users do) and then later realize what a pain that is and want to merge them all together. Another common reason is that they want to bring in contacts from a colleague's database (say, if one salesperson takes over another salesperson's territory).

To import records from another ACT! database

1. From the File menu, select the Data Exchange submenu and the Import command.

   This brings up the first screen of the Import Wizard (**Figure 15.1**).

2. If necessary, select ACT! 3.0 and 4.0 (*.dbf) from the File Type drop-down list (it should be the default).

3. In the Filename and Location text box, type the name and path of the ACT! file you want to import, or use the Build button (the one with the three dots) to select the file from an Open dialog box.

4. Click the Next button.

   If the database you are importing from is password-protected or is a multiuser database, you will be prompted for your name and password (**Figure 15.2**).

5. At the second screen of the Import Wizard (**Figure 15.3**), select the type of records (contact, group, or both) that you want to import.

6. If you want to change the import options, click on the **Options** button and make any desired changes in the Merge Options dialog box (**Figure 15.4**).

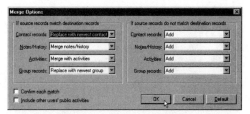

Figure 15.4 Options, options, options! Fortunately, the default settings here work in just about all circumstances.

On the left side of the dialog box, select what action ACT! should take if an imported contact record, Notes/History entry, activity, or group record already exists in the database. Your options are generally to merge the two, replace the existing one with the imported one, or leave the existing one as is.

On the right side, specify what ACT! should do if there is no match. This should always be set to Add, as that is the whole point of importing the data in the first place.

The two other options are "Confirm each match," which is a safety feature that can quickly get tedious, and "Include other users' public activities," which will import all activities from other users, except where they have specifically set them as private.

Generally, the default settings for these options are best for just about everyone and shouldn't be changed unless you have specific needs (and know what you are doing).

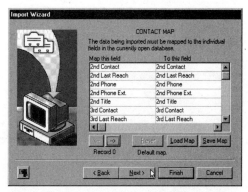

Figure 15.5 A contact map is used to make sure the correct data goes into the correct fields.

7. Click on the **Next** button to get to the third screen of the Import Wizard (**Figure 15.5**).

This is the Contact Map screen, where you set which imported fields are placed into which existing fields. Since you are bringing one ACT! database into another, the fields will almost always match up correctly. (We'll look at these map settings in detail later in this chapter.)

8. If all of the fields that contain data are mapped correctly, click the **Finish** button to complete the importing process. (If not, refer to the *Mapping fields* section on page 269.)

> ### New terms you should know...
>
> **Import:** The process of bringing data into an application from a file, usually one created in another application. By importing data you can use already existing data from another application rather than having to re-enter it. Formatting is often lost, but the data comes in intact.

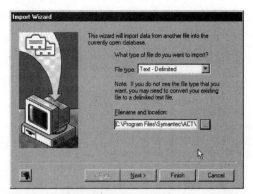

Figure 15.6 If ever, oh ever, a wiz there was, the wizard of imports is one because...

Figure 15.7 Select the type(s) of records you want to import.

Importing data from other applications

Importing data from other applications is very similar to importing data from other ACT! databases, with two big exceptions: The data must be saved in an acceptable format, and it usually needs to be mapped to make sure it gets into the desired fields in the recipient ACT! database.

To import data from another application

1. Open the source file (in the application that it was created in) and save or export the file in **tab delimited text**, **.csv** (comma separated values, a valid but little-used format), **dBASE III-V**, or **Q&A 4.0 to 5.0** format.

2. Close the application and launch ACT!, opening the database into which you want to import the data.

3. From the File menu in ACT!, select the Data Exchange submenu and the **Import** command.

    This brings up the first screen of the Import Wizard (**Figure 15.6**).

4. From the File Type drop-down list, select the file format you used to save your file in the other application.

5. In the Filename and Location text box, type the name and path of the ACT! file you want to import, or use the Build button (the one with the three dots) to select the file from an Open dialog box.

6. Click the **Next** button.

7. At the second screen of the Import Wizard (**Figure 15.7**), select the type of records (contact or group) that you will be importing.

8. If you want to change the import options (which is usually unnecessary), click on the **Options** button and make any desired changes in the Import Options dialog box (**Figure 15.8**), then click the **OK** button to return to the second Import Wizard screen.

In the Import Options dialog box, you can select either comma or tab separated (that is, whether the blocks of data in the file are separated with commas or tabs), choose the character set (Macintosh or Windows), and specify whether or not you want the first record imported (if it contains values and not field labels, as is often the case) If you aren't sure, go ahead and import the first record. You can always delete it if it contains field names or other bogus information.

9. Click the **Next** button.

10. At the next screen of the Import Wizard (**Figure 15.9**), select the "Use a pre-defined map" option and select the appropriate application from the list if *you are importing data from one of the listed applications*. If not, select the "Don't use a predefined map" option.

11. Click the **Next** button.

This brings up the final screen of the Import Wizard, the Contact map screen (**Figure 15.10**).

12. If you selected a predefined map in the previous step, you probably don't need to do any mapping. Click the **Finish** button to complete the importing process. If you didn't select a predefined map, you will definitely need to map your data. Refer to the *Mapping fields* section on the next page to map your data, then click the **Finish** button to complete the importing process.

Figure 15.8 This options screen appears for all types of imported data except Q&A files (which don't need it, since they save data in a similar fashion to ACT!, being another Symantec product).

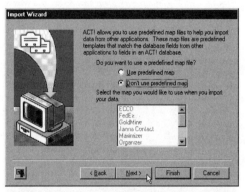

Figure 15.9 If you can use a predefined map, do so. It'll make things a lot easier.

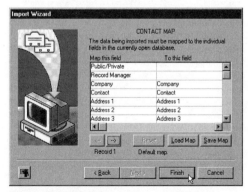

Figure 15.10 When you import non-ACT! data, contact maps are invaluable.

IMPORTING DATA FROM OTHER APPLICATIONS

Figure 15.11 Select the desired source field from the list of imported fields.

Figure 15.12 Select the field you want to data to go into from this list.

Mapping fields

The ability to map fields is useful when you're importing data from other ACT! databases, and invaluable when you're importing data from other applications. Mapping fields is really just a matter of telling ACT! where to put stuff. You select a field that is being imported and tell ACT! which field in your database is equivalent to it. This is crucial when you import data from other applications, as the field order of the imported data will almost never match the field order of your ACT! database.

Once you have mapped the data correctly, you can even save the map for later use. This way, if you ever need to import another file that's in the same format, you can just load the map and all of your data will go straight into the correct fields.

To map fields

1. Follow the steps in the *Importing records from another ACT! database* or *Importing data from another application* sections earlier in this chapter to get to the Contact Map screen of the Import Wizard.

2. If you want to use an existing map, click on the **Load Map** button and open the map as you would open any file.

3. Select the field that you want to map (we'll call it the "source field") from the list of imported fields (the left-hand list, labeled "Map this field") (**Figure 15.11**).

4. To choose a destination in your database for the data in the selected field, double-click on the field immediately to the right of the source field (in the "To this field" column).

   Double-clicking will open a drop-down list of available fields (**Figure 15.12**).

5. Select the desired destination field from the list by clicking on it.

   If you do not want to import data from the selected source field, choose the Do Not Map option from the list.

6. Repeat steps 3–5 for each field in the left-hand list for which you want to set a different destination ACT! field.

7. If you want to save the map for later use, click on the **Save Map** button. Save the map as you would any other file.

8. If you completely mess up your field placement, click on the **Reset** button to reset all field assignments.

✔ Tip

■ These maps are saved as regular files on your hard drive. This means that you can give them to other users by copying them onto floppies or sending them as e-mail attachments. Once you've gone to all the trouble of mapping an often-used source, there is no reason that everyone in your company should have to do the work all over again. Simply send them the appropriate .map file and have them drop it into their ACT! folder.

New terms you should know...

Map: In ACT!, a map is a list that matches imported fields with existing fields, allowing ACT! to rearrange imported data so that the correct information is placed in the correct fields. Also called a *data map* or a *field map*.

MAPPING FIELDS

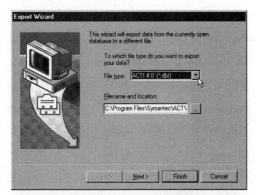

Figure 15.13 Just as Heat Miser had his Snow Miser, the Import Wizard has its Export Wizard. (Refer to the classic *The Year without a Santa Claus* for more information on these two delightful chaps — Heat Miser and Snow Miser, that is, not the Import and Export Wizard.)

Exporting records to another ACT! database

As you might expect, the procedure for exporting records from one ACT! database to another is virtually identical to the procedure for importing records from one ACT! database to another. You use the Export command instead of the Import command, and you have one extra screen in the wizard, but other than that, there is no difference.

Exporting is used more often when you need to select the specific records that you want to transfer, while importing is used most often when you just want to bring in everything from another source.

To export records to another ACT! database

1. To export a single record, go to that record. To export a set of records, create a lookup of those records. To export group records, go to the Groups window before exporting.

2. From the File menu, select the Data Exchange submenu and the **Export** command.

   This brings up the first screen of the Export Wizard (**Figure 15.13**).

3. If necessary, select ACT! 4.0 (*.dbf) from the File Type drop-down list (it should already be selected, since it is the default).

4. In the Filename and Location text box, type the name and path of the ACT! file you want to export to, or use the Build button (with the three dots) to select the file from an Open dialog box.

5. Click the **Next** button.

   If the database you are exporting to is password-protected or is a multiuser database, you will be prompted for your name and password.

6. At the second screen of the Export Wizard (**Figure 15.14**), select the type of records (contact, group, or both) that you want to export.

7. If you want to change the export options, click on the **Options** button and make any desired changes in the Merge Options dialog box (**Figure 15.15**).

These options are exactly the same as those for importing data, which are discussed on page 267.

8. Click on the **Next** button to get to the third screen of the Export Wizard (**Figure 15.16**).

9. Select the records you want to export (the current record, current lookup, or all records) and click on the **Next** button one last time to get to the final screen of the Export Wizard.

This is the Contact Map screen (**Figure 15.17**). Since you are exporting from one ACT! database into another, the fields will almost always match up correctly, with the possible exception of customized user fields. Changing these map settings was covered earlier in this chapter (on page 269).

10. If all of the fields that contain data are mapped correctly, click the **Finish** button to complete the exporting process.

Figure 15.14 Select the type(s) of records that you want to export.

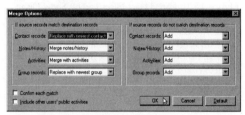

Figure 15.15 These options are the same whether you are importing or exporting.

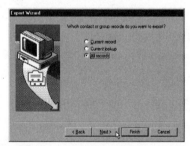

Figure 15.16 This seems like an awful lot of dialog box for just these three little choices.

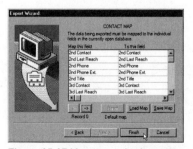

Figure 15.17 Mapping works the same way whether you are importing or exporting.

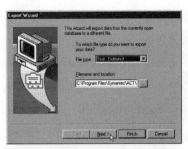

Figure 15.18 As always, select the file type and specify the name of the export file you want to create.

Figure 15.19 Select the type of records that you want to export.

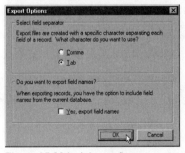

Figure 15.20 Let's hear it for easy options!

New terms you should know...

Export: The process of saving data in a file format that is easily read by another application.

Exporting records for use in other applications

ACT! is a great program, but it can't do everything. If you need more robust mail-merge capabilities or you need to move your contact data into a relational database, you will need to export your ACT! data to another application.

As you are probably expecting by now, ACT! has a wizard that walks you through the process of exporting your data in a format that is readable by other applications. The Export Wizard, which we looked at previously on page 271, serves this purpose as well. But unlike exporting to another ACT! database, which is simply a matter of mirroring the importing process, exporting data for use in another application is somewhat complex.

To export records for use in another application

1. From the File menu, select the Data Exchange submenu and the **Export** command.

2. In the first screen of the Export Wizard (**Figure 15.18**), select **Text—Delimited** as the file type for your exported data.

3. Type the name and path for the exported file (or use the Build button to specify the location with a dialog box).

4. Click the **Next** button.

5. At the second Export Wizard screen (**Figure 15.19**), select whether you want to export contact or group records.

   As always, you can set options here as well by clicking on the Options button. Fortunately, the options for delimited text are rather... well, limited. (**Figure 15.20**).

6. Click the **Next** button.

7. Choose which contact or group records you want to export (**Figure 15.21**) and click the **Next** button again.

8. In the last screen of the Export Wizard (**Figure 15.22**), specify the fields to be exported and the order in which you want your fields to appear in the exported file (unless you like the order as it is). You do this by clicking on a field and then either clicking the **Insert Field** button to add a field before it (you select which field you want to add from a drop-down list) or clicking the **Remove Field** button to remove it.

These field lists can be saved and loaded just like any other field maps.

9. Click the **Finish** button to export your data. Since you've saved it as delimited text, you should be able to open the new file in just about any application.

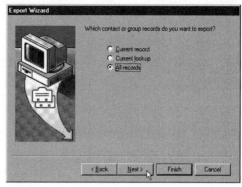

Figure 15.21 So much room, so few choices.

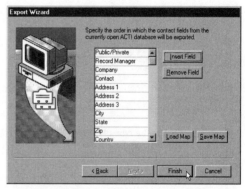

Figure 15.22 This is a sort of field mapping, but instead of matching fields, you are just specifying which fields to export and in what order.

EXPORTING RECORDS FOR USE IN OTHER APPLICATIONS

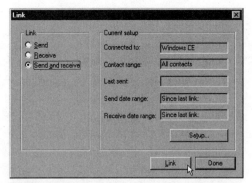

Figure 15.23 If you didn't have to set up the link, this would be easy.

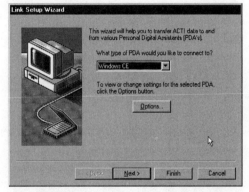

Figure 15.24 Another wizard, but boy, are they helpful!

Exchanging data with palmtop computers or electronic organizers

You can link an ACT! database on your desktop computer with an ACT! database on a hand-held computer capable of running Windows CE, a Psion Series 3a palmtop computer, or an Apple Newton MessagePad. Linking the two databases lets you exchange data between them so that both databases are as up-to-date as possible at all times. Obviously, you'll need to have a copy of ACT! for Windows CE running on the handheld device.

Exchanging data between your desktop computer and a portable machine involves a rather involved set-up process, after which the actual exchange of data involves only a single click of a button.

To set up a link between desktop and handheld ACT! databases

1. Create a lookup of all records that you want to exchange with the handheld device.

   To exchange a single record, you do not need to create a lookup, just go to the desired record.

2. From the File menu, select the **Link with Handheld Device** command.

3. The Link dialog box (**Figure 15.23**) appears.

   In the upper-left corner, select whether you want to send, receive, or both send and receive data. (Unless you are using a Newton, in which case the only option available is "Send and Receive.")

4. Unless the options under "Current setup" exactly match your actual setup (wouldn't that be great?), click on the **Setup** button. This brings up yet another wizard, the Link Setup Wizard (**Figure 15.24**).

5. Select the type of handheld device that you want to connect with from the drop-down list. If your device does not appear on the list, make sure that it is properly connected and that the interfacing software (if any) has been properly installed.

6. Click the **Options** button to set options for the type of PDA you just selected.

The options vary depending on the type of PDA, but generally relate to the port and speed of the link or (for a Windows CE device) whether you want the existing database deleted before the download occurs.

7. Click the **Next** button to access the next screen of the Link Setup Wizard (**Figure 15.25**).

8. Select what kind of information you want to send to your PDA, then click on the **Next** button.

In the "Contact selection" section, choose the current contact, current lookup, all contacts, or a selected group.

In the "Data selection" section, use the drop-down lists to specify if you want to send notes/history and activities for all entries; the last two, four, or eight entries; or no entries.

In the "Additional items to send" section, select "Field labels" to send any new field labels to your PDA or "Field drop-downs" to send any newly defined field drop-down lists.

9. Click the **Next** button.

10. In the final screen of the Link Setup Wizard (**Figure 15.26**), specify the time periods for which you want to exchange data.

Your options for both sending and receiving are "All dates," "Since last link," and "Date range:". Choosing "Date

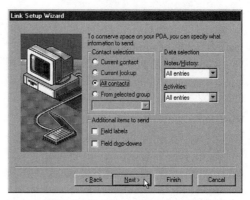

Figure 15.25 Because the space on most handheld devices is so limited, it's important to specify exactly what information you want to send.

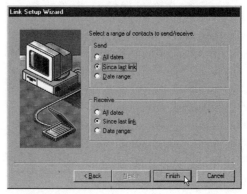

Figure 15.26 Again, because space is at a premium on handheld devices, you should specify only the dates you really need.

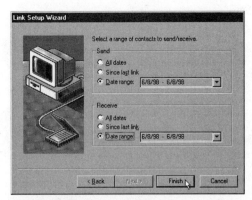

Figure 15.27 This mini-calendar works like the mini-calendars used for filtering dates.

range:" will give you a pop-up calendar within which you can specify an exact range of dates (**Figure 15.27**). Use the "All dates" option sparingly, as ACT! data can quickly fill up the limited storage space on most handheld devices.

11. Click the Finish button to complete the setup process.

12. Click the Link button to perform the actual data exchange and you are done!

16

ADVANCED REPORTS

In Chapter 10 we discussed the basics of creating reports and editing report templates. However, because some aspects of these topics are more technical than the everyday user may ever want or need to delve into, we have broken those aspects into their own chapter —this chapter.

Advanced report creation and template editing are usually the province of the database administrator or technical support team, rather than the casual user. That doesn't mean that this chapter is just for techies, though! All the tasks have been broken down into the simplest, most easily understood steps. Anyone who can do simple template editing will be able to follow along here; it's just that these topics are generally only of interest to the more technically oriented ACT! users.

Understanding report sections

As discussed in Chapter 10, all report templates are divided into sections to organize how data is presented in the report. All templates start with at least three sections: Header, Contact, and Footer. Additional sections can be added as needed, giving you the ability to completely customize the look of your reports and the information that they contain.

However, those three are just the beginning of the available sections. ACT! offers the following section types:

♦ **Header** or **Footer**: A Header or Footer section defines what data should appear at the top or bottom of every printed page, just like a header or footer in a word-processing document.

♦ **Title Header** or **Title Footer**: These are like regular Header and Footer sections, but appear only on the first page (the "title page") of a report. A Title Header or Title Footer section replaces the regular Header or Footer section for the first page.

♦ **Contact** or **Group**: These sections make up the body of the report. They work the same way, but a Contact section displays fields from a contact record and a Group section displays fields from a group record. The data in a Contact or Group section is then repeated for each contact or group record. Each report can contain either a single Contact or a single Group section. A report cannot contain both section types, nor can it contain multiple Contact or Group sections.

♦ **Group Subsection** or **Contact Subsection**: If you are creating a contact-based report (that is, your body is made up of a Contact section) and you want to include a few fields from a group record, then adding a Group Subsection is the only way to do it. This would let you list a contact's group affiliations as part of a contact report, for example. By the same token, a Contact subsection would let you include data from contact fields in a group-based report.

◆ **Notes/History** or **Activities**: As you might expect, these sections allow you to include data from the Notes/History or Activities tabs of a contact or group record in your reports. These sections can only be added to reports that already include a Contact or Group section.

◆ **Summary**: A Summary section includes one or more fields that summarize the data in the body of a report. (The "body" of the report is all of the data displayed in the Contact or Group section of the report.) These summary fields can display counts, totals, averages, or highest or lowest values of the data presented in the body of the report. Summary fields are discussed on page 218 of this chapter.

◆ **Summary Sorted By**: This section type is similar to a Summary section, but gives you the additional option of selecting the field by which the data is sorted.

✔ Tip

■ A Summary Sorted By section doesn't have to be used just to sort summary data. For example, by placing an empty Summary Sorted By State section in a Contact section, you can sort all of the contacts in your report by state without summarizing any of the data.

New terms you should know...

Section: An area of a report template within which text, graphics, and field placeholders can be placed. Some sections, such as Header or Footer, simply determine where in the report data appears. Other sections can be used to include additional fields or to summarize report data.

Adding sections

You can add any of the sections discussed in the previous pages to your report templates fairly easily. The tricky part isn't adding the sections, but rather understanding what sections to add and why. Make sure that you feel comfortable with the purposes of the different sections (refer back to *Understanding report sections* on page 280 if necessary), then just follow these steps to add functionality to your report templates.

Figure 16.1 Just about everything having to do with sections is done from this dialog box.

To add a section to a report

1. If you are not already in the Report Designer, use the **Edit Report Template** command in the Reports menu to open the report template you want to work with.

2. From the Edit menu, select the **Define Sections** command. The Define Sections dialog box appears (**Figure 16.1**).

3. Click on the **Add** button.

4. From the Sections listing (**Figure 16.2**), click on the section type that you want to add.

5. Select any desired options by clicking on the appropriate checkboxes in the lower-left corner.

   "Page break before each section" will create a forced page break at the beginning of the section.

   "Allow section to break across multiple pages" will prevent ACT! from inserting a page break before the section if the data in the section won't fit in the remaining space on the current page.

   "Collapse blank lines" and "Collapse blank sections" will eliminate lines or entire sections that contain no data or duplicated data.

6. Click the **OK** button to exit the Add Sections dialog box.

Figure 16.2 Select section types and other options here.

ADDING SECTIONS

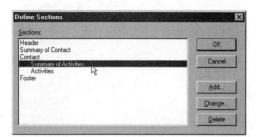

Figure 16.3 Summary Sorted By sections can only be created for Contact or Group sections or subsections.

Figure 16.4 You can sort by any field in this list.

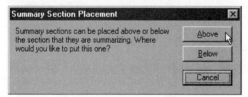

Figure 16.5 Summary Sorted By sections can go above or below the original section.

Adding sorting sections

As mentioned earlier in this chapter, one section type (Summary Sorted By) can be used to sort the data within a report. Adding Summary Sorted By sections is similar to adding regular sections, with a few extra options.

To add a sorting section to a report template

1. If you aren't already in the Report Designer, open the report template you want to work with.

2. From the Edit menu, select the **Define Sections** command.

3. In the Define Sections dialog box, select the section you want to add the Summary Sorted By section to.

   This must be a Contact or Group section, or a subsection of one of those two sections (**Figure 16.3**).

4. Click on the **Add** button.

5. Click on the **Summary sorted by** option in the Sections listing.

6. From the list of available fields on the right side of the dialog box, click on the field that you want to sort by (**Figure 16.4**).

7. From the Sort Order drop-down list, select either ascending or descending order and click on the **OK** button.

   A dialog box (**Figure 16.5**) will appear, asking whether you want the Summary Sorted By section to appear above or below the originally selected section.

8. Click the **Above** or **Below** button to specify where you want to place the Summary Sorted By section.

Deleting sections

Sections that you no longer need (or that were added to a report template during a moment of excess-cough-syrup-induced euphoria) can easily be removed from a report template. You do this using the same Define Sections dialog box you used to add the sections.

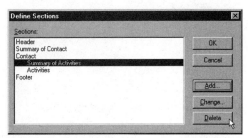

Figure 16.6 Empty sections can be deleted with the click of a button.

To delete a section from a report template

1. If you are not already editing the report template from which you want the section deleted, open it.

2. From the Edit menu, select the **Define Sections** command.

3. In the Define Sections dialog box, click on the section that you no longer want, then click the **Delete** button (**Figure 16.6**).

   If the section is not empty or contains subsections, ACT! will present you with a warning dialog box (**Figure 16.7**).

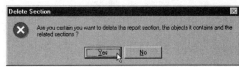

Figure 16.7 Sections that contain data won't deleted without a warning.

4. In the warning dialog box (if it appears), click the **Yes** button.

   The section is deleted from the layout.

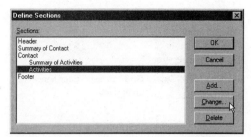

Figure 16.8 Be sure to select the section you want to change.

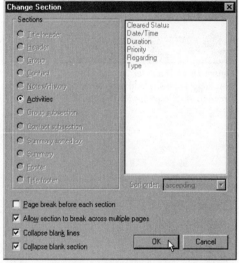

Figure 16.9 Change section parameters in this dialog box.

Editing section settings

When you create or edit a report template, you should test the template with different sets of data and print copies of the reports that the template generates. During the course of this testing you will undoubtedly find that you need to go back and change settings for certain sections. This can be accomplished via that wonderfully versatile Define Sections dialog box.

To edit section settings

1. As always, if you are not already in the Report Designer, open the report template you want to work with using the Edit Report Template command in the Reports menu.

2. From the Edit menu, select the **Define Sections** command.

3. In the Define Sections dialog box, click on the section you want to work with, then click the **Change** button (**Figure 16.8**). The Change Sections dialog box opens (**Figure 16.9**). It looks a lot like the Add Section dialog box we saw earlier. The main difference is that you cannot change the section type.

4. Change any desired parameters—such as where page breaks occur, whether blank lines or sections are collapsed, or what field Summary Sort By sections are sorted by— then click the **OK** button.

Using rulers and grids

ACT!'s rulers and grids are invaluable tools for any ambitious template design or editing. The rulers let you precisely position objects on the report template and help you design your reports to fit company stationery or fulfill other positioning requirements.

Grids are designed to help you position objects in a reliable, visually consistent manner. Many reports or other documents have an unprofessional look to them that is the result of very small errors in positioning and aligning elements. Grids take care of that problem by assuring that all template objects line up at precise grid intervals.

The following steps assume that you have already opened a report template and are editing it.

To activate or deactivate the rulers or grid

1. To turn the ruler on or off, choose the **Show Ruler** or **Hide Ruler** command from the View menu.

2. To turn the grid display on or off, choose the **Show Grid** or **Hide Grid** command from the View menu.

3. To activate the grid, select the **Snap to Grid** command from the View menu.

   A checkmark will appear next to the command (**Figure 16.10**), indicating that it is active. While it's active, all objects will "snap" to the nearest spot on the grid. Selecting the command again will deactivate the grid.

To change ruler settings

1. From the View menu, select the **Ruler Settings** command.

2. In the Ruler Settings dialog box (**Figure 16.11**), select the measurement type

Figure 16.10 With "Snap to Grid" on, everything lines up perfectly.

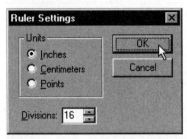

Figure 16.11 The Ruler Settings dialog box . Help! I'm being held prisoner and forced to write captions for this book!

USING RULERS AND GRIDS

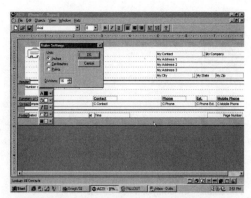

Figure 16.12 The spacing of the ruler ticks and grid points is determined by the value in the Divisions box.

(inches, centimeters, or points).

Most users are familiar with points as a vertical measure of font size. In case you are not familiar with them, points are a unit of measurement used in typography. There are 72 points in an inch.

3. If desired, change the Divisions value by clicking on the up or down arrows, or by simply selecting the current value and typing a new value over it.

The Divisions value determines the number of divisions in the rulers and the spacing of the grid points. For example, the default setting of 16 divisions for inches means that you will have tick marks every 16th of an inch on your ruler and your grid points will be 1/16th of an inch apart (**Figure 16.12**).

4. Click the **OK** button to close the dialog box.

New terms you should know...

Grid: An invisible set of lines which, when activated, pull all nearby objects to them, forcing alignment and creating a uniform visual look for a report template. Grids are a common feature of all object-oriented drawing and page-layout programs.

Adding summary fields

A summary field is pretty much what you would expect: a field that summarizes data. Specifically, a summary field can be used to display the count (the number of records that have data in the selected field), total, average, or highest or lowest value of any numeric, date or time field in your database (text values cannot be computed, obviously).

Summary fields can only be added to Summary or Summary Sorted By sections. If you do not already have one of these sections in your report, you will need to create one before adding a summary field.

These steps assume that you have a report template that includes a Summary or Summary Sorted By section open.

To add a summary field to a report template

1. Click on the Field tool in the tool palette (**Figure 16.13**).

Figure 16.13 The Field tool creates fields, including summary fields.

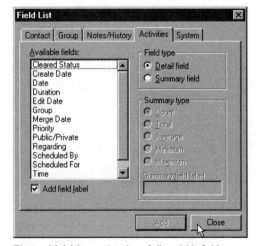

2. Position the crosshair cursor where you want your summary field to begin and press and drag to the right to define the size of the field.

As soon as you release the mouse button, ACT! will present you with the Field List dialog box (**Figure 16.14**).

3. In the "Field type" section of this dialog box, click on the Summary Field option.

The "Summary type" section now becomes active.

4. Click on the type of summary field you want to create (Count, Total, Average, Minimum, or Maximum).

Count returns the total number of records that contain data in the selected field; Total returns the sum total of all values in the selected field; Average returns the average

Figure 16.14 A complete list of all available fields.

ADDING SUMMARY FIELDS

Figure 16.15 Text fields are unavailable unless you select the Count option.

of all the values in the selected field; and Minimum and Maximum return the lowest or highest value in the selected field.

5. If you want a label for this summary field, enter it in the Summary Field Label text box.

6. In the Available Fields list, click on the field that you want ACT! to use to calculate the specified summary.

   If you selected anything other than Count in step 4, only numeric, currency, date, or time fields are available, since text cannot be totaled, averaged, and so on (**Figure 16.15**).

7. Click the **Add** button to add the field to your template.

8. Repeat steps 3–7 to create additional summary fields, or click the **Close** button to exit the dialog box.

ADDING SUMMARY FIELDS

Defining filters

One of the options people most frequently overlook when creating or editing report templates is the ability to predefine filters. As you may recall, whenever a report is run, the Run Report dialog box appears, with a Filter tab (**Figure 16.16**) for filtering out unwanted data. As a report designer, you can set these filtering options ahead of time.

A perfect example of this (and also a very easy and useful edit of a report template) is a report listing all overdue phone calls for an assistant to take care of when you get swamped. You could do this by simply opening the Task List report template, changing the filtering options to include just phone calls with past dates, then saving the template as something like "Overdue Phone Calls." A report generated from this template will only list phone calls that should have already been made.

Keep in mind that changing filtering options in the template does not prevent the Run Report dialog box from appearing, nor does it prevent the user from changing filtering or other options. Basically, defining filters for report templates just lets you change the default options in the Run Report dialog box.

To define filters for a report template

1. Open the desired report template (if necessary).

2. From the Edit menu, select **Define Filters**.

3. In the Define Filters dialog box, change any options on the General or Filter tabs (**Figure 16.17**) as desired.

   These options are discussed in detail in the *Filtering reports* section of Chapter 10 (page 169).

4. Click the **OK** button to save the changes and exit the dialog box.

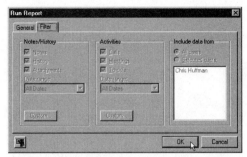

Figure 16.16 The Run Report dialog box.

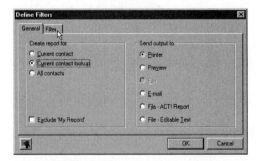

Figure 16.17 Any options selected here become the default for all reports generated from this template.

17

SYNCHRONIZING DATA

The concepts, preparation, and procedures involved in synchronizing two or more databases probably cause more confusion than any other aspect of ACT!. To help make things as easy as possible, we'll start this chapter with a fairly lengthy discussion of the concepts and processes involved, then move into the different ways of setting up ACT! for data synchronization, and finally discuss the synchronization process itself.

The ACT! 4.0 User's Guide covers these subjects in greater detail, but for a truly great source of additional information on synchronizing data (and other subjects that frequently fall at the feet of database administrators), be sure to print out and read the ACT! Administrator's Guide, which is located on the ACT! installation CD (you can access it from the main installation screen, under "View Documentation").

Understanding data synchronization

Data synchronization is the process of transferring contact information from one database to one or more other databases.

One example of a situation requiring synchronization would be when a user has both a laptop and a desktop computer. Without synchronization, every time the user returns to the office from a business trip, he or she would have to locate all records created on the laptop and reenter them into the desktop machine (and vice versa to get desktop records onto the laptop). If the user synchronized the two databases, both databases would be updated to include all records, and even to reflect any changes made to existing records.

Another example would be a group of sales personnel who share clients and contacts. In order for each salesperson to have up-to-date information on contacts entered by the rest of the group, the databases have to be synchronized on a regular basis. In this example, rather than databases being synchronized directly, the data can be sent to a shared folder on a network drive that everyone has access to, or even sent via e-mail for salespeople who are out of the office or based elsewhere.

These two examples of when to synchronize are also good examples of the two different types of synchronization: direct and remote. *Direct synchronization* refers to the transfer of data directly from one database to another. Direct synchronization can only synchronize two databases at a time and requires access to both databases simultaneously (usually over a local area network). You must have Administrator privileges for both databases in order to synchronize them.

Remote synchronization occurs when data is sent from one database to an intermediate location, and then from there to the destination database. The advantages of remote synchronization include the ability to synchronize more than two databases and the fact that all databases (and their users) do not have to synchronize at the same time.

You can do remote synchronization by using a shared folder on a hard drive accessible to all users (usually over a local area network (LAN) or a wide area network (WAN)), by sending synchronization data via e-mail, or even by sending information directly over a modem. We do not recommend the modem-to-modem method for several reasons, chief among them the extreme inconvenience of trying to schedule and then establish a modem-to-modem connection also long-distance charges, down-time, and possible line problems can make modem-to-modem synchronization very unattractive. In this chapter we'll take you through the two recommended methods for remote synchronization, via a shared folder and through e-mail (as well as direct synchronization, of course).

During a direct synchronization, the data is sent to and received from the other database virtually simultaneously. During a remote synchronization, update information is sent to an intermediate location (such as an e-mail server or shared folder) and is picked up and applied when convenient for the users with whom you are synchronizing.

Before you can synchronize your data, you must go through a rather involved setup process, and before that, you really should set up your synchronization preferences. You will also need to create "synchronization users" for your database (which is slightly different than just adding users to your database). All of these processes are discussed in detail on the following pages.

New terms you should know...

Direct synchronization: The exchange of contact information between two databases. Update information is sent virtually simultaneously from one database to the other, with no intermediary, such as an e-mail message or a folder on a shared disk, between the two.

Remote synchronization: The exchange of contact information between two or more databases via e-mail, a shared location, or a modem connection. Remote synchronizations are the only way to synchronize more than two databases or users.

UNDERSTANDING DATA SYNCHRONIZATION

Setting synchronization preferences

The first step in preparing ACT! for data synchronization is to set up your synchronization preferences. The choices you make here will determine the default settings for many of the choices that you will have to make over and over again when setting up for synchronizing or performing an actual synchronization.

To set synchronization preferences

1. From the Edit menu, select the Preferences command.

2. Click on the **Synchronization** tab to bring up the Synchronization preferences screen (**Figure 17.1**).

3. In the "When synchronizing" section, select whether you want to "Send updates," "Receive updates," or both.

   You can also select neither, but then your synchronizations will be kind of pointless.

4. In the "Data to synchronize" section, select Activities, Notes/Histories, both, or none (to send only data from the main contact fields, such as name, company, address, etc.).

5. If you will be synchronizing with other users via a shared folder, in the "Location to receive synchronizations" section, click on the Browse button and locate and select the folder where you want received synchronization updates and reports to go (**Figure 17.2**), then click on the Select button to return to the Synchronization preferences screen.

   See the note about this folder, below.

6. If you will be sending and receiving synchronization updates via e-mail (or modem), select the correct modem from the Modem Settings drop-down list.

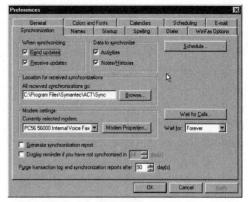

Figure 17.1 The Synchronization screen of the Preferences dialog box.

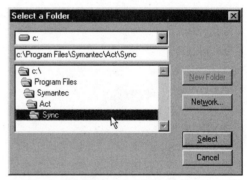

Figure 17.2 Specify a new shared folder for shared-folder remote synchronizations.

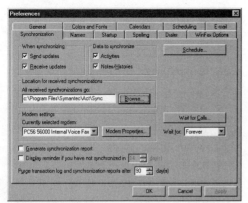

Figure 17.3 Make your life easier by reading up on automating synchronizations, then clicking this button.

If you have already set up your modem for other modem-related ACT! tasks, such as calling or faxing clients, it should already be selected.

7. If you want reports generated for synchronizations, click on the "Generate synchronization report" checkbox.

8. If you want a reminder to synchronize, click on the "Display reminder if you have not synchronized in..." checkbox and specify the number of days before the reminder appears.

9. If desired, change the number of days for the "Purge transaction log..." option.

10. Click the **OK** button.

The Schedule button (**Figure 17.3**) is used to automate the synchronization process and is discussed in *Automating synchronizations* (page 308). The Wait for Calls button (and the Wait For drop-down list) are only used when receiving modem-to-modem synchronizations, which we don't recommend. They tell ACT! to wait for the phone to ring when you are expecting a synchronization call, and how long to wait.

✔ Warning

■ If you want to synchronize via a shared folder the folder selected in step 5 *must* be available to all users who will be sending you synchronization updates (that is, pretty much anyone you want to synchronize with). Make sure that the correct privileges have been set up for the folder so that everyone who needs to access it can do so. You may want to have your IS or database administrator create a folder for you specifically for this purpose.

SETTING SYNCHRONIZATION PREFERENCES

Setting up for direct synchronization

Direct synchronization refers to an unmediated data exchange between two databases. This is the simplest kind of synchronization to perform, but does require Administrator-level access to both databases, as mentioned earlier in this chapter.

You set up for a direct synchronization by activating the Synchronization Setup Wizard and selecting options in its many screens. The process is somewhat lengthy, but you won't have to do again, unless you decide to synchronize with a different database.

To set up for direct synchronization

1. From the File menu, select the **Synchronize Setup** command.

2. At the Introduction screen, click the **Next** button.

   You may want to click on the "Don't show this screen in the future" checkbox to hide this screen for future setups.

3. At the next screen (**Figure 17.4**), select the **Database to database** option and click the Next button.

4. At the next screen (**Figure 17.5**), click on the **Browse** button.

   This brings up a standard Open dialog box.

5. Navigate in the Open dialog box to locate and select the database file you want to synchronize with, then click the **Open** button.

6. Click the **Next** button to advance to the next screen of the wizard (**Figure 17.6**).

7. Select whether you want to synchronize Notes/Histories, Activities, both, or neither, then click the **Next** button.

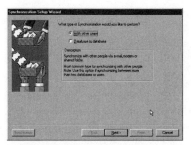

Figure 17.4 Select the type of synchronization you want to set up.

Figure 17.5 You must locate the database that you want to synchronize with.

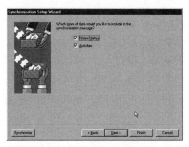

Figure 17.6 If you select neither option, you will synchronize only basic contact data such as name, address, etc.

Figure 17.7 Select which records you want to synchronize.

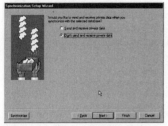

Figure 17.8 You probably will not want to send and receive private data (well, receive maybe, but definitely not send).

Figure 17.9 Be conservative when it comes to field definitions. You never know how the person on the other end of the synchronization may have modified their database fields.

Figure 17.10 The Schedule button lets you automate synchronizations.

The default settings here are based on your settings in the Synchronization preferences dialog box.

8. Select whether you want to synchronize All groups and contacts or just Selected groups. If you choose to synchronize only selected groups, select the desired groups from the list (**Figure 17.7**).

9. Click the Next button.

10. Select whether or not you want to send and receive private data (**Figure 17.8**) and click the Next button.

11. Select whether or not you want to send and receive database field definitions (**Figure 17.9**). If you do choose to send field definitions, select which definitions you want to be applied (those from your database, those from the other database, or the newest definitions).

We really don't recommend sending field definitions unless you are a database administrator and have created or modified field definitions for your users. Field definitions can safely be received as long as you know and trust the ACT! skills of the person with whom you are synchronizing (such as your database administrator or the ACT! "whiz kid" in the office.).

12. Click the Next button.

13. Select whether or not you want to automate the synchronization process by scheduling a time for ACT! to send and receive synchronizations for you (**Figure 17.10**), then click the Next button.

If you select Yes, refer to the *Automating synchronizations* section on page 308 of this chapter. For now, we will assume that you are leaving the No option selected.

14. Select whether you want to **Send only changed records** or **Send all records...** (**Figure 17.11**) and click on the Finish button.

If you want to start an immediate synchronization, click the Synchronize button in the lower-left corner, which starts the synchronization process without displaying the Synchronize dialog box.

When you complete the Synchronization Setup Wizard, ACT! assumes that you want to actually synchronize your data, and displays the Synchronize dialog box for you, within which you can change Synchronization options before starting the actual data synchronization process. Refer to the *Synchronizing data* section on page 306 for instructions on this next step in the synchronization process.

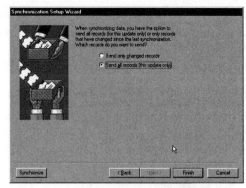

Figure 17.11 Select which records you want to synchronize, and you can click the long-awaited Finish button.

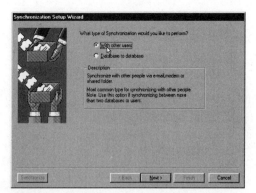

Figure 17.12 The all-important question; the type of synchronization you select determines what you will see from here on out.

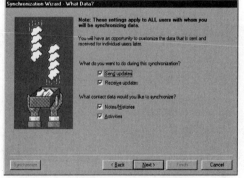

Figure 17.13 "To send, or to receive," that is the question (with apologies to Hamlet).

Setting up for remote synchronization

The process of setting up for remote synchronization (that is, synchronization via shared folder, e-mail, or modem connection) is the most involved effort that ACT! will ever require of you. That is the bad news. The good news is that you can set up a mind-boggling number of users for synchronization in one pass through the Synchronization Setup Wizard. Once you have things set up, a few mouse clicks will initiate synchronizations for all of these users while you sit back and watch the show.

As with direct synchronization, setting up for remote synchronization is a matter of activating the Synchronization Setup Wizard and selecting options or entering information in each of the screens as they are displayed.

To set up for remote synchronization

1. From the File menu, select the Synchronize Setup command.

2. If you have not already disabled the Introduction screen (by clicking the "Don't show this screen..." checkbox), click the Next button to move past it.

3. At the next screen (**Figure 17.12**), select the "With other users" option and click the Next button.

4. At the What Data? screen (**Figure 17.13**), select whether you want to "Send updates," "Receive updates," or both. The default setting is based on your settings in the Synchronize preferences dialog box.

5. Select whether you want to synchronize Notes/Histories, Activities, both, or neither.

Again, the default setting is based on your settings in the Synchronize preferences dialog box.

6. Click the **Next** button.

7. At the With Whom screen (**Figure 17.14**), select the people with whom you want to synchronize data by selecting them from the Contacts or Users lists on the left side of the dialog box and then clicking on the **Add** button. You can remove mistakes by selecting the person from the right-hand list and clicking the **Remove** button.

Don't forget about using Shift-click and Ctrl-click to select multiple users.

8. If you need to send to a user who has not yet been set up, click the **New User** button, enter their name in the New User dialog box, and click **OK**. Repeat this step for each new user you need to create.

9. Once you have the desired users selected and moved to the Sync list, click the **Next** button.

10. In the How dialog box (**Figure 17.15**), select the users from the "users to synchronize with" list one at a time and specify how you want to connect to each one.

To synchronize via e-mail, click on the "Use e-mail" option and enter the correct e-mail address, if it is not already present in the "E-mail address" text box. (The address used by default is the contact's or user's primary e-mail address from their contact record.)

If you will be synchronizing via a shared folder, select the "Use shared folder" option and specify the folders to be used for both sent and received synchronization updates.

If you are going to use a modem-to-modem connection, select either the

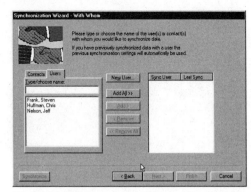

Figure 17.14 You must select all users with whom you want to synchronize data.

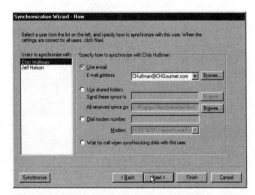

Figure 17.15 If a user has not already been set up for synchronizations, you must do so here.

SETTING UP FOR REMOTE SYNCHRONIZATION

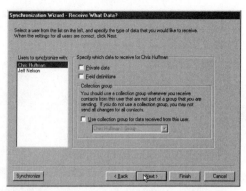

Figure 17.16 Receiving private data and (especially) field definitions is usually not a good idea.

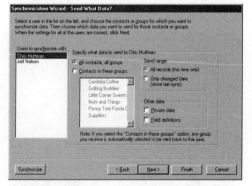

Figure 17.17 Select what records you want to send to each user.

"Dial modem number" option or the "Wait for call..." option. (If you will be initiating the call, you will also need to specify the number to be dialed and the modem you will be using.)

11. Click the **Next** button to get to the Receive What Data? screen (**Figure 17.16**).

12. For each user in the "Users to synchronize with" list, specify whether you want to receive private data or field definitions.

13. Click on the "Use collection group..." checkbox unless you know that you will not be receiving any contact records from the selected user that do not belong to a group that you already have. (In other words, contacts that belong to groups that exist in his or her database, but not in your own.)

14. If you selected the "Use collection group..." option in step 13, select a group from drop-down list of available groups. Any new contacts you receive from the selected user which belong to groups that don't exist in your database will go into this collection group.

    If you do not want these "orphaned" incoming records to go into any of your existing groups, select the "<user's name>'s Group" option, and a new group will be created just for these records.

15. Click the **Next** button to get to the Send What Data? screen (**Figure 17.17**).

16. Again, for each user in the "Users to synchronize with" list, select whether you want to send "All contacts, all groups" (the default) or only "Contacts in these groups" by clicking the appropriate button. If you choose "Contacts in these groups," then select the groups whose contacts you want to send from the list of available groups.

17. In the "Send range" section select either the "All records..." option or the "Only changed data..." option.

18. In the "Other data" section, select "Private data," "Field definitions," both, or neither.

19. Click the Next button.

20. Select whether or not you want to automate the synchronization process by scheduling a time for ACT! to send and receive synchronizations for you, then click the Next button.

If you select Yes, refer to the *Automating synchronizations* section on page 308 of this chapter. For now, we will assume that you are leaving the No option selected.

21. Click the Finish button!

When you complete the Synchronization Setup Wizard, ACT! assumes that you want to actually synchronize your data, and displays the Synchronize dialog box for you. Refer to the *Synchronizing data* section on page 306 for instructions on this next step in the synchronization process.

Figure 17.18 The Define Users dialog box.

Creating users for remote synchronization

Before you can synchronize data remotely with another user, they must exist as a valid user of your database. Even if the person will never see or access your database, you still must create them as a user of the database.

The Define Users command can be used to create users for synchronization just as it is used for creating regular database users. The difference here is that you must fill in all of the send and receive data for each synchronization user. For extra security, you may also define the user as one with whom you will be synchronizing data, but who cannot log onto your database.

To create or define synchronization users

1. From the File menu, select the **Administration** submenu and the **Define Users** command.

2. In the Define Users dialog box (**Figure 17.18**), click the **Add User** button to create a new user.

   If you do not want to create new users, but only to set up existing users for synchronization, skip to step 8.

3. Enter a name for the user in the User Name text box.

4. Enter a password for the user (if desired) in the Password text box.

5. Select a security level for the user from the Security Level drop-down list.

   "Administrator" gives the user full access to all ACT! features, including database modifications, adding and deleting fields, etc.

"Standard" lets the user see, edit, add, and delete records and perform database synchronization. This is your most likely choice here.

"Browse" only allows the user to view database records.

6. If this user is being created only to receive synchronizations (and not to actually access this database), click on the Enable Logon option to turn it off.

7. Click on the Enable Synchronization checkbox to turn it on.

   Repeat steps 2 through 7 for each new user you want to create.

8. Click on the **Send** tab to activate the Send screen and its options (**Figure 17.19**).

9. Select the user whose synchronization settings you want to define or change from the list on the left side of the dialog box.

   This is unnecessary if you are working with a user you just created, as that user's name will still be selected in the list.

10. From the Connect Via drop-down list, select a connection method for sending synchronization updates.

    "Shared Folder" is used for shared-folder synchronizations (obviously) and "Modem" is used for modem-to-modem synchronizations. All other choices result in e-mail synchronizations.

11. In the "E-mail address or location" text box, enter the user's primary e-mail address or the location of the shared-folder.

12. In the "Groups" section, either select "All contacts and groups" or select "Selected groups" and specify from which of the selected groups contacts are to be sent.

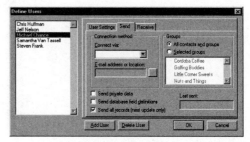

Figure 17.19 Specify what data will be sent and how it will be sent for each user.

Figure 17.20 You must also specify how to receive data from each user.

13. Select or deselect the "Send private data," "Send database field definitions," and "Send all records..." options as desired.

14. Click on the **Receive** tab to activate the receiving options screen (**Figure 17.20**).

15. If desired, select a group from the Collection Group drop-down list to receive all incoming contacts who belong to groups that don't exist in your database.

16. If you want to receive private data or accept database definitions from this person, click on the appropriately labeled checkboxes.

17. Click the **OK** button.

If you need to define synchronization settings for other users, go back to step 8 and select the next user you want to work with.

✔ Tip

- Remember, you can also create new synchronization users from within the Synchronization Setup Wizard itself. Simply click on the New button when you get to the With Whom screen of the wizard and enter the names of all the users that you want to create. The rest of the wizard will allow you specify all necessary information for these new users, as explained in the *Setting up for remote synchronization* section (page 299).

Synchronizing data

Compared to setting up for synchronization, the process of actually synchronizing data is extremely simple. All you have to do is open the Synchronize dialog box, select a few options, then click on a button, and ACT! will do the rest. (Speaking of rest, by now you probably deserve one, so follow these steps to start your synchronization, then lean back and put your feet up for a bit. Just don't nod off, fall over and fracture your skull. You don't want to end up with synchronized data, but a de-synchronized brain.)

To synchronize data

1. From the File menu, select the Synchronize command.

   The Synchronize dialog box appears (**Figure 17.21**).

   If you go through the Synchronization Setup Wizard, the Synchronize button on the latter screens or the Finish button on the last screen will also bring you here (**Figure 17.22**).

2. In the "Choose an action" section, select whether you want to "Send updates," "Receive updates," or both by clicking on the appropriate checkbox(es).

3. In the "Select type of synchronization" section, click on either the "With other users" option or the "Database to database" option.

4. If you have not already gone through the Synchronization Setup Wizard to configure ACT! and your users for synchronization, click the Setup button.

   This will launch the Synchronization Setup Wizard. Refer to either the *Setting up for remote synchronization* section (page 299) or the *Setting up for direct (database to database)* synchronization section (page 296), depend-

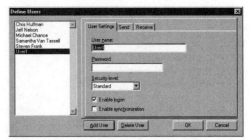

Figure 17.21 The Synchronize dialog box.

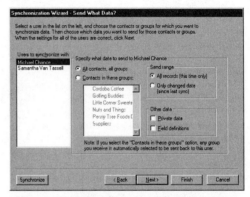

Figure 17.22 The Synchronize and Finish buttons in certain Synchronization Setup Wizard screens will take you to the Synchronize dialog box as well.

SYNCHRONIZING DATA

Figure 17.23 One user in a modem-to-modem connection will have to wait for the call (and hopefully won't get stood up).

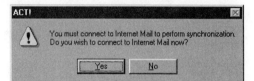

Figure 17.24 If you are not already connected to all the drives and e-mail systems that are required for the synchronization, ACT! will let you know.

ing on whether you selected the "With other users" option or the "Database to database" option in step 3.

5. Select the "Clear the synchronized records to be deleted" option if you want ACT! to delete from your database all records that have been deleted in the database(s) that you are synchronizing with.

If you don't select this option, ACT! creates a lookup of these records so that you can look at them before deciding to delete them.

6. Select the "Lock database upon synchronizing" option if you want to lock out other users of the database for the duration of the synchronization process.

Synchronizations are faster if no one else is using the database. Anyone using the database when the synchronization starts will be warned that the database is about to be locked, and will be logged off automatically, if necessary, when the synchronization begins.

7. If someone else will be calling you to initiate a modem-to-modem synchronization, click on the Wait for Calls button and tell ACT! how long to wait for the call (**Figure 17.23**).

8. If you are initiating the synchronization, click on the Synchronize button.

ACT! will prompt you to make any necessary connections (to the Internet for e-mail synchronizations, or to a networked drive for shared-folder synchronizations, for example) (**Figure 17.24**).

Automating synchronizations

As we've seen, synchronizing data is much easier than setting up for synchronization, but it's even easier if you don't have to do it at all!

By automating the synchronization process, you can make ACT! send and receive synchronization updates for you at specific times (such as during the middle of the night when phone rates are lower or while you are at lunch and not using your computer anyway) and on specific days (like on the weekend, when database synchronization is the last thing on your mind). Your database will always be up to date (as will your colleagues') without your ever having to think about synchronizations again.

To automate the synchronization process

1. From the Edit menu, select the **Preferences** command.

2. In the Preferences dialog box, click on the **Synchronization** tab to access the Synchronization preferences screen (**Figure 17.25**).

3. Click on the **Schedule** button.

4. In the Synchronization Schedule dialog box (**Figure 17.26**), select the day(s) when you would like automatic synchronizations to occur by clicking the appropriate checkbox(es).

5. Select the time(s) when you want synchronizations to occur, and click the **Add** button to add the times to the "Synchronize at" list.

6. Click the **OK** button to return to the Preferences dialog box, then click **OK** again to return to the main ACT! display.

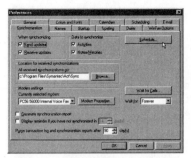

Figure 17.25 The Synchronization preferences screen.

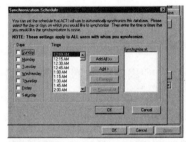

Figure 17.26 Scheduling synchronizations is a pretty straightforward affair.

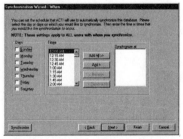

Figure 17.27 A "Yes" choice here inserts a step in the Synchronization Setup wizard for scheduling automated synchronizations.

✔ Tip

■ You can also set up automatic synchronization from the When screen of the Synchronization Setup Wizard (**Figure 17.27**) by selecting the Yes option, then clicking the Next button.

AUTOMATING SYNCHRONIZATIONS

PREFERENCES

If you've taken a peek at ACT!'s Preferences dialog box (and you probably have or you wouldn't be reading this), you may have felt a bit overwhelmed. Just the first screen (or page or tab, or whatever you want to call it), for setting General preferences, has 15 separate options on it. And there are ten other screens to deal with!

For your convenience we have set aside these next few pages to explain everything that needs explaining when it comes to changing your ACT! preferences. Because this is a purely information-based section (rather than being task-oriented, like the rest of the book) preferences are dealt with in this appendix.

General preferences

The General preferences screen (**Figure A.1**) contains several unrelated preferences that can be set. Most of these are self- explanatory.

In the "Default applications" section, select the word processor and faxing software that you want ACT! to use. Your word-processing choices are always the same three programs, but the "Fax software" list will include any fax software that ACT! finds on your system.

"Move between fields" lets you choose which key will take you to the next field in the Contacts window, Groups window, or any other window.

You can use the "Attaching contacts/activities to messages" section to select the file format(s) for contacts or activities that are attached to e-mail messages.

The "Default locations" section lets you change where ACT! stores all of the files that your create as you use ACT!. With the possible exception of word- processing documents, we don't recommend changing this.

The rest of the options are all self-explanatory. Most of the rest of the options are fairly self-explanatory. "Prompt before exiting" will just ask you if you are sure you want to exit ACT!, 'Remember password" will save you the trouble of typing in your password every time you open the database, "Remind me to backup every ___ days" lets you set an interval for the reminder dialog box that you need to back up your database, etc.

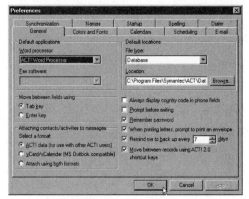

Figure A.1 The General preferences screen.

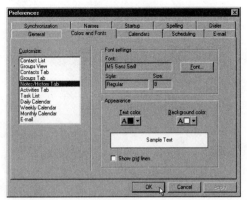

Figure A.2 The Colors and Fonts preferences screen.

Colors and Fonts preferences

If you never change any of the Colors and Fonts preferences (**Figure A.2**), you'll save yourself countless hours of showing others how to do it, (since people will notice if you change the text in your Contacts screen to 14-point, fuschia Ridiculous Script, and they will undoubtedly (don't ask me why) want to do it, too).

The "Customize" list on the left lets you select which aspect of ACT! you want to customize. The "Font settings" section lets you pick a font, font size, and font style, and the "Appearance" section lets you change text and background color, and also show gridlines.

Calendar preferences

It should come as no surprise to anyone that the Calendars preferences screen (**Figure A.3**) lets you change calendar settings.

Most of the options here are pretty self-explanatory ("Calendar week starts on" either a Sunday or a Monday, etc.).

The purpose of the "Calendar increments" section may not be immediately obvious, though. These values determine the size of the time blocks in your daily and weekly calendars. By default they are set at 30 minutes for your daily calendar and one hour for your weekly calendar, which is why your time blocks are the size they are on those calendars.

The "Show full day banner for activities with duration of ___ or longer" option simply determines how long activities are *displayed* on your calendar. It has no other effect.

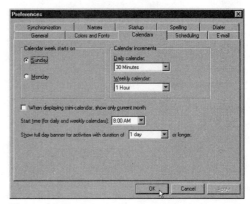

Figure A.3 The Calendars preferences screen.

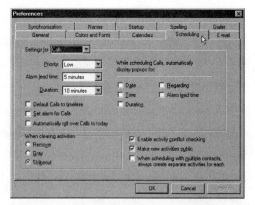

Figure A.4 The Scheduling preferences screen.

Scheduling preferences

With the Scheduling preferences screen (**Figure A.4**) we are getting into deeper territory. Some of these options not only require a little explanation, but also they can significantly change the way you schedule activities in ACT!

The drop-down list in at the top of the "Settings for ___" section lets you choose whether you will be altering preferences for calls, meetings, or to-dos. Once you have picked an activity type, the rest of the options in this section change how your activities are scheduled. You can change the default priority, lead time, and duration;, whether or not the activity type is timeless or has alarms set automatically; and if you want all overdue activities to automatically "roll over" to today (which reschedules them from the overdue date to today's date). You can also check any of the "...automatically display popups for:" checkboxes to choose dates, times, and so on from pop-upshave screns pop up for date, time, etc, selection, instead of specifying these parameters in the Schedule Activity dialog box.

The "When clearing activities" section determines the appearance of cleared activities on calendars and the Task List.

If "Enable conflict checking" is selected, ACT! will warn you whenever one scheduled activity conflicts with another. "Make new activities public," well, makes new activities public (rather than private) by default., and "When scheduling with multiple contacts, always create separate activities for each" does pretty much what it says, creating a separate activity for each contact, rather than one activity for all contacts. This determines how many activities show up on calendars and the Task List.

E-mail preferences

If you don't use ACT! to send and receive e-mail, you don't need to bother with this screen. If you do send and receive e-mail with ACT!, though, you really should spend a few minutes setting up your e-mail preferences (**Figure A.5**). It will make your e-mailing a little faster and easier.

The "E-mail system" section consists of two items: a drop-down list where youto select the e-mail system you use, and a button you click to set up ACT! to work with that system. Clicking the "E-mail System Setup" button launches the E-mail Setup Wizard, which consists of three dialog boxes (**Figures A.6 – A.8**) within which you select an e-mail system and enter all of the necessary information necessary to enable ACT! to connect to it. You will need information from your Iinternet service provider to complete this wizard.

In the "New message settings" section you can enter signature text (text that appears at the end of all of your e-mail messages), and set whether you want ACT! to automatically create history entries for sent messages, request return receipts, attach sent messages to contact records, or use "typeahead" (a feature where you simply type the first few letters of a contact's name when addressing a message and ACT! will locates the correct contact and adds his or her name).

The "Inbox settings" section is very basic, with options to confirm message deletions and set new message notification.

The largest section on the E-mail preferences screen is the "Attaching messages to contacts" section, within which you can specify how ACT! deals with attached files attached to incoming messages, and where messages are stored on disk. It also contains a button for purging (deleting) old messages.

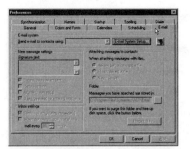

Figure A.5 The E-mail preferences screen.

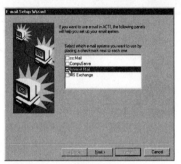

Figure A.6 The first screen of the E-mail Setup Wizard for Internet mail.

Figure A.7 Screen two of the Wizard (this is the ugly one).

Figure A.8 The final screen of the E-mail Setup Wizard.

E-MAIL PREFERENCES

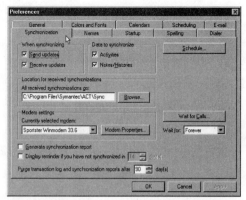

Figure A.9 The Synchronization preferences screen.

Synchronization preferences

The options on the Synchronization preferences screen (**Figure A.9**) are only used (obviously) for synchronizing data with other users. If you work alone or never share data with other users, you will never need to look at this screen. But if you are going to be synchronizing databases, you will definitely want to set up everything up here to match your specific needs.

The "When synchronizing" and "Data to synchronize" sections let you specify whether you want to send or receive data (or both) and if you want to work with activities and/or notes and history entries.

The "Location for received synchronizations" is exactly what it says, and offers a Browse button for selecting a different destination, if desired.

"Modem settings" lets you set which modem you want to use and offers a button for changing modem properties.

At the bottom left are three options for generating reports each time you synchronize data, displaying a reminder at specified intervals (every ___ days), and purging logs and reports after a specified number of days.

There is a button in the upper right for scheduling automatic synchronizations (this is discussed in Chapter 17, *Synchronizing data*).

Lastly, the "Wait for Calls" button and "Wait for: Forever" drop-down list do not reflect your social life (at least not intentionally) but rather are used to tell ACT! how long to wait for a call when a colleague is sending you synchronization data via modem. (Again, see Chapter 17 for more details.)

SYNCHRONIZATION PREFERENCES

Name preferences

The Names preferences screen (**Figure A.10**) is a very straightforward affair. The "Name prefixes and suffixes" section contains lists of first- and last- name prefixes and last-name suffixes. This helps ACT! to know how to split a contact name into first and last name sections. The Add and Remove buttons are used to add new items or to remove incorrect or unneeded items.

The "Salutation" section contains three options for creating a salutation from the information you type into the "Contact" field.

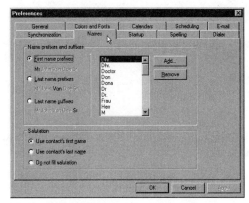

Figure A.10 The Names preferences screen.

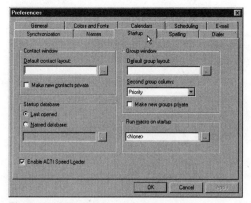

Figure A.11 The Startup preferences screen.

Startup preferences

The Startup preferences screen (**Figure A.11**) is where you set the default layouts and startup settings for ACT!.

The "Contact window" and "Group window" sections let you set default layouts for the Contacts and Groups windows, and specify whether or not you want new contacts and groups to be private by default. Additionally, you can select the second group column (important since only two columns are usually visible in the Groups window).

The "Startup database" section lets you specify that ACT! open a particular database each time you start it, rather than simply reopening the last open database.

The "Run macro on startup" option is used to specify (hold onto your hats) a macro to be run on startup.

Finally, the "Enable ACT! Speed Loader" option puzzles a lot of people. If this option is selected, ACT! keeps certain important data stored in your computer's memory so that your computer doesn't have to read as much information from disk in order to launch ACT!. If your computer is low on memory, you may want to turn this option off.

STARTUP PREFERENCES

Spelling preferences

The smallest preferences screen (in terms of options), the Spelling screen (**Figure A.12**), deals exclusively with the spelling dictionaries. You can change your main dictionary to another language, set the desired dialect within the language you are using, or open, create, or modify supplementary user dictionaries. These tasks are all covered in detail in Chapter 9, *Word Processing in ACT!*.

The only other option is "Auto suggest spelling changes,", which tells ACT! to automatically suggest possible correct spellings for words that it doesn't recognize.

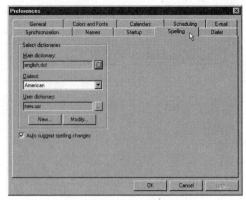

Figure A.12 The Spelling preferences screen.

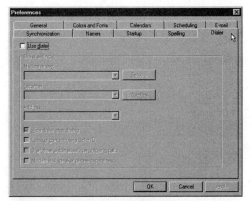

Figure A.13 The Dialer preferences screen.

Dialer preferences

In order for you to use ACT!'s dialer abilities, your computer and telephone systems need to meet certain criteria. If they don't meet these criteria, it will be difficult or impossible for you tor use of ACT! as a telephone dialer. These requirements (and a step-by-step walk-through of setting up the dialer) are described in Chapter 11, *Staying in Contact*.

You use the dialer preferences screen (**Figure A.13**) is used to set up your dialer configuration initially and also to change settings as your dialing needs change.

The "Use dialer" checkbox turns ACT!'s dialing features on or off.

The "Dialer settings" section lets you select and set up a modem as well as, choose and configure a location (useful for those of you who use ACT! on laptop computers and may be dialing out from several different locales). Also in the "Dialer settings" section is a drop-down list labeled "Address," which is used to tells ACT! which extension you want to use on a phone line with multiple extensions.

You can also choose whether to hide the dialer dialog box after dialing the phone, look up contact records for incoming calls using caller ID information, or start a timer for all outgoing calls automatically, and finally, you can let ACT! know that if your modem has speaker-phone capabilities.

WinFax options

Because Symantec has designed WinFax to
work very closely with ACT!, there are a
number of options that can be set in the
WinFax Options preferences screen (**Figure
A.14**) that will enable WinFax to modify
records in your ACT! database.

The first option is labeled the "Use the
currently open ACT! database as a WinfFax
phonebook" and does exactly what it says.
This option must be selected in order to
access the other options on this screen.

The options in the "When WinFax sends to
an ACT! contact" section let you specify for
what types of events Notes/History entries
will be created, and if you want reminder
activities created for unsuccessful fax
attempts.

The "Notes/History attachments" section
contains a single option to attach a "link"file
to the contact record that links to the fax that
was sent or attempted. This allows you to
open and edit the actual WinFax fax file from
within ACT! by double-clicking on the
attached file in the Notes/History tab of the
Contacts view.

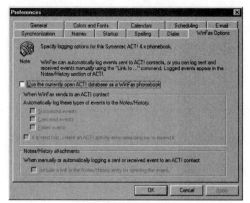

Figure A.14 The WinFax Options screen.

WINFAX OPTIONS

HELP AND SUPPORT

This appendix is designed to help all ACT! users increase their support base by introducing or emphasizing some of the great help features that ACT! has, as well as some other sources of support that are available to everyone.

Some portions of this appendix are designed for administrators and some for users, but everyone can benefit from the information in these next few pages.

Getting the most from online help

ACT! comes with two resources for getting help while you're actually using ACT!. These are the application help system that all Windows programs use and the Viagrafix online tutorials.

You can access the application help system by simply clicking on the Help menu and selecting the desired command (Help Topics gives you a listing of all available help topics, and is a good first step toward locating information about whatever it is that you are having trouble with).

Symantec has done a very nice job of enhancing the standard Help menu choices with some genuinely helpful additional choices.

There is a help system just for Symantec Online Support, accessed via the command of the same name (**Figure B.1**). LiveUpdate ensures that you always have the latest version of ACT!, and the QuickStart Wizard is used to create a new database or change basic settings such as your preferred word processor, e-mail system, and fax software.

An Adobe PDF (portable document format) version of both the *entire* ACT! 4.0 User's Guide and the Moving to ACT! 4.0 guide are very thoughtfully included on the ACT! CD and can be accessed from the Online Manuals submenu (**Figure B.2**). Both of these documents are located on the ACT! CD, so the CD must be in the drive, but enterprising users will copy the files directly to their hard drives for access anytime (they don't take up all that much space, considering what you are getting).

The Help menu also includes a Getting Started with ACT! 4.0 submenu, from which you can access any of Viagrafix's video tutorials for ACT!. You can also access these tutorials from within many ACT! dialog boxes by

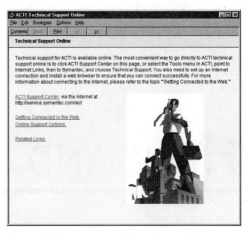

Figure B.1 The Symantec Online Support help system.

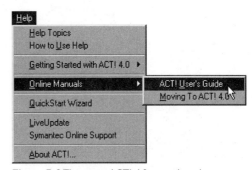

Figure B.2 The entire ACT! 4.0 manual can be accessed via the Online Manuals submenu.

Figure B.3 The Viagrafix logo in a dialog box

clicking on the Tutorial button (**Figure B.3**) whenever it appears in a dialog box.

These tutorials are a nice addition to ACT! and are especially useful for less experienced users, but do suffer from two problems. The first, and most troublesome, problem is that the ACT! CD must be in the drive for you to see any of the tutorials. This is problematic for many businesses who have site licenses or for individual users who do not carry the CD around with them (or can't find it, even when they are at their desk). Unlike the PDF manual, the video tutorials are too big and too little used to justify copying them to the hard drive. The second problem is that clicking on the Tutorial button in certain dialog boxes will, rather than giving you help on what you are trying to do in the dialog box, launch the more general (and usually more basic) video tutorial on the subject matter in general. The tutorials are best used as a one-time primer immediately after you install ACT! (which may very well be their raison d'être in the first place).

Making your users more self-sufficient

If you are a system administrator in charge of an ACT! database, there are five things you can do to help create a self-sufficient cadre of ACT! users.

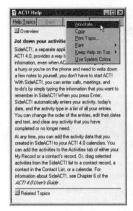

Figure B.4 Notes can be added to any help topic in any Windows application.

♦ Have every user copy the ACT! 4.0 User's Manual PDF file onto their hard drive, make sure they have the Adobe Acrobat Reader properly installed, and make sure they understand that they now have the *entire* ACT! manual at their fingertips.

♦ Make sure your users know how to annotate the application help files. (From within a help topic, click on the Options button and choose the Annotate option.) (**Figure B.4**). This will allow them to keep track of all the tips, tricks, and warnings that you share with them or they pick up on their own.

♦ Training, training, training!

Be sure to factor in the cost of adequately training your users in the fundamentals of ACT! whenever you consider, for example, the cost of computerizing your sales force. And make sure you give them adequate ACT! and Windows training *before* turning them loose with their laptops. (An ounce of prevention, and all that.)

✔ Tip

■ By the way, you can make yourself much more self-sufficient by checking out the excellent ACT! Administrator's Guide, which is located on your ACT! CD (in PDF format) and is chock-full of great information about administering one or more ACT! databases smoothly.

Tech support do's and don'ts

Symantec has a marvelous bunch of technical support specialists waiting in breathless anticipation of your call. These fine souls want nothing more than to help you to be happy and productive with your Symantec products. All they ask in return is a few simple things:

- Have your computer already on and ACT! up and running (if possible) when you call.

- Open your computer's config.sys file so that you can refer to it if they ask you questions about its contents (which they frequently need to do).

  You can open this file by launching any word processor and using the Open command from the File menu. The file is located at the root level of your C: drive. (When opening the file, you may need to tell your word processor to list *all* files, not just its own.)

- If you have called tech support before and have been given an ID number, have it handy. One way to make sure you always have it is to add it and the Symantec tech support phone number to the bottom of your standard layout (as mentioned in Chapter 13, *Productivity Power Tools*).

TECH SUPPORT DO'S AND DON'TS

Accessing Symantec's web site

Symantec's Web site is, not surprisingly, a terrific source of help for us ACT! users. Point your browser to **www.symantec.com**.

If you are in ACT!, the easiest thing to do is to go to the Tools menu, then select the Internet submenu, the Symantec submenu, and the ACT! command. This will take you straight to the ACT! page of the Symantec Web site (**Figure B.5**). From there, just follow the links to access the files or information that you need.

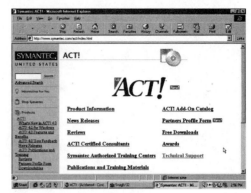

Figure B.5 The ACT! page of Symantec's Web site, our home (page) away from home.

Figure B.6 The first screen of the LiveUpdate wizard.

Using LiveUpdate

To connect to a LiveUpdate server and automatically update your version of ACT! to the most recent version (this isn't for major updates, like moving from 3.0 to 4.0, but for minor updates and bug fixes), select the LiveUpdate command from the Help menu. This will launch the LiveUpdate Wizard (**Figure B.6**). Select your connection method, if desired (the "Find device automatically" option works just fine) and then click the Next button. After LiveUpdate connects to a server, it will show you a list of all available updates. Select the ones you want and click the Next button again to start the download. Sit back and relax (it will take a little while) and then just follow the rest of the prompts to complete the updating process.

Getting the most out of a consultant

For small or customized training needs, or if you need help in creating sophisticated report templates, a consultant is often the most cost-effective solution.

You can find a listing of Symantec-certified ACT! consultants in the box that ACT! came in, but a more up-to-date listing is available from the ACT! page of Symantec's Web site. You can look through all of the available consultants or narrow the list down by geographical area (country or state).

Once you have located a consultant or three, call them up and ask them two questions. One will be the name of a former client or two who you can contact as a reference. Any good consultant should have plenty of happy customers, and a few that he or she regularly uses as a reference.

The second question should be some small but legitimate question about ACT! that you really would like answered. Consultants make their living by answering questions for money, so don't expect a free lesson over the phone, but the consultant should be able to answer a simple question in a reasonable amount of time and in a way that makes sense to you. And don't expect them to have the manual memorized. You are looking for someone who can teach you what you need, or perform the work you want to contract them for. But if their answer or style confuses you or puts you off over the phone, thank them for their time and hang up. An on-site consultation is going to leave you more frustrated and confused than ever, plus a couple hundred bucks poorer.

THE ACTDIAG UTILITY

The best-kept secret of ACT! is the Actdiag (short for "ACT! diagnostic") utility that ships with every version of ACT! Actdiag is installed on your computer during the normal ACT! installation, so if you have ACT!, you have Actdiag.

Actdiag is a terrific little utility program for solving some of the most common technical problems that plague ACT! users. It was written by Duane Anderson (way to go, Duane!) and is absolutely invaluable for any ACT! administrator (and pretty darn useful for all but the most casual users of ACT!, as well). With Actdiag you can diagnose databases for possible problems, reset databases that ACT! cannot open, undelete those "gone forever" records, and much more.

One thing to keep in mind, though, is that Actdiag was developed as a technical support and database administration tool. It has some very powerful abilities, some of which can have undesirable effects if not used properly.

Adding an Actdiag shortcut to your ACT! program items folder

Actdiag is installed on your computer as part of the installation of ACT!, but no shortcut is added anywhere to help you access it. If you are going to be using Actdiag with any frequency at all, it makes sense to create a shortcut for it by following these steps:

1. From the Windows Start menu, select the **Setting** submenu and the **Taskbar & Start Menu** command.

2. In the Taskbar Properties dialog box (**Figure C.1**), click on the **Start Menu Programs** tab to make that the active screen.

3. In the Start Menu Programs screen, click on the **Add** button.

   This brings up the Create Shortcut Wizard (**Figure C.2**).

4. Click on the **Browse** button and navigate through the standard Open dialog box to locate the Actdiag file.

   From the root level of your hard drive, open the Program Files folder, then the Symantec folder, then the Act folder.

5. Select the Actdiag file and click on the **Open** button.

   This returns you to the Create Shortcut Wizard.

6. Click on the **Next** button.

7. At the Select Program Folder screen, click on the ACT! 4.0 for Windows folder (**Figure C.3**). (You may first need to open the Programs folder by double-clicking on it.)

8. Click the **Next** button.

Figure C.1 The Taskbar Properties dialog box.

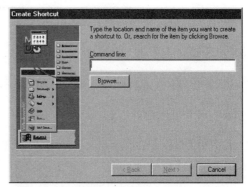

Figure C.2 The first screen of the Create Shortcut wizard.

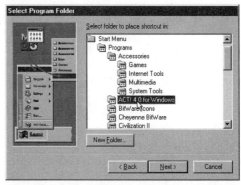

Figure C.3 Select the ACT! 4.0 for Windows folder to place the shortcut in the same location as ACT! itself.

ADDING AN ACTDIAG SHORTCUT

Figure C.4 Now Actdiag is available anytime.

9. If desired, enter a new name for the Actdiag shortcut, then click the **Finish** button.

10. You can now open the Actdiag program at any time as easily as you would open ACT! itself (**Figure C.4**).

Diagnosing a database

Within Actdiag, the Diagnose button cries out to be clicked on. (Well, maybe not "cries out," but it is pretty prominent.) Whenever you want to check the integrity of a database, especially one that has been giving you problems, use the Diagnose button, like this:

1. Click the **Diagnose** button.

2. Actdiag presents you with a standard Open dialog box, conveniently pointed at your ACT! Database folder (**Figure C.5**).

3. Click on the database that you want to diagnose, then click on the **Open** button.

4. Actdiag does a quick diagnosis of the database and displays the database's statistics in the center of the Actdiag window, with any problems listed at the bottom of the window (**Figure C.6**).

   If a problem is listed, you may be able to solve it using one of the commands in the Options or Reset menus, or you may need to call technical support for guidance, but at least you'll be aware of—and able to identify—the problem.

The Options menu

The Actdiag Options menu (**Figure C.7**) contains eight commands, all of which perform single, quick actions and don't really require any instructions as to how they are used. (That is, you simply select the command, and Actdiag does its magic.) A little information on what these commands are used for, though, will be helpful.

Over the course of time, the index files for your databases are going to become inefficient at the very least, and can become badly corrupted if not properly maintained. The Remove Index File command removes the index file completely for the selected database (thus removing any potential problems).

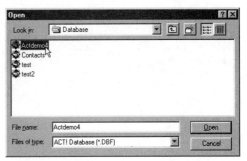

Figure C.5 Select the database you want diagnosed.

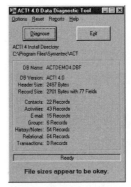

Figure C.6 The Actdiag window displays the statistics of the selected database.

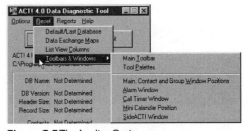

Figure C.7 The Actdiag Options menu.

DIAGNOSING A DATABASE

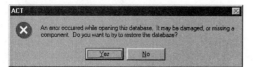

Figure C.8 The lack of an index causes this error message.

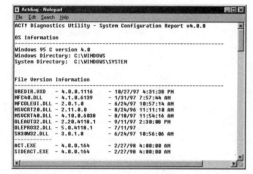

Figure C.9 The Database Maintenance dialog box.

In order to use the database again, you will need to reindex it. *Symantec technical support recommends removing the index file and reindexing at least once a month.* Here are the steps to follow from within Actdiag to perform this indexectomy:

1. From the Options menu, select the **Remove Index File** command.

2. Select the desired database file in the standard Open dialog box and click the **Open** button.

3. Click the **Yes** button in the first confirmation dialog box and the **OK** button in the second confirmation dialog box.

4. From the Reset menu, select the **Default/Last Database** command.

5. Exit Actdiag.

6. Launch ACT!

7. Because you reset the default/last database, ACT! opens to an empty screen.

8. From the File menu, select the **Database Maintenance** command.

9. Select the same database file that you selected when deleting the index file in steps 1 and 2, then click the **Open** button.

10. Because there is no index file for the database, you will get an error message (**Figure C.8**). Click the **Yes** button to continue.

11. In the Database Maintenance dialog box (**Figure C.9**), select the "Compress and reindex database" option and click the **OK** button.

This completes the maintenance of the database.

The Remove Unapplied Sync Packets command removes any sync packets left behind by unsuccessful modem-to-modem synchronization attempts. If such an attempt is made and is unsuccessful, quite often the sync

DIAGNOSING A DATABASE

packet is left behind and interferes with any future attempts. Removing the sync packet removes the problem.

The Remove TEMP Files command removes Windows temporary files from the Windows TEMP directory. These temporary files are used by Windows to keep track of data while a program or file is in use. If the program or file is not properly shut down, the temp files are not cleared from the TEMP directory and can cause problems down the road. Even if these temporary files never cause noticeable problems, they take up valuable hard drive space. The Symantec technical support record was set by a caller whose TEMP folder contained over 5,000 files taking up over 18 megabytes of hard drive space.

The Failed Conversion Check command is used to correct problems with LiveUpdate. If LiveUpdate is interrupted or fails for any reason during an attempt to update ACT!, this command will reset LiveUpdate so that you can attempt another update. (The problem arises when LiveUpdate is interrupted after it tells itself that the new version has been downloaded, but before it actually gets to update ACT!. LiveUpdate then won't download the new version because it thinks you already have it.)

The Back Up ACT! Registry command provides a quick and easy way to make a backup copy of the ACT! registry file before a technical support specialist has you start making changes to it. The backup file is saved as "actreg.reg" and is located in the Windows folder of your primary hard drive.

The Opportunistic Locking on NT Server command is used only when ACT! is loaded onto a Windows NT server. In this case, Actdiag should be run immediately after installation and this command used to prevent Windows NT from corrupting the index files of any ACT! databases that are created.

Figure C.10 Actdiag gives you this warning before undeleting records.

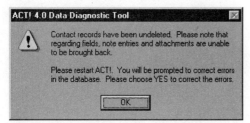

Figure C.11 Another helpful dialog box, courtesy of Actdiag.

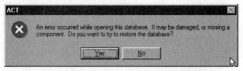

Figure C.12 Again, ACT! warns you of something Actdiag has done. But Actdiag knows what it's doing.

For more information on Windows NT opportunistic locking, contact your friendly neighborhood IS administrator. For more information on this command (or Actdiag in general) call Symantec Tech support.

Probably the best part of Actdiag (at least for most users) is the Undelete Records command. If you (or one of your users, if you are administering a database) accidentally delete records *but have not yet done a compression and reindex of your database*, the Undelete Records command will restore all contact information from the lost records (unfortunately, there is no guarantee that notes, activities, and history entries will be 100% complete). Once a database is compressed and reindexed, however, not even the Undelete Records command can recover lost records, as compressing and reindexing a database purges the database of all deleted information. Follow these steps to undelete lost records:

1. In ACT! make a backup of the database to which you want to restore records.

   You never know what might happen, and it may be that you will be less happy with the restored database than you are with as is.

2. Launch Actdiag and select the **Undelete Records** command from the Options menu.

3. Click the **Yes** button and the warning dialog box (**Figure C.10**).

4. From the standard Open dialog box, select the database with the missing records and click the **Open** button.

5. Click the **Yes** button at the resulting dialog box (**Figure C.11**).

6. Exit Actdiag and launch ACT!.

7. At the error message dialog box (**Figure C.12**) click the **Yes** button to have ACT! restore the database (you may need to log

DIAGNOSING A DATABASE

in to the database during the course of the restoration process).

Your database will open with all deleted records restored.

The Exit command is used to exit Actdiag. Selecting this command is the same as clicking the big Exit button in the Actdiag window.

The Reset menu

The Reset menu (**Figure C.13**), as the name implies, is used to reset various aspects of your ACT! databases. Most of the commands in this menu are fairly self-explanatory, but the uses of a few of them might be a little unclear.

The Default/Last Database command resets the flag in ACT! that keeps track of the last database opened (or the database that is set to be opened on start-up, if you have set one in the Preferences dialog box). This is invaluable when the last or default database has become damaged and every time you start ACT! it tries to reopen the damaged database, and can't. By resetting the flag, you will be able to open ACT! without opening the database.

The Data Exchange Maps command resets the default maps used when you import or export data from ACT!'s Import and Export dialog boxes. The only time you will need this is when those maps become corrupted. This doesn't happen too often, but when they do become corrupted, this is the only way to fix them.

The List View Columns command resets all list view columns in the Contacts, Groups, Task List, and all other views back to their default settings.

All of the commands in the Toolbars & Windows submenu are used to reset various toolbars and window views back to their default settings.

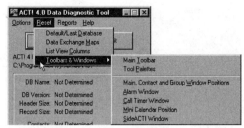

Figure C.13 The Actdiag Reset menu.

DIAGNOSING A DATABASE

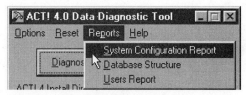

ACT! 4.0 Data Diagnostic Tool
Options Reset Reports Help
System Configuration Report
Database Structure
Users Report
Figure C.14 The Actdiag Reports menu.

Actdiag - Notepad
File Edit Search Help
ACT! Diagnostics Utility - System Configuration Report v4.0.0
OS Information
Windows 95 C version 4.0
Windows Directory: C:\WINDOWS
System Directory: C:\WINDOWS\SYSTEM
File Version Information
VREDIR.VXD - 4.0.0.1116 - 10/27/97 4:31:38 PM
MFC40.DLL - 4.1.0.6139 - 1/31/97 7:57:44 AM
MFCOLEUI.DLL - 2.0.1.0 - 6/24/97 10:57:14 AM
MSVCRT20.DLL - 2.11.0.0 - 8/24/96 11:11:10 AM
MSVCRT40.DLL - 4.10.0.6038 - 8/18/97 11:54:16 AM
OLEAUT32.DLL - 2.20.4118.1 - 9/11/97 2:30:08 PM
OLEPRO32.DLL - 5.0.4118.1 - 7/11/97
SH30W32.DLL - 3.0.1.0 - 6/24/97 10:56:06 AM
ACT.EXE - 4.0.0.164 - 2/27/98 4:00:00 AM
SIDEACT.EXE - 4.0.0.164 - 2/27/98 4:00:00 AM
Figure C.15 A report created by Actdiag.

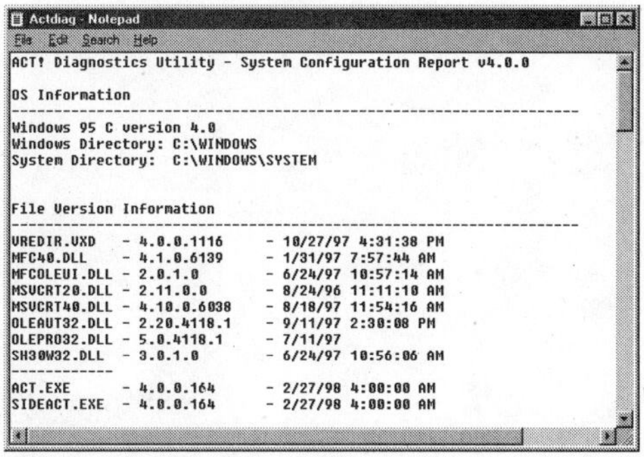

The Reports menu

The Reports menu (**Figure C.14**) contains only three commands, System Configuration Report, Database Structure, and Users Report, all of which generate text reports for use primarily by Symantec technical support (**Figure C.15**). While a database or IS administrator might find these reports informative, they are usually only run when a Symantec technical support specialist asks a user to run one in the course of a technical support call.

INDEX

INDEX

INDEX

INDEX

INDEX

T